D1597467

AFRICAN SAFARIS

AFRICAN SAFARIS

by

Major G. H. ("Andy") Anderson, M.C.

late 18th Royal Hussars (Queen Mary's Own)
and a foundation member of the
East African Professional Hunter's Association

With a FOREWORD by

The Rt. Hon. Lord Cranworth, K.G., M.C.

Safari Press Inc.
P.O. Box 3095, Long Beach, CA 90803-0095, USA

Anderson, Major G. H..

Safari Press Inc.

1997, Long Beach, California

ISBN 1-57157-074-8

Library of Congress Catalog Card Number: 970-67708

10 9 8 7 6 5 4 3 2 1

Readers wishing to receive the Safari Press catalog, featuring many fine books on big-game hunting, wingshooting, and sporting firearms, should write to Safari Press Inc., P.O. Box 3095, Long Beach, CA, 90803, USA. Tel: (714) 894-9080, or visit our web site at http://www.safaripress.com.

CONTENTS

CONTENTS (Continued)

FOREWORD

By LORD CRANWORTH

I FEEL proud indeed to be asked to write a Foreword to these reminiscences of that great big game hunter and splendid sportsman Major " Andy " Anderson. This the more since, while the author stresses at times that his recollections are of a bygone age, my own are even older.

It is, I should think, improbable that there lives today any white man who has had the intimate experience of the big game of Africa, and more especially of elephants that Andy possessed, and one must stand amazed that he was able to combine it for so long with an active career in a cavalry regiment. Roughly speaking one may say that when there was any possibility of fighting he was a soldier, and when there was none he was a hunter. The arrangement seems to have been eminently satisfactory to his Commanding Officer, which is surely the highest tribute to his fighting qualities and one which his record abundantly justifies. Another remarkable thing is this: at the outset of his hunting career in 1908 he, like so many in the early days of the century, was very badly mauled by a lion —which brings to my mind the unexplained problem as to why these accidents have tended to decrease to such a great extent—and suffered from a stiff leg ever afterwards. Elephant hunting calls for great exertion on foot over protracted periods and how he overcame this disability is a tremendous testimony to his courage and determination. Later he added another handicap in the form of deafness, but this again he just took in his stride.

As regards elephants Major Anderson's name will always be linked with that of his great friend Jim Sutherland, of whom he has much to write, and to all African big game hunters these two will for long remain household words of almost legendary repute. One of the many reasons for their success was, no doubt, that they hunted at the back of beyond, always a little farther than the other people, and as their hunting grounds became known, they sought fresh territory even more remote from civilisation. There is alas today not much farther that one can go, and so there can never be in Africa a repetition of the experiences herein related.

If the shooting of elephants demands high qualities of courage and endurance, the next adventure described calls for even more. This was the expedition undertaken with the object of filming elephants in their native haunts, and more especially to obtain " close-ups " of elephants charging. The illustrations show the success achieved and, writing as one whose strictly limited experience found even the rumbling of an elephant's stomach in close proximity highly disturbing, I regard the feat of photographing an elephant provoked into charging at a few yards range with awe and admiration, which only the positive proof would have convinced me to be possible.

This phase was brought to an end in 1914 by the outbreak of war, and since the filming was taking place in the heart of German East Africa, the Germans at once sent a force to arrest the two men, which no doubt they regarded as an easy task. Their escape is described, but I fear that I must draw attention to a defect, albeit a pleasant one, of the writer through excessive modesty. I was in East Africa at the time, and this escape through trackless bush, at some 40 miles a day, pursued by German askari who knew the country well, was regarded throughout our forces as a feat verging on the incredible. No one reading this account would guess this, but it is a proof that what is written throughout is an under-statement rather than highly coloured.

After reaching safety Major Anderson at once struck out for France, travelling by devious routes, and rejoined his regiment, I should judge most irregularly, outside Ypres. With them he served with great distinction, received the M.C. for gallantry in action, was mentioned in despatches, and finally severely wounded. Later General Northey applied for his services on his staff in Nyasaland and German East Africa, and there he did fine work on Intelligence for which his knowledge of the country well fitted him.

In 1919 he retired from the Army with the rank of Major, married, and settled in Kenya where he had a coffee farm outside Nairobi. His heart, however, was not really in farming but in East Africa's big game which he knew so well, and he became one of the most distinguished of the numerous White Hunters of that decade. He conducted many parties, including two Royal parties, with invariable success and without mishap. In 1930 he was largely instrumental in founding the East African Professional Big Game Hunters' Association of which for many years I have had the honour of being president. Major Anderson has, and rightly, many good words to say of these fine men. Indeed they have a splendid record of sportsmanship, courage and devotion to their clients' safety. This work, interspersed with some more elephant shooting, occupied him till 1939 when he came Home on holiday. Perhaps he smelt the battle from afar! At the outbreak of war his age and infirmities frustrated his desire for yet more active service, but he did his full share as a Sergeant-Major in the Home Guard, coupled with work in a war factory. In 1945 he returned to

Kenya and, in April 1946, he conducted his last safari to the Northern Frontier when he shot his last elephant with tusks of over 200 lbs. the pair. On this expedition he contracted a severe illness. He went south, to Johannesburg, to recuperate, but died there of pneumonia following a chill.

It is, I think, obvious that these experiences comprise more than enough material to produce a fascinating book and to me they have emphatically done so. The author would never have pretended to be, indeed he would have strenuously denied being, a polished writer. He was definitely a man of action. But I cannot think that this book suffers in any way thereby. He states his facts clearly and with humour, and gives, all too modestly, descriptions of what he has seen and done, while his views on African game and their habits clearly show the hand of a master of his craft.

Major Anderson has now again gone on, blazing the trail through unknown territory. No more will he watch his beloved game at dusk winding down to their waterholes to drink. He leaves a host of friends; few men had more. Among them he will always be remembered as a splendid soldier, a gallant English gentleman and among the dozen finest hunters that Africa has ever known — a select list which includes Selous, Sir Frederick Jackson, " Karamoja " Bell, Major Stigand, his friend Jim Sutherland, R. J. Cunninghame and one or two more.

It is nice to know that he had a good life, happy in his marriage, his friends, his soldiering, and his sport. If this book gives pleasure to his readers it would have made him happy too. And that it will do so I am well assured, for it is the simply-told record of one of the finest sportsmen of my generation.

To

My Wife

Lorna Anderson

NOTES IN APPRECIATION
OF MAJOR G.H. "ANDY" ANDERSON

I T IS a great honor and pleasure for me to write this new introduction to Major G.H. "Andy" Anderson and his book *African Safaris*. Without a doubt it is one of the most interesting, pleasing, and informative books ever written about hunting in Africa.

We few lucky ones who were fortunate enough to read Anderson's original work can appreciate how the author's qualities as a person, hunter, and military man made him someone to follow. All the virtues of the Victorian gentleman came together in him, and his life and experiences under the African sun were unique.

G. H. Anderson was born in England in 1878, and he grew up and was educated there. In 1899, at the age of twenty-one, he enlisted in the Paget Cavalry Regiment to fight the Boers in South Africa. Later he joined the 18th Royal Hussars as a second lieutenant, launching a brilliant military career that included many commendations and decorations, among which was the Military Cross. He retired in 1919 with the rank of major.

In 1907 he made his first hunting expedition in British Somaliland, which at the time was one of the best-known areas of Africa for this kind of activity. He was accompanied by Dr. Harold Brooks. Earlier, Anderson had taken part in some smaller hunts while he was stationed in northern Nigeria, and these had whipped up his appetite for hunting and his desire to take the major species of African fauna.

On this first expedition he took a leopard and several antelopes, and he decided to return the next year to go after lion, which were so abundant at the time. But he was unlucky in that the first one he shot, a lioness, was only wounded and attacked him before he could stop her with the second barrel of his .450 Nitro Express. The animal took a bite out of his right knee, and he never recovered full use of his leg. The leg remained stiff for the rest of his life and the natives gave him the Swahili nickname of "Bwana Muguu," or "Mister Leg."

This handicap, which would have dampened another person's enthusiasm, didn't discourage Anderson who started hunting again as soon as his wounds healed. He never let himself be slowed down by the limp, and he spent his life "carrying on" as if nothing had happened. Once, at the beginning of World War I, he marched 300 miles to escape the German patrols who wanted to capture him in what was then German East Africa (now Tanzania).

In 1912 during a visit to Europe, he met the famous elephant hunter James Sutherland on board a German ship at the port of Tanga. The friendship lasted throughout both of their lives and led to numerous elephant-hunting expeditions, with Anderson becoming an expert and taking many impressive trophies.

In 1919 when Anderson retired from the army, he married, and he and his wife, Lorna, began running a coffee plantation near Nairobi. He also devoted himself to hunting and leading sporting safaris. He became one of the most famous "White Hunters" of all time. In 1924 he and another professional, Pat Ayres, were chosen to take the Duke and Duchess of York—later King George VI and Queen Elizabeth of England—on safari in Kenya. In 1930 he and fellow professionals Bror von Blixen and Denys Finch-Hatton took the Prince of Wales and later the Duke of Windsor on safari.

Like all real hunters, Anderson was always interested in protecting wildlife and in following hunting regulations. In 1934 he collaborated in the creation of the East African Professional Hunters Association and remained its vice-president until his death.

Thanks to the decision by Safari Press to reissue Major Anderson's magnificent *African Safaris*, present and future generations of hunters can enjoy his incredible adventures in a book that is rare and almost impossible to find today. Even if one can be found, the price is usually unaffordable since most of the 400 copies originally printed in 1946 have probably vanished with the passage of time.

Through a cruel trick of fate, Anderson never saw his book published. At the beginning of April 1946, he led a safari in the Northern Frontier District of Kenya, planning to photograph elephants. It was here that he took his last trophy, an old bull with tusks weighing more than two hundred pounds. During this safari, he contacted a severe case of malaria, which ruined his health.

When he was able, he finished the book and delivered it to Nakuru Press in Kenya for publication in May 1946. On medical advice he went to Johannesburg, South Africa, to see if the change of climate would help him recover. It did not, and he died of pneumonia on 15 July 1946, at the age of 68, far from his beloved Kenya.

Tony Sanchez-Ariño
Valencia, Spain
March, 1997

PREFACE

BEFORE reading this book, I ask that the Preface be read, for that will help to understand what follows. It is quite impossible to record the very many safaris which I have undertaken in Africa, and in most instances there would be nothing of outstanding interest to the general reader.

When relating some of my hunting experiences and other episodes in Africa several friends have urged the writing of a book of reminiscences. Not being of a literary turn of mind, all writing being an effort, and knowing that so many books of this kind have already been written I could not bring myself to do this. Then, owing to ill-health, I returned to England just before the outbreak of World War II. I was rejected for further Army service by a Medical Board and served in the Home Guard, from start to finish, as well as, from 1944 to 1945, doing a part-time job in a war factory. In order to pass the long and dreary winter evenings I wrote down some of my experiences on safari in Africa, and this recalled many happy memories of a life that I love so well.

I have divided up the matter into distinct episodes, so that it may interest the general reader no less than those who have been associated with big game hunting. To this end, I have given a brief sketch of my life so as to lend a certain degree of cohesion as well as convey to the reader that what I have written is the truth, to the best of my knowledge, and *not* fiction. I do not wish to convey an impression of posing as a mighty big game hunter, for there are others who have had more experience of big game than myself.

I first touched the shores of Africa in the April of 1900, serving during the South African war as a trooper in Paget's Horse (Imperial Yeomanry) and, shortly after my return to England in the June of 1901 I was commissioned in the 18th Royal Hussars (Queen Mary's Own). For financial reasons, and longing to see more of Africa, I was seconded from my regiment in 1904 to the Mounted Infantry of the West African Frontier Force. Rejoining the 18th Hussars at the beginning of 1906, I afterwards went on other semi-official expeditions in Africa. To my Commanding Officers, the late Colonel W. P. M. Pollok-Morris, C.M.G., D.S.O., and the late Colonel the Hon. H. S. Davey, C.M.G., I owe a debt of gratitude for granting me the necessary leave and also for encouraging me in my travels.

On my return from a safari in German East Africa (now Tanganyika Territory) at the beginning of 1912, I resigned my commission in the Army to join forces with the late Captain Jim Sutherland, the well-known elephant hunter. I returned to Africa with him on an expedition into the Belgian Congo after ivory, and also to take up hunting as a profession. Having settled in Kenya Colony during 1919, two years later I became a professional White Hunter, and later had the honour to be selected as one of the White Hunters on the safari of Their Majesties the King and Queen when, as the Duke and Duchess of York, they visited Kenya in 1924-1925. I also had the honour to act in the same capacity when the Prince of Wales (now the Duke of Windsor) visited Kenya in 1930. When I was not employed on safari as a White Hunter, I was often away on my own after elephants and taking photographs of big game. Since my return to Kenya Colony in the March of 1945 I have been in charge of a permanent camp in connection with Army Welfare work for the East African Command, which was established for the purpose of showing members of the Forces serving in East Africa some of the big game in the wonderful game country at Amboseli, mentioned in my book.

To my very old friend Colonel H. A. Cape, D.S.O., the Adjutant of my regiment when I first joined and who later commanded the 5th Royal Irish Lancers, I owe a deep debt of gratitude for all his encouragement and also for the trouble he has taken in reading all my notes; and I am also indebted to another old friend, Major W. R. Foran, an " old-timer " of East Africa, for putting together these notes and helping me in the preparation of the manuscript. To Mr. F. S. Joelson, Founder and Editor of *East Africa and Rhodesia,* I convey my thanks for allowing me to quote from the brief sketch of the life of the late Major Philip J. Pretorius, C.M.G., D.S.O.; also for his many hints and the encouragement given me to write this book. My thanks are also due to Lieut.-Colonel C. R. S. Pitman, D.S.O., M.C., Game Warden of Uganda, for allowing me to quote from his book, *A Game Warden Takes Stock,* the incident of the lion in Northern Rhodesia.

G. H. ANDERSON.

Nairobi, Kenya Colony.
May, 1946.

BRITISH SOMALILAND — 1907

I AM recording this short account of a safari in British Somaliland because it really started me off on this shooting profession, although I had done a little shooting in Northern Nigeria, when serving with the Mounted Infantry of the West African Frontier Force from 1904 to 1906. It was then commanded by Colonel T. A. Cubitt (afterwards Lieut-General Sir Thomas Ashley Cubitt, Governor and Commander-in-Chief of Bermuda, who died in 1939). Tom Cubitt, as he was affectionately known to all "West Coasters," was one of the most brilliant and clever men whom I have ever met; he was also a splendid Commanding Officer to serve under. He had, at that time, a keen lot of British officers and a certain number of British N.C.O.s, both seconded from British regiments. They certainly were a lively lot and a good number of hard cases amongst them, both officers and N.C.O.s; but no one knew better than Tom Cubitt how to deal with them, and he was greatly beloved by his Officers, N.C.O.s and the Native soldiers. Tom Cubitt had the best flow of language that I've heard from any man.

I served again under him, when he was Brigade Major of the Cavalry Brigade at the Curragh in Ireland and lived in our Mess. He proved himself a most able and efficient Brigade Major, and was deservedly popular with all ranks. I have often heard the men, when the Brigade was all drawn up mounted, whisper to each other as Cubitt rode on parade: "Here comes bloody old Tom!" but this was not meant to be in any way disrespectful, but more of a term of endearment, as they would do anything for him. A great personality, and the type of man who would do well at any job that required leadership. I met him again in England, several years ago, when he was commanding a Division at Aldershot. The Governorship of Kenya Colony was at that time vacant, and I said to him: " You'd better come out to Kenya as Governor. That's the job for you!" He replied: " I once was asked by Sir Frederick Lugard, when he was Governor of Northern Nigeria, to go into the Civil Service, but would not do so, as I wished to continue soldiering; and I've made, more or less, a success of it. If I had gone into the Civil Service, I should have been a blinkin' Duke by now and with Orders hanging down to my toes!" (Only he did not say toes.)

I am afraid that I have rather digressed from the shooting trip to British Somaliland; but once knowing Tom Cubitt, one would never forget him. He certainly was a character.

The little shooting I was able to get in Nigeria made me terribly keen to do some more in Africa. When stationed at York with my regiment during 1907, through a mutual friend I was introduced to Dr. Harold Brooks who had done a shooting trip to British East Africa, and also two trips to Canada. Like myself, he had served as a trooper in Paget's Horse (Imperial Yeomanry) during the South African War; but we did not know each other at the time, for we were in different squadrons. During the trip we became great friends. He was a first-rate fellow and a good sportsman, but I don't know what he was like as a doctor. I think sport was more in his line!

At the time I met him, he was making arrangements for a shooting expedition to British Somaliland and asked me if I would join him. I was mad keen to accompany him but two chief difficulties to overcome were, firstly, to get leave from my regiment; and, secondly, the question of £.s.d. In those days we were allowed two and a half months' long leave in the winter; and my Commanding Officer, Lieut.-Colonel W. P. M. Pollok-Morris, a real good soldier and keen sportsman, granted me extra leave. By going overland, there would be time for the shoot.

I suppose that the general public would say: "What the devil do the officers do in the way of work? They always seem to be on leave!" That is entirely wrong. During the winter months about half the N.C.O.s and men were on leave; it was only possible to get the horses exercised, and little or no training could be carried out during that period.

As to the £.s.d. question, I went into this very carefully with Brooks. He had already worked out the expenses with a friend of his who had been in Somaliland, and found that it could be done fairly cheaply, the heavy expenses being the passage there and back. Anyway, I decided to go with Brooks.

We left at the end of December, and by going overland to Brindisi, we caught one of the two boats which ran in connection with the P. and O. mail-steamers at Port Said. These two boats were called the *Isis* and *Osiris*. They were small and built on the lines of a destroyer, and averaged a speed of over 20 knots an hour; it did not matter what the weather was, they simply drove them through it all at full speed. It was on the *Isis* that we went over to Port Said. She was commanded by Captain Armitage, who had been Sir Ernest Shackleton's second-in-command on the *Nimrod* during his Antarctic Expedition. A very nice and interesting man he was.

Arriving at Port Said we transferred to the P. and O. steamer and travelled on to Aden, where we again transhipped to a small steamer which ran weekly from Aden to Berbera. There were two very small coasting-steamers, owned by a Parsi firm (Messrs. Cowarjee and Dinshaw and Brothers), one steamer named the *Snipe* ran to Jibuti (French Somaliland) and the other, the *Woodcock,* to Berbera in British Somaliland. We travelled on the latter after spending a night at Aden and embarking the following evening. The *Woodcock* arrived at Berbera next morning. We found all our camp equipment and stores awaiting us at Berbera. The camp equipment we had sent out from England, but the stores had been ordered from Cowarjee and Dinshaw, who did us very well and cheaply.

Berbera, the capital of the British Somaliland, then consisted of a few houses occupied by officials, and was built on a flat, sandy plain near the sea. It was as hot as Hades. Brooks had written to his friend at Berbera, so we found that he had engaged a very good lot of Somalis and a most excellent headman named Harshi Jama. Owing to the kindness and help we got from local officials, we were enabled to get away after two and a half days. We purchased 10 camels at an average price of about 50 shillings each; and also bought a pony each, for riding, the price being about £5 a pony.

We were advised by officials to make for Hargeisa — 100 miles due west of Berbera and towards the Abyssinian frontier — and hunt in that area. After trekking across the maritime plain, south of Berbera, for about 20 miles, we climbed the Golis Mountains by the Hargeisa caravan route and thus gained a plateau about 4,000 feet up, where the climate was delightful and a great change from the sweltering heat near Berbera. Our marching hours were from about four a.m. to nine a.m.; and again from one p.m. to five p.m. The camels were allowed to graze during the midday heat and for about half an hour before sunset. Every night when making our camp, the Somalis made a zariba of thorn-bushes for protection from lions. We never had any trouble with our boys about turning out in the morning, and they were past-masters in loading up the camels.

What I remember of the country through which we passed was that sometimes it was open plain but at others covered with low thorn-bush and practically waterless. In fact, all British Somaliland is the same. The only water obtainable is from a few wells in dried-up river-beds. Everything in that country seemed to exist on very little water. Watering the camels about every five days is sufficient to keep them in condition; but they will go, at a pinch, for as much as 10 days without water. We carried a certain amount in tanks for the use of ourselves and boys. The Somalis can do with very little water and do not require anything like the same quantity as the Natives of East or Central Africa; this also applies to the ponies, but even more so to the wild animals. The latter,

3

I am certain, go for months on end without drinking. It is all a question of environment.

On several occasions we passed Somali *karia* (villages) with thousands of camels, sheep and goats on the march to other grazing grounds, and this was a really wonderful sight. These *karia,* when not on the move, are often as much as 40 miles from the nearest water-holes and the Somalis send their camels to fetch water when required. These water-holes are generally in a dried-up sandy river-bed, and often 30 to 50 feet in depth, the water being obtained in calabashes by men in the water-hole, who pass it up from man to man until finally it is emptied into a mud-trough. The water-holes are narrow, and niches are cut in the bank for men to stand one above the other, maybe three or four men being required in the well just according to its depth. As one can imagine, this is a long and tedious job. Often, also, it is the cause of fights between different tribes who come to water their camels, sheep and goats.

Brooks and I got a certain amount of shooting *en route* to Hargeisa in the way of Soemmering's gazelle, Speke's gazelle and dik-dik.

I remember on the way to Hargeisa passing a large mosque-shaped building, which had been erected by the late Lord Delamere during one of his shooting expeditions to Somaliland, situated on the edge of an arid and waterless plain; personally, I thought it a God-forsaken place. It was occupied by some Somali Chief. Whatever made Lord Delamere put up that building I cannot think; it must have been more or less a headquarters from which to run his safaris. He was badly mauled by a lion in British Somaliland during one of his expeditions, but completely recovered from it.

Lord Delamere, as all East Africans know, was one of the earliest and the leading settler in Kenya; and he meant to Kenya what Cecil Rhodes meant to Rhodesia. Nobody did more for the development of Kenya Colony than Lord Delamere. He died on November 13th, 1931, in the country which he so much loved, having spent a fortune on experiments with stock-raising and farming; but little he got in return, as it was all so much in the experimental stage. The present settlers owe Lord Delamere a great debt, for they are now benefiting from his experience, and that grand country Kenya is going ahead by leaps and bounds. It is not for me to say what a great man Lord Delamere was, as his life, and what he did for Kenya, has been so well described by Elspeth Huxley in her delightful book, *White Man's Country: Lord Delamere and the Making of Kenya* (1933).

On arrival at Hargeisa we met Captain (now Lieut.-Colonel) F. W. Bell, V.C., who was the District Commissioner and the only white man in the place. The nearest other white man was at Berbera, 100 miles distant. He was most kind to us, giving a lot of help and useful information concerning the shooting. He was a hard-bitten looking Australian, who had come from Australia with a Mounted Corps to the South African war, when he had won the Victoria Cross, and afterwards joined the Colonial Civil Service, in Somaliland. The next place I ran into him was at Ypres in the December of 1914, when he was attached to the 4th Dragoon Guards; again I was to meet him at Narok in Kenya Colony where he was District Commissioner. That was in 1921.

I was at the time on safari with my wife and remember it so well as we were trekking with an ox-wagon, and got caught in a devil of a thunderstorm about four miles outside Narok. The wagon was hopelessly bogged right up to the axles, so we rode on into Narok and ran into Bell. Again he was most kind, put us up for the night in his bungalow, fitted out my wife and myself with pyjamas and clothes, as we were both soaked to the skin. About a year and a half after Brooks and I had met Bell at Hargeisa, he was very badly mauled by a lion, which gave him a real bad doing, and he was laid up for months.

Hargeisa itself was quite a pretty spot with a certain amount of grass about, as it was situated on a river, not at that time running. There was a plentiful supply of good water, and a large number of permanent huts.

We had a real good shoot in the Hargeisa area and towards the Abyssinian border, our bag including lion, leopard, Beisa oryx, greater and lesser kudu, gerenuk (or Waller's gazelle), Soemmering's and Speke's gazelle, Swayne's hartebeest (in Somali called *sig*), and wart-hog. Somaliland, in those early days, was a real good sporting country to shoot in. Of course, you did not get anything like the variety of game obtainable in East Africa and had to work fairly hard for some of the trophies. But one great consideration was that it could be done cheaply for transport cost very little, and the camels could always be sold on finishing the safari and you dropped very little on them. This was where we had the luck to have such a good headman as Harshi Jama, who did all this for us and also all our interpreting, as he spoke quite good English, too.

The only bit of excitement I had was with a leopard after putting out a " kill " and wounding it when shooting from a *boma* at night. The leopard came on to the " kill," a dead Soemmering's gazelle pegged down about a yard outside the *boma*, which latter was made of thorn-bushes with just enough room inside for myself and gun-bearer to lie down with a small hole made in the thorn-bushes to shoot through. The leopard came on the " kill " about midnight. I fired and wounded it, and we heard it growling in the bushes some little distance off. Not knowing much about the game in those days, my gun-bearer and I lit a hurricane-lamp and went poking about outside the *boma*, trying to locate the wounded leopard in the bushes. Luckily for us, we did not find it.

Next morning, with my gun-bearer and a few local Somalis, who happened to be there, we spoored the leopard for about a quarter of a mile and then lost the blood-spoor. After about an hour and when just about to abandon the search, a Somali (about 30 yards to my right) threw a stone into some thorn-bushes, with the result that the leopard sprang out and nearly landed on top of the Somali. They both rolled over together. Another Somali, who was standing beside his pal, luckily beat off the leopard with his spear; and at once the beast came straight for me, but I dropped it a few yards away. The Somali was not badly mauled and had only a few claw wounds round his shoulder, which I dressed and then gave him a present. He went off quite happy and shortly afterwards I heard that he had completely recovered. The Natives do not seem to suffer from blood-poisoning in the same way that Europeans do.

I only give this as an instance of a damned silly thing to do — to go looking for a wounded leopard in the bush at night. No animal is so quick or so hard to see, for they will lie absolutely concealed and immobile until there is an opportunity to charge. There is no more plucky animal than a wounded leopard, and they will practically always charge if wounded and followed. Although it is the duty of every sportsman to follow up an animal which he has wounded, yet not on a pitch-dark night and in the bush with the gun-bearer only holding a hurricane-lamp. Wait until the morning and then follow it up. Knowing what I do now, nothing could induce me to follow a wounded leopard on a pitch-dark night in bush. That is just how a great many of the accidents occur: pure ignorance and over-keenness.

I did not get a lion on this trip, but Brooks bagged quite a good maned lion which he spoored and came upon when lying down just outside some bush.

After finishing our shoot, we made our way back to Berbera, this time via Bulhar, which is 40 miles west of the capital and on the sea coast. On arrival at Berbera we sold all the camels, ponies, water-tanks and so forth, and over this business we did quite well. Only one camel had died, the others being in very good condition with hardly any sores, caused by bad loading. This was entirely due to the good camel-man we had.

There is certainly something fascinating about the country; the early morning march and the intense silence in the dark when trekking with camels, only broken by the occasional mournful howling of the hyena or the grunting of a leopard. Very seldom did we hear lions roaring, this being probably due to a great extent, to their following Somali *karias* in the hope of picking up stray camels and cattle. This, with the beautiful sun-rises, and knowing one is miles away from civilisation, all adds to the charm of the wandering life.

The Somali is no doubt a wonderful bushman, and on several occasions, with a couple of mounted Somalis, I have cut right through light thorn-bush, with not a landmark such as a hill in sight, for about eight to nine miles; but they brought me straight back to the camp, never hesitating for a moment, and all this done at a canter. The Somali is a far superior tracker to the average Native of East or Central Africa. This, no doubt, is accounted for by their upbringing, as from earliest childhood they spend their time in herding camels, cattle, sheep and goats; and thus, if any go astray, it is second nature for them to follow a spoor.

The Somali has many sides to his character. He is very intelligent, cheerful and tireless on the march, and often reckless when after dangerous game. In fact, I think in many cases it is due to this recklessness of a white man's gun-bearer that so many accidents occur when after dangerous game; more especially when the white man is inexperienced. But against that, many a white man's life has been saved by a Somali gun-bearer beating off a lion with the butt-end of his master's second rifle.

These people have the devil of an opinion of themselves, are very conceited and excitable, and their dignity is easily hurt. But, from what I saw of them, they are excellent to have on a safari in their own country. They are of slight build with good features, and many of them are fine looking men. I don't know what their history is, but they seem to have a lot of Arab blood in their veins; while I have heard that they are of Arab descent, probably originating from the Yemen or Hadramaut of Southern Arabia. Their life is purely nomadic. They spend most of their lives tending the numerous herds of camels, cattle, sheep and goats, while wandering from one grazing ground to another. A certain amount of intermittent fighting used to go on in the interior between the tribes, and this was regarded by the Elders as a healthy pastime and as affording the young men something to do.

After settling up everything at Berbera, where we were kindly entertained by some of the officials, Brooks and I left for England. The only thing I remember about the voyage is that we had a really rough trip between Port Said and Brindisi in the *Osiris*.

7

II

SOMALILAND AND ABYSSINIA — 1908-9

SHORTLY after rejoining my regiment at the beginning of 1908, which in the meantime had moved to the Curragh Camp in Ireland, I had the offer to go on a semi-official job to British Somaliland and Abyssinia for six months during the " leave season " of the next winter, provided I could get leave from my Commanding Officer. As you can imagine, I was terribly keen to go.

I went on the line, before asking for leave, of always jokingly saying that I was off again somewhere in the following winter, and if you do this, people will take it for granted that you are going. But if you suddenly put in for six months' leave without preparing the ground beforehand, in nine cases out of ten you would have no hope of having it granted. The first I had to tackle was my Squadron Officer, Major C. H. Corbett, so watching him like a cat watches a mouse, I got him when he was in a real good humour with himself and broached the subject of six months' leave. He kindly granted my request, and the Colonel did the same.

I left at the end of September, overland, and caught the P. and O. boat at Marseilles, having sent all my camp equipment on ahead by sea. On the voyage from Marseilles I met Anthony F. Wilding who, at that time, was the world's tennis champion. He was on his way home to New Zealand, and we became quite friends. He was a fine figure of a man, a most cheery fellow, and kept himself very fit. Every evening we used to go to the upper deck and skip. A great man with the ladies, and I don't wonder at it as he was very good looking, he was without an atom of side. I played tennis with him in a double at Port Said. When Wilding served, the ball came over the net like a bullet out of a gun. What a hope! He, like so many other good sportsmen, joined up in the Great War of 1914-18 and was killed on May 9th, 1915.

On arrival at Aden, I was met by my old headman, Harshi Jama, who told me he had got all the boys and camels marked down for me and ready to start from Berbera as soon as we arrived. Visiting Messrs. Cowarjee and Dinshaw and Brothers, I was informed that all my stores and equipment had been forwarded to Berbera. Again they did me well.

I crossed over to Berbera on one of their small coasting boats, the only other European passenger being a Government official in the Somaliland

Civil Service and his newly wedded wife. The bride only arrived at Aden on the same day as the bridegroom from Berbera, and they were married straight away in Aden. Of all the places to spend a honeymoon, one of those small steamers must be about the worst! The cabins were about the size of a large dog-kennel, as hot as Hades at that time of the year, so practically everyone slept on deck for coolness' sake. In the morning the bridegroom appeared about six o'clock, followed shortly by the bride; and they both looked more dead than alive. I don't wonder at it, as the heat in the cabins was terrific, and no punkahs or electric fans. The captain, a European, semed to spend all his time in pyjamas and looked as if suffering from alcoholic poisoning.

On arrival at Berbera I went straight off and reported myself to the Commissioner of Somaliland, Captain H. E. S. Cordeaux, C.B., C.M.G. (the late Major Sir Harry E. S. Cordeaux, K.C.M.G., C.B.), who said that he was expecting me but my permit to enter Abyssinia had not yet arrived. He advised me to return to Aden and see Colonel Sir John Harrington (then British Consul at Addis Ababa, capital of Abyssinia). As I had just missed the boat back to Aden, he kindly arranged for me to get a passage on H.M.S. *Fox,* which happened to be at Berbera.

The *Fox* was a gunboat employed in patrolling the Persian Gulf and Somaliland coast to prevent gun-running and for the suppression of the slave-trade from the northern coast of Africa to the Persian Gulf. She was commanded by Captain Hunt, R.N. (later Admiral Sir T. Hunt, K.C.B.). He was a well-known sportsman, and spent a great deal of his service on the East Coast of Africa and never missed the opportunity of a shoot. There was not a man in the Royal Navy who had done so much shooting. Captain Hunt and his officers were most kind to me, and I stayed on board as their guest while at Aden, going ashore with Captain Hunt to play tennis or squash rackets.

After six days in Aden, I met Sir John Harrington, who was on his way to England on leave from Abyssinia. Sir John said that he knew all about me but had been unable to get me the permit from King Menelik, as the latter was very ill and said to be dying. Sir John gave me chits to the Acting-Governor of Harar, a Greek who was acting British Consul there, also to Abdulla Taker, an Arab who was Governor at Jigjiga, the frontier post on the Somaliland-Abyssinian border. Sir John was most kind, and furnished me with a great deal of useful information, and so I decided to return to Berbera. As I had just missed the weekly coasting boat, I fixed up a passage on an Arab dhow and left Aden on the same evening.

Since those days I have made several trips by dhow, which are quite all right for a short journey but, when you have to spend a night or more on them they are no " joy-ride " and the sanitary arrangements are not of the best. I should have been only one night on the dhow but, owing to the lack of wind, we were becalmed for a whole day just in sight of the barren rocks of Aden. It was very hot. There was only just room enough to lie down on my blankets and no shelter from the sun, so glad I was to see the last of the dhow when reaching Berbera early on the second morning out of Aden.

On seeing Captain Cordeaux, he told me that reports had reached him from Harar, mostly from Greeks, to the effect that they thought they were all going to be murdered. In fact, they all seemed to have the wind-up. Owing to the illness of King Menelik, Ras Makonnen, the Governor of Harar, had gone to Addis Ababa and there was no law or order in Harar. Ras Makonnen, a nephew of King Menelik and father of Ras Tafari —now the Emperor Hailie Selassie of Ethiopia—was a very good friend to the British and had great influence in Harar. He was a first-rate Governor and a just ruler.

Before I left Berbera, Captain Cordeaux told me to send him a report of what I thought about the situation at Harar, and offered to let me have two mounted askari, dressed in the ordinary kit of a Somali complete with a couple of spears and a small round shield, which most Somalis carry on a journey. They would bring back my report to him at Berbera, after I had learned what was the true situation in Harar.

In the meantime, and whilst I had been away at Aden, the faithful Harshi Jama had fixed up my caravan, having bought eight camels, mats, rope, water-tanks, and all the other small things which are required for a camel caravan. I also bought quite a nice Somali pony for myself.

On the second day after my return to Berbera I was able to send my camels off under Harshi Jama, with orders to await me at a camp about 20 miles distant. All the officials were most kind and helpful during my stay at Berbera and, on my last night there, I dined with Captain Cordeaux. He very kindly let me have a fast trotting-camel to ride out to my caravan; also a mounted Somali askari to accompany me and bring back the camel. This was my first experience of riding a camel, and I found it most comfortable. Anyhow, after an excellent dinner and plenty of good drinks, I felt like riding anything; and saying good-bye to my kind host, I hit the road for Harar—which is about 240 miles from Berbera via Hargeisa.

It was a glorious moonlight night and a grand feeling to be off again into the wilds, that free and wandering life that has such a charm. After three hours' ride I picked up my caravan, and had a rest for three hours, and then started off with the caravan. We followed the same caravan route to Hargeisa that Brooks and I had used during the previous year, arriving there after six days' trek. There was a District Commissioner at

Hargeisa, the only white man, and he very kindly put me up for the night.

After another five days I struck the Abyssinian frontier-post of Jigjiga, which is situated on an open plain and, from what I remember of it, just a wooden stockade with about 100 Abyssinian soldiers stationed there. On arrival at Jigjiga, I camped on the plain, a bleak and arid spot and about a quarter of a mile from the stockade. The first person to come out and visit me was the Governor of the district, Abdulla Taker, who was a most intelligent and enlightened Arab. We carried on our conversation through Harshi Jama, who acted as interpreter, giving him Sir John Harrington's letter of introduction. I explained that it was my wish to visit Harar. He said it was impossible to let me proceed until permission had been obtained from the Abyssinian Governor of Harar; also that I should have to see the Abyssinian officer in charge of the soldiers at Jigjiga. So I went over with Abdulla Taker to the stockade and was shown into a mud-hut, about six Abyssinians all sitting round. The Abyssinian officer in charge fairly put me through it in the way of questions, asking me the reasons for my wish to visit Harar and what was I doing in the country. I explained that I was on a shooting trip and having heard what a fine city Harar was, wished to see that town before going on to shoot. After about half an hour the conversation faded out. I returned to my camp.

In the evening Abdulla Taker came to my camp and said that, after a lot of trouble with the Abyssinians, they had allowed him to send a mounted messenger to the Governor of Harar to ask his permission for me to go there, but in the meantime I had to remain at Jigjiga. I knew that Abdulla Taker had done all possible, and it struck me that he had very little use for the Abyssinians. I spent about eight days at Jigjiga waiting for an answer from the Government of Harar, and was thoroughly fed-up with the place. There was nothing to do, except go out for a ride in the mornings and evenings; and every time two armed mounted Abyssinian soldiers accompanied and gave me clearly to understand that I must not go far away from my camp. On the ninth day, Abdulla Taker came to my camp and said I had permission to go on to Harar.

I struck camp at once and started off, still having the two Abyssinian soldiers with me. About 30 miles from Jigjiga I camped for a couple of days to try and shoot a greater kudu, but did not see any; and on returning to camp, found another four Abyssinian soldiers there. They told me that I could not go along the route then being followed to Harar, but must practically go back on my own tracks and take another route. There was nothing for it but to do so.

Shortly after leaving the plains around Jigjiga one strikes into a very hilly country, and the scenery completely changes, plenty of good streams in a valley and well wooded. It was a nice change after the waterless and arid country through which I had passed. After about the third day the terrain became more mountainous, and it was no country for the poor old camels, which were sliding and slipping all over the place. The Abyssinian soldiers advised me to send them by another road, much longer but better going. They said that if we left early—the Abyssinians and myself—on the following morning, we could arrive at Harar in the evening; and if we did not reach it by sundown, we could not get into the town as all the gates were closed at that time, Harar being enclosed by a large mud wall with the only entrances at the gates of the City.

I left on the following morning at dawn, taking only a toothbrush. The distance to Harar was about 35 miles, but it took us all our time to get there before sundown, as the so-called road was nothing more than a track covered with large boulders, up and down the most appalling hills. But some parts of the country were quite lovely, intersected by good streams; and with large herds of cattle and sheep grazing in the valleys. We reached Harar just before the gates were closed, but I was held up temporarily by some Abyssinian soldiers at the gates. They proved rather truculent. Anyhow, they let us pass after a short time, and I went direct to the house of the Acting British Consul, situated in the middle of the town. The British Consul at that time was a Greek, and he very kindly asked me to make his house my headquarters during my stay.

Harar looked very much like a large Arab town in North Africa, which after all, is only natural, as the Egyptians were in possession of it from 1874 to 1884. It is situated on a plateau at from 5,000 to 6,000 feet altitude, with small broken hills around it. A great deal of coffee was grown in the vicinity, and real good coffee it was. The town itself consisted of a series of narrow streets, while sanitary arrangements simply didn't exist. The most curious spot was a square, for, on one side of the walls surrounding it was a large gateway, surrounded by two wooden lions of extraordinary shape and with several elephant tails nailed to the top of the doorway.

There were a good number of Europeans resident at Harar: mostly Greeks and Armenians, but a few French and Germans, the former living far more like Natives, a good number of them working for the Abyssinians and the others being small traders. The Native population consisted mostly of a mixture of Galla and R'hotta races, who called themselves Harari. There were not a great many Abyssinians, mostly soldiers of those holding posts of authority. All the nabobs of Harar used to meet in the evening at a place they called the Club, which consisted of one large and dirty room, with a broken-down billiard-table and lit by a few smoking lamps. I used often to go down in the evening and play a so-called game of billiards, very often with an Austrian, who was living just outside Harar. He seemed quite a good fellow, but I never could get much out of him about his past history. He, at one time, served as an officer in an Austrian cavalry regiment, and probably left the homeland for his country's good.

In the meantime I did my utmost to ascertain the true situation at Harar for the promised report to the Commissioner of the British Somaliland Protectorate. After a few days I came to the conclusion that the information received by Captain Cordeaux had been greatly exaggerated. There was a certain amount of unrest owing to Ras Makonnen being away at Addis Ababa, but this was caused only by what we would call a gang of hooligans.

After five days my caravan arrived at Harar and camped outside the town. As soon as it arrived I sent back the two mounted Somali askari to Berbera with a report to Captain Cordeaux stating that I did not think there was any truth in the rumours to the effect that all Europeans would be murdered; but that most of them seemed to be suffering from " nerves." The only evidence I knew of such a likelihood was that one night, when at dinner at the Greek's house where I was staying, there was a crash and a large stone came hurtling through the window. It landed on the table while we were seated there. Three other Greeks, also dining with my host, were very frightened. Shortly after arrival they had been rather badly beaten up by some of the local Natives, one of their Somalis being severely hurt.

I stayed for six weeks at Harar and in its vicinity, during which time I paid a brief visit to Diredawa, then the railhead of the Jibuti-Addis Ababa railway, and about 35 miles to the north-west of Harar.

Before leaving Harar I went with our Consul to pay my respects to the Abyssinian Acting Governor, who lived in a rather dilapidated house in the town. We were admitted by an Abyssinian soldier and had to climb up a ladder through a sort of trap-door into a large room, in which the only furniture consisted of a few broken chairs. The Abyssinian Governor was not at all an impressive personality, and it was hard work to make any conversation, even with the help of many glasses of *tej*, the Abyssinian drink, made from native mead or fomented honey, mixed with water. So the visit did not last long, and I came away very unimpressed. During my stay at Harar I often saw minor Abyssinian Chiefs coming in from the outlying districts. They were always mounted on mules, with an escort of about a dozen followers, armed with modern breech-loading rifles. They appeared to be rather truculent and to have no atom of respect for a white man.

I was not sorry to leave Harar, although it certainly was a rich and fertile district, with a good climate. On the return journey I went by a different route, the same by which my caravan had come, and on arrival at Jigjiga my Abyssinian soldiers left me.

III

SOMALILAND AND ABYSSINIA — 1908-9 (Continued)

AFTER recrossing the Somali-Abyssinian frontier, it was my intention to strike south. I hoped to get some shooting, more especially lions.

Now the most usual way of hunting the lion in Somaliland is by putting a " kill " outside a thorn-bush zariba (or *boma,* as this is called in Eastern Africa), and then waiting there for a lion to come on to the " kill " at night. This is not a very sporting way of shooting, and has now rightly been stopped by the Game Departments of East Africa; but, in those days, it was how a great number of lions were shot and it was then regarded as quite a legitimate way of bagging a lion. Of course, if a lion was wounded you often had all the excitement wanted when spooring it up on the following morning.

There are two other methods. One to obtain some mounted Somalis to try and locate a lion and then bring back news to the hunter, whilst leaving about six or eight Somalis to prevent the lion breaking away; and if the lion tries to break, they gallop round and head him off thus compelling him to take cover in some thorn-bush. The hunter then goes out as quickly as possible in an endeavour to get a shot at the lion. If it breaks cover on his approach, the Somalis gallop round and bring him to bay; thus giving the hunter an opportunity for a shot as the lion's attention is concentrated on the horsemen. The other method is to get on to a fresh spoor with a gun-bearer, and generally one or two Somalis, and then track down the lion, as they nearly always lie up during the heat of the day, under the shade of some thorn-bushes. As I said before, most Somalis are excellent trackers and seldom lose the spoor.

Lion-hunting often means hanging about Somali *karias,* with crowds of natives around your camp; also countless camels and sheep filling the air with dust and sand, and one gets very tired of it. Looking back, after my many years' wandering in Africa, the Somali lion, as a general rule, seemed to me bolder than most lions encountered in other parts. I think this is probably due, as I already stated, to their following up the Somali *karias* on the chance of killing a stray camel or cattle; and there were a great many cases of lions jumping over the thorn-zariba at night, and taking sheep and often a sleeping Somali; also there were a great many white men who got mauled. This probably was due to the fact that there were more sportsmen going to Somaliland in those days.

Two days after crossing the frontier into Somaliland I made my camp near a Somali *karia,* and a native reported that there were lions around the *karia* every night. I asked if there were many of them, and, like all African natives, he answered: " Oh! There are ever so many. You don't have to look for them, as they look for you! " On the following morning I found this statement only too true, as I will now relate.

I made a thorn-zariba and put out a " kill," pegging it down to prevent it being dragged away. The " kill " was only about two feet away from the zariba. After an early dinner, I, with my gun-bearer, went into the zariba just after sundown. Nothing came on to the " kill " until about eleven o'clock, and then some jackal came sniffing around. Shortly afterwards hyena appeared, and the jackal immediately cleared off. Suddenly, the hyenas left, a sure sign that there were lions about; and, without a sound of its advent, we heard a lion on the " kill."

It was a very dark night, so I waited for about five minutes to try and get the outline of the lion. Even at such a short distance I could not make out which was his fore and which his aft portion. Unfortunately, I fired at the aft end of the beast. There was a " Woof, Woof," and the lion cleared off. We heard a lot of growling some little distance away, and the gun-bearer insisted that the beast was dead. Anyway, I had learned more sense since the leopard episode, so I waited until daylight before getting out of the zariba.

Not a sign of a dead lion, only a certain amount of blood. Shortly afterwards I was joined by some of my men from my camp, who had heard me shoot. They all came armed with spears and sticks, and also my syce with my pony. Telling my syce to keep well in the rear of us with the pony, we followed up the blood-spoor for about two miles through scattered thorn-bush; and then a lioness suddenly bolted out of some bushes, from about 60 yards distant. I could not get the chance of a shot, owing to the density of the bush. She made a half-circle and came back, lying down in some thorn-bushes about 70 yards distant from me. I could only see her head and part of the neck, as the rest of her body was hidden by bush. I saw her tail swishing and realised that she was a damned angry beast.

Thinking that, at this short range, a bullet could be put into the base of her skull (I was using a double-barrelled .450 rifle, lent to me by an officer), I fired the first barrel and just grazed the skin, as I found out afterwards. She gave a growl and came straight for me at a terrific speed, galloping like a dog with its mouth open. Mind you for a short distance (say, about 50 yards) a lion can go as fast as a horse galloping " all out." It never entered my mind that I could not stop her with the

16

second barrel, so I fired my second at a distance of about eight yards and hit her (I found out afterwards) in the chest but too low down. My Somali gun-bearer stood up like a man beside me, but made an even worse shot than myself, hitting her near the root of the tail.

She hit me with her mouth just above my knee, sending me flying on to my back; and, at the same time, swung round on me, and knocked over my gun-bearer. She took me up in her teeth by the thigh, and shook me like a rat, at the same time giving short growls very much like a dog worrying a bone. I held on to my rifle and drove it down on to her head to protect my knee. She did this several times and then suddenly caught me by the arm with her mouth, so I rolled over on my face and put my hands over the back of my neck to protect it. I remember wondering where next she was going to bite me. But nothing happened. In the meantime the gun-bearer picked himself up and lambasted her with the butt-end of my second rifle which he was carrying. The other Somalis, including the faithful Harshi Jama, very pluckily rushed up with spears and sticks, beating her off. She ran off for about 20 yards into some bush, and tried to charge again, but was very sick and my gun-bearer finished her off with my rifle.

All this was only a matter of seconds. Although it happened over 34 years ago, I can clearly remember every single detail of the mauling. The stock of the rifle, with which the gun-bearer hit the lioness, had a chip knocked out of it with the force of the blows. I have often been asked what my feelings were when the lioness got hold of me. All I can say is that I felt no pain, except at the first bite which was like a red-hot needle being pushed into me, and after that I felt nothing. This was probably due to the severe shock. I have asked several other men who have suffered a mauling from a lion, and they all said the same thing.

I was perfectly conscious of everything that happened and very surprised, after she had left me and I sat up, to find I had about 20 wounds on my legs and right arm. Most of them, of course, were only superficial, many being mere scratches. The worst bites were in my right leg near the knee, caused by her fang teeth. The right leg of the trousers was nearly torn off, and I cut off the remains with a knife. Unfortunately, I had practically no dressings and only some iodoform. I washed the wounds as well as I could with the contents of my water-bottle; then I put on some iodoform, which is really worse than useless, and with the help of my boys,] bandaged my wounds.

I found it was difficult to stand on my feet but, with the help of my Somalis, I mounted the pony and rode back to the camp, where I set to and had a real good breakfast. I was feeling quite well in myself and in no pain. I wrote a note to the District Commissioner at Hargeisa, and

17

asked him to telegraph to Berbera for a doctor, sending this off by one of my boys. At that time I was about 40 miles from Hargeisa and 140 miles from Berbera, and there were no aeroplanes or motor-cars to take one off to a hospital in those days. After breakfast, I was not feeling quite so good while the wounds in my leg had begun to touch me up a bit.

I got the boys to strike camp, and started off for Hargeisa. As I could not ride my pony, the boys strapped my valise on a baggage-camel and I was half-sitting and half-lying on it, but not too comfortable as it was necessary to hang on in order to prevent myself falling off. I went on all day and did not halt until the evening. When the Somalis helped me off the camel I nearly fainted, so shouted for my boy to bring some whisky and a chair, into which I flopped. Anyway, the whisky did the trick and I came to life again; and, as soon as they had got the tent pitched, tumbled into my camp-bed. My gun-bearer skinned the lioness and brought the skin along with me: afterwards I had it mounted and it is still in my possession. The following morning I got a message from the Native clerk at Hargeisa to say that the District Commissioner was at Berbera on Christmas leave; but, he had opened my letter, sent a telegram to Berbera for a doctor, and was sending out a Native dresser at once.

The following morning I could not move out of bed, so I got my boys to cut two poles and lash them to the bed so that four men, two at each end of it, could carry me. The trouble was that I had only ten men, which made us very short-handed with the camels; but my head-man Harshi Jama rose to the occasion and divided them up into reliefs for carrying me. Everyone knows how all Somalis loath carrying any loads, as it is regarded' by them as an indignity to do so, but I must say they were excellent and played up well. On passing several caravans I gave my rifle to Harshi Jama, who held up some of the men, compelled them to carry me, and so relieved my own men. Otherwise I could never have got any distance that day. On the third day I met the Native dresser and so made camp. He syringed and cleansed my wounds, doing all he could for me.

Captain D. S. Skelton, Medical Officer of the Somaliland Political Department, reached me on the fourth day after I was mauled, having come up from Berbera on a trotting-camel. I think, he covered the distance in two days. He was most kind and did everything possible for me under the circumstances, and doped me with morphia most nights. I was carried all the way on my bed, and it was a devil of a trip: cold in the morning, and terribly hot when the sun got up. As it was not feasible to rig up any shelter over my bed, I got an awful lot of pain from my wounds. Anyhow, it was no joy-ride and I don't think I was very far from being planted en route. I met Captain (now Major-General) Skelton again in 1914 at Zanzibar, where he was Medical Officer of Health, when en route to German

East Africa with Jim Sutherland; and he assured me that he thought I would never get to the coast alive. I shall always remember his kindness to me as I must have been a cursed nuisance to him as well as damning and cursing all the time with pain; but he was always patient with me and most sympathetic and understanding.

We arrived at Berbera about the ninth or tenth day, and there I was put into a bungalow to await the coasting boat to take me to Aden. All of the local officials did everything they possibly could for me; while Dr. Skelton and Harshi Jama sold off all my camels, pony, etc. Two others to whom I owe a deep debt of gratitude were my faithful headman, Harshi Jama, and the gun-bearer, whose name I forget.

On the arrival of the coasting boat for Aden, I was put on board on a stretcher. I remember being slung on to the deck by the ship's derrick and then sleeping on deck. On the following morning I arrived at Aden, and was taken straight to the Civil Hospital near Steamer Point. I remained there for nearly three weeks.

The Nuns, who did the nursing, looked after me very well, but I can't say much for the Anglo-Indian doctor. The pain in my knee got worse and it was really damnable. I told the doctor. He said that my knee must have been twisted when the lioness knocked me over and there was water on the knee as it was terribly swollen. But I told him that I had had water on the knee several times through football injuries, but never had the pain been anything to compare with this.

The only incident I remember in hospital at Aden was when the Army Medical Board, composed of three officers—one, I think, a Colonel—came to visit me and report my case. They were dressed up in swords, Sam Browne belts and spurs, and it looked to me more like having a Board to cast an old troop horse than a Medical Board on an officer patient. They did not cheer me up, as I was then feeling far more dead than alive, and that was the last I saw or heard of them.

Eventually we arrived at Tilbury Docks, and I was very lucky to get there, being told afterwards that I was nearly slipped overboard on the voyage. I have to thank the doctor for his kindness and the most efficient way in which he looked after me. The Captain of the ship used to visit me daily and did everything he possibly could for me, allowing a steward or stewardess to be on duty most of the time. Cecil Waudby,. my old friend and brother officer, came to meet me at Tilbury Docks and did everything he could for me. I was put on a stretcher but it was impossible to get me out of the cabin as they could not turn the stretcher into the alley through the cabin-door, so the ship's carpenter came and removed part of the door-way. I was still causing trouble to everyone!

They took me in an ambulance direct to the King Edward VII Hospital, better known as Sister Agnes' Home, in Grosvenor Gardens. This home was established and run by Miss Agnes Keyser at the beginning of the Boer War for the benefit of Officers of the Navy and Army. Sister Agnes was the best friend they ever had. She was at the hospital every day—morning, noon, and night—never missing attendance at an operation, and also expending a great deal of her private money on the hospital. Her sister, Miss Fanny, also visited us every afternoon and kept us all supplied with books, etc. It could not have been possible to find a more comfortable or efficient hospital, as everything was simply excellent. I shall never forget the kindness I received, not only from Sister Agnes and her sister, Miss Fanny, but also from all the staff.

I remained there for close on five months, nearly all the time in bed and doped with morphia every night. After being in the home for about five weeks I had, as a stable-companion in the next bed, Captain H. M. Craigie Halket, who had been serving with the King's African Rifles in Uganda. He had been very badly injured by an elephant which had caught him whilst hunting, I believe in the Lado Enclave of the Belgian Congo, now the West Nile district of Uganda. As far as my memory serves, Craigie Halket told me that he fired at a bull when a cow elephant rushed at him from long grass, knocked him over and jabbed a tusk through part of his thigh, and inflicted another very bad wound in the upper portion of his body. How he survived, I don't know! But Craigie Helket was a pretty tough fellow. I met him again at Mongalla in the Southern Sudan. In the Hospital Craigie Halket and I were respectively nicknamed "the Elephant Puncher" and "the Lion Tamer." I must admit that I did not feel much like a lion tamer at that time.

During my stay at Sister Agnes' Home the late King Edward VII visited the Hospital. He was a great friend of Sister Agnes and took a genuine interest in the Home. On this occasion I had the honour of meeting him. I remember it so well. He came in one afternoon, with an Equerry, and had a chair pulled up beside my bed; and, after shaking hands, said: " Now, my boy, will you tell me all about what happened to you?" This I did. He asked what sort of a doctor I had in the ship coming home from Aden. I told him that he was a splendid doctor who had looked after me very well indeed. He also asked me if I had seen Sir John Harrington; and what sort of rifle I was using when mauled, adding that he had done some big game shooting when in India. He also asked for Craigie Halket but he unfortunately had just had an operation that day and been moved into another ward. His Majesty was most kind and sympathetic, putting me at my ease at once. He was talking to me for about ten minutes; and, on leaving, shook hands and said: " You're a lucky fellow to be alive!" I inwardly agreed.

Another person who visited the hospital was the late Admiral Lord Charles Beresford. I remember him as a genial, breezy and typical sailor. I also had a chat with him.

After nearly five months' stay at Sister Agnes' Home and as soon as able to use crutches, I said goodbye to all my friends there and left for the Officers' Convalescent Home at Osborne in the Isle of Wight. A little time before leaving I was told by Sir Anthony A. Bowlby, the great surgeon who had looked after me so well and also operated upon my leg, that I should always have a stiff knee owing to the blood-poisoning. Sir Anthony died on April 7th, 1929, having been created a Baronet in 1923.

So I was left with a " swinger." This was a great blow as I thought it would mean having to leave my Regiment and prevent me taking any active part in sport or games; but, in after years, I found it was not such a great handicap as at first anticipated.

IV

BRITISH EAST AFRICA (NOW KENYA) — 1909-10

JUST before leaving Osborne Convalescent Home, I went before a Medical Board, and was granted six months' leave. Having touched up the Insurance Company for nearly £200—and in those days £200 was £200 and one got full value for it, very different from these times— I was most anxious to visit British East Africa (now Kenya Colony), and had two good reasons for doing so. First, I had grave doubts about a Medical Board passing me fit on account of my leg and I had hopes that in this country I might have the opportunity of getting some congenial job, and second, to see the game of the country and at the same time do a little shooting if fit enough.

Shortly afterwards I found myself on board the *Adolph Woermann*, of the German East Africa Line, and this was one of the most cheery and interesting voyages I had out to those parts. Probably, I was more impressed as it was my first, and so I will give a short description of the voyage. The passengers were represented by a dozen or so different nationalities, bound for all sorts of places in East and Central Africa, but the majority were German officers and officials.

First and foremost was Sir Percy Girouard, the newly-appointed Governor of British East Africa. He was a grand type of man and at that time about 42 years of age. He was born in Canada and knighted in 1900 for his splendid work in building railways in the Sudan, and as Commissioner of the Central South African Railways. At that time he had just come from Northern Nigeria, where he had been Governor. He was, without doubt, one of the most popular and best Governors that British East Africa ever had: always most genial, cheery, efficient, far-sighted, and forceful. I met him again on several occasions in later years and he was always the same.

On his staff he had two officers, Captain W. K. (" Pat ") O'Brien, Queen's Bays, as Private Secretary; and Captain John Murray, Coldstream Guards, as A.D.C. " Pat " O'Brien I knew well before, as we had served together in the Mounted Infantry of the West African Frontier Force in 1904-5. He was a lively lad and a first-rate sportsman. After Sir Percy Girouard had finished his time as Governor, " Pat " took up land in British East Africa and became a settler. After going through the Great War of 1918 poor " Pat " died about 13 years ago. John Murray was another splendid type who, like " Pat " O'Brien, became a settler in British East Africa; but, on the outbreak of the Great War in 1914, he rejoined the Coldstream Guards and was killed at the beginning of the War. He was most popular with everyone and, if he had lived, would without doubt have become one of the leaders of the Colony.

There were two professional elephant-hunters on board, Bill Buckley and Pickering. Both were going to the Lado Enclave, now the West Nile District, which at that time was in process of being handed over by the Belgians to the British but was still a sort of no-man's-land; it was first-rate elephant country in those days. Some of it is now part of the Southern Sudan, and the other is the West Nile district of the Uganda Protectorate. Bill Buckley was an old hand at the game and he had shot a great number of elephants in different parts of Africa.

In his early days he served during the Matabele War of 1893 and the rebellion of 1896, and told me that he had been detailed to accompany Major Alan Wilson's Shangani Patrol, but had gone down with a bad go of fever just before and so did not accompany it. The patrol was surrounded by the Matabele *impis* on the Shangani River on December 5th, 1893, and wiped out to a man.

Bill was a man with a great sense of humour. The last time I saw him was in 1934, when passing through Kampala (Uganda) with a couple of lorries to Butiaba in order to meet a party coming down the Nile for a shoot in Uganda. I pulled up at the hotel for a cup of tea and saw old Bill Buckley sitting on the veranda. I said, "Hullo, Bill, how are you?" " Oh," says Bill, " I've come up here for a holiday. I've got a kink in my neck from looking up at the coconuts." Bill at that time had a coconut shamba down on the Coast near Mombasa.

One amusing incident happened whilst going through the Red Sea, when it was very hot, as it can be at the end of August. Everybody was sleeping on mattresses on deck. Up came Pickering about 1 a.m., feeling very merry and bright. Seeing what he thought was his old pal Bill Buckley asleep on his mattress, Pickering started to roll him up and down on the deck, but instead it was a fat Hun. You have never heard such a row as there was afterwards, for the Germans took it as a personal insult. The trouble is they have no sense of humour. The feeling on the boats in those days was not good, the German and British keeping themselves to themselves. I always thought after the last War that the feeling between the two nations, whenever I travelled on a German boat, was ever so much better amongst the older Germans who had fought in the Great War; but some of the younger ones were out and out nasty Nazis.

There was a party of very nice Americans on board, all going to a shoot together in British East Africa: Mr. and Mrs. Carl Akeley, Mr. Stephenson, and Mr. John T. McCutcheon, the well-known cartoonist of *The Chicago Tribune*. Carl Akeley was very well-known, both in America and England, as a wonderful taxidermist. His work for the Natural History Museum of New York could not be beaten, and I saw some of it in New York during 1913, when Jim Sutherland and I visited the Museum. Akeley's groups of animals — such as elephants, buffaloes, etc. — were absolutely life-like and the work of a true artist. He was also a very fine hunter. During his many expeditions when collecting for the Natural History Museum of New York, Akeley had been badly mauled by a leopard and on another occasion nearly killed by an elephant. He completely recovered from both accidents. A man of rather reserved personality, but a charming character and as hard as nails, Akeley died about 1938 in the Kivu district of the Belgian Congo, when collecting gorilla for the Museum. His wife, Mrs. Mary L. J. Akeley, was also very charming and accompanied him on many of his expeditions.

Mr. Stephenson was a genial giant, standing over 6 feet 5 inches, and built in proportion, one of the best of good fellows and most popular with everyone on the boat.

Last, but not least of the party, was John T. McCutcheon, who wrote a most amusing account of the safari called *In Africa* and a copy of which he very kindly gave me. He made a caricature sketch of myself in his book. Always most cheery and bright, I met him in London just after the Armistice in 1918. He had been serving with the American Army. I found him just the same cheery good fellow.

Another amusing American party were on board — that of Mr. W. D. Boyce, the Chicago newspaper owner, with his American Balloonograph Expedition. The object of the expedition was to take photographs of game from the balloon. The party consisted of Mr. W. D. Boyce, his son Ben, and two professional cameramen. On arrival at Nairobi they gave a trial run to the two small balloons they had with them. One of the first to go up was Stephenson, who weighed about 230 lbs., but after getting into the basket and all the ballast had been released, the balloon only got up a few feet. Stephenson then threw his boots overboard and managed to get up about 40 feet.

This expedition was in charge of that well-known White Hunter, Bill Judd, who had been hunting for years and knew the country real well. He, like many another hunter, met his death by an elephant near Mason-galeni, not far from Voi. He was a man of great experience with all game, and what happened no one quite knows. I believe the elephant charged him, he failed to stop it, and was instantly killed. As far as I remember, this occurred about 1926. Judd had told several of his friends that this

24

was going to be his last safari, as he was then no youngster.

There was another amusing incident on the voyage which again goes to show how Germans lack a sense of humour. In the smoking-room of the *Adolph Woermann* was a bronze bust of Mr. A. Woermann, owner of the D.O.A. Line, presented by himself. One night after leaving Port Said some light-hearted Britisher placed a slouch hat at a rakish angle on the head of the bust, the result being really funny and giving him the appearance of having just come aboard after a "night out" at Port Said. The Germans again took it as a personal insult to their nation and that did not improve the feeling between ourselves and the Germans on board.

If you went to visit the barber's shop on the boat to have your hair cut, he would ask if you would have it done African style, which means, completely shaved and leaving not a hair on your head. Most of the Germans adopted this style, the result being that it made them look more like "square-heads" than ever. After leaving Aden we had the usual deck sports — cock-fighting, pillow-fighting on the spar, chalking the pig's eye. On arrival at Kilindini (the port of Mombasa), Sir Percy Girouard, and his staff, landed in full uniform to take up his appointment as Governor; and practically all the British passengers got off the boat en route for up-country. So that was the end of a most cheery and interesting trip.

Nairobi, in those early days, was very much in the pioneering stage; mostly tin shacks, with very few stone buildings, vastly different from the present time with its countless motors, modern hotels, and several others on the outskirts.

After a short stay at Nairobi, I collected a few porters, and a mule to ride, through the old and well-known safari outfitters, Messrs. Newland and Tarlton (afterwards Safariland Ltd.). Alas, Safariland, like so many old landmarks in Nairobi, has disappeared. Little did I think, at that time, that I should be so much connected with them in later years as I often used to go out as hunter to some of their parties. N. and T., as it was known to everyone in the country in those days, was run by two Australians, V. M. Newland and Leslie J. Tarlton. Newland returned to Australia a good many years ago, but Leslie Tarlton is still with us and going strong. In those days Leslie was a mighty hunter of lions and, with the late R. J. Cunninghame (then a well-known and leading White Hunter) accompanied ex-President Theodore Roosevelt and his son Kermit-on the memorable safari in British East Africa and other parts of Africa. Leslie did not go with them beyond Kenya, but "R.J.C." took the party through Uganda, the Belgian Congo and the Sudan.

With my porters I made my way to Mukuyu, about 45 miles from Nairobi, to stay with Mervyn Ridley. There I made my headquarters.

Mervyn could not do enough for me during my stay. He is now one of the oldest settlers, and to him and many others Kenya Colony, and the present-day farmers, owe a great debt. At that time all farming was in the experimental stage and there were many setbacks, often a lot of money being lost over these experiments. Mervyn is now one of my oldest friends in the Colony, and never seems happy unless he is ploughing up the land and putting it under cultivation. I always tell him he is spoiling Africa. But it was owing to these old pioneers that Kenya Colony played such a big part in supplying foodstuffs, pigs, cattle, and so on, for the troops in the late War. Mervyn and I had a lot in common, as he was also just recovering from a mauling by a lion, which left him with a stiff arm at the elbow. He again dropped into more trouble, joining up as a trooper in the East African Mounted Rifles and then getting a commission in the Grenadier Guards. He was badly wounded in France in the Great War of 1914-18.

There were two other grand pioneers, Randall Swift and Ernest Darley Rutherfoord, who lived at Punda Milia (Swahili for zebra) and quite close to Mukuyu. They were growing sisal and farming, having come to the Colony a few years previously. Never have I met two men who worked so hard or were so full of energy, working on the farm from dawn to dusk, day in and day out. Occasionally they would come into Nairobi to attend a race meeting, and this was done with the aid of one bicycle, which they owned between them. One rode, the other walked, the one riding leaving the bicycle on the roadside for the other, and then walking on. The distance from Punda Milia to Nairobi was 49 miles. More often than not, they danced all night, hit the road again in the morning, and off straight to work on the farm.

Randall Swift now lives a bit beyond Nyeri, where he hunts a pack of hounds and does a little farming. It was only just recently that he and his wife were staying with my wife and myself and he was as fit as ever, even with his arm in a sling, having just broken his collar-bone for the umpteenth time, as his pony came down with him whilst out hunting.

Rutherfoord now manages Sisal Limited at Punda Milia and is to be seen most evenings playing a real good game of tennis, running round the court like a two-year-old. And, mark you, they are both well over 70!

Mukuyu and the surrounding country in those years was full of game: masses of zebra and wildebeest, and a good number of lions. In the Ithanga Hills, which are quite close, were to be found rhino, buffalo and roan antelope. I did not do any serious shooting, but was out practically all days and thoroughly enjoyed it all. One of the first days out from Mukuyu I was riding the mule, when my gun-bearer suddenly said: " Simba, bwana! (Lion, master!)." I nearly fell off the mule with fright as I saw what I thought was a lion in some rather long grass, about 14 yards away. It turned out, however, to be a young kongoni. The shock was simply due to my nerves still being in a pretty rotten state, after my recent experience in Somaliland.

When it was time for me to return to England, I felt a very different person and left this splendid country with the greatest regret but determined to come back there again. Kenya Colony, as it is now called, has had some very bad propaganda owing to a few unfortunate instances. Also some politicians and others in England seem to do their best at every opportunity to run down the settlers, making them out to be nothing but a lot of slave-drivers, in a mild form, of the African and to have taken all the best land from them, which charges are quite untrue and unjust. In the most cases this is done by people who have never been near Kenya and know nothing of the local conditions. In fact, whenever such people write or talk about Kenya it always reminds me of an old rhino who won't learn any sense and suffers from a bad liver.

On rejoining my regiment in Ireland, I was passed fit by a Medical Board and I put this down, to a great extent, to the few months I had spent in British East Africa.

V

JIM SUTHERLAND: THE LAST OF THE "OLD-TIME" PROFESSIONAL ELEPHANT HUNTERS

THE late Captain James ("Jim") H. Sutherland, author of *The Adventures of an Elephant Hunter* (1913), was, without a doubt, one of the greatest elephant hunters of all time.

I first met Jim Sutherland aboard a German steamer at Tanga in the beginning of 1912. Having just returned from a safari through German East Africa (now Tanganyika Territory) with Captain Sloane, an old Rugby "Blue" of Oxford University, I was then on my way Home. At first, I could not place him at all. Jim was a man of about five feet eight inches in height, very compact and well-made, with a most springy walk, and wearing spectacles· as the result of spirillum fever. He looked exactly like a hard-bitten parson, his English got all mixed up with Swahili (the language of the East African Coast), and I put him down as a missionary returning Home on leave from some out-of-the-way spot in Africa. On asking a German Officer, whom I happened to know, who was the missionary aboard, he replied: "Oh, that's *Bwana Sutherlandi.*"

As I was to find out later, few men had led a more adventurous life than Jim. Born during 1872 in the north of Scotland, he inherited all the love of wandering and adventure for which Scotsmen are renowned; and also had that dogged determination of his race. He left Scotland in 1896 for South Africa with only £500 capital and no idea as to what sort of career he would take up after arrival in Africa. As he stated in his book, Jim inherited the wanderlust from his father, who had spent his early days as a gold-digger in New Zealand and Australia. Of his first 24 years lived in Scotland I know very little, except that Jim was an exceptionally fine amateur boxer. Whilst on the voyage out to South Africa he met Kid McCoy, who was then the middle-weight Champion of the World. Kid McCoy gave a sparring exhibition on the liner before arrival at Capetown, but found difficulty in finding anyone aboard to spar with him until Jim volunteered to do so.

Shortly after landing in South Africa Jim was "broke." All I know about that period of his life is that he was laid up in hospital with a bullet wound which, I think he told me, was due to an accident when cleaning a revolver. He went to Johannesburg and once again met Kid McCoy who asked him to come to his training quarters as one of the sparring partners.

Jim must have been really first-class at the game, as McCoy offered to take him to the United States to fight as a professional prize-fighter; but, as he told me, it was obvious that he was drifting into a very tough crowd, so he decided to cut it all out and start something fresh. He fought several fights as a professional in Johannesburg. Jim, however, was always most reticent about his fights and I could never get much out of him about them; and I never heard him talking about his boxing days or even that he knew anything about the game. He always looked and acted as if the most inoffensive person.

From Johannesburg he worked his way to Beira, the port of Portuguese East Africa, bossing up a gang of Native labourers on the Beira Railway. In those early days Beira was a lively spot, judging by all Jim told me and from what I have heard from the " old-timers." While at Beira, after a good deal of persuasion, he agreed to fight the ex-Heavy-weight Champion of India (an old soldier, he did tell me his name but I have forgotten it) for a stake of £200. I cannot now remember all the details of that fight but, from what I heard and Jim told me, he knocked out the ex-champion in the ninth round; and this, after giving away nearly two stone in weight. In those days Jim weighed about 11 stone. As far as I am aware, that was his last fight.

Shortly afterwards he got into trouble with the Portuguese authorities at Beira, who tried to arrest him for some silly thing and take him to the police-station. Jim promptly knocked out the Portuguese policeman, who had to retire to hospital. He was then about to sail to Chinde *en route* for British Central Africa (now Nyasaland); he made all haste, got all his kit together, and boarded the British steamer. He did not go ashore again at Beira!

On arrival in British Central Africa he started trading with the Natives and was doing quite well until the death of his bull-terrier Brandy. Jim was passionately fond of dogs, more especially of bull-terriers. I cannot do better than quote extracts from the story of Brandy's death as related by him in his book. The whole episode was typical of Jim Sutherland, whose nature was full of romance and sentiment. He wrote:

" One night, one of glorious tropical moonshine, I had Brandy chained up at the door of my tent, while close to the tent was a fire by which sat the watchman, who replenished it through the night as the fire burned low. I had also arranged cut thorn-bushes in such a way that any prowler of the night would have to pass close to the fire ere he could reach the door of the tent and, feeling everything was secure, had gone peacefully to sleep. I was awakened some hours later by the yell of a frightened human being and the snarling growls of a leopard. Instinctively seizing my magazine pistol, which I always keep under my pillow, I jumped out of bed to find a leopard and my bull-terrier in the throes of a fierce encounter, the faithful watchman having long since made himself scarce. Now Brandy was endowed with all the pluck and fighting instinct of his breed, besides being fully trained to take care of himself; and at the very outset of the combat had, with his usual tactics and extreme quickness, managed to fasten his teeth into the side of the leopard's neck. Here he hung on like grim death, his own neck fortunately being protected by a broad brass-studded collar.

"Afraid of wounding my dog, I fired two shots in quick succession into the leopard's hip and another into its shoulder; but these failed to finish it and the conflict continued as fiercely as ever. As they writhed and fought, I could see every movement of the leopard in the bright tropical moonshine; and, seizing the first favourable opportunity, sent a bullet through its head to kill the leopard instantly. Even then, Brandy clung to his opponent as if determined to avenge himself for the mauling he had received. It was some time before I could coax the plucky dog into loosening his hold. When I did so, I found that my bull-terrier's chest and left hip were terribly torn by the leopard's sharp claws. Very gently I cleansed, disinfected and stitched up the warrior's wounds and made him as comfortable as possible, but so badly had he been lacerated in the struggle that it took him two months to recover thoroughly from the effects.

"Poor Brandy, he afterwards succumbed to the bane of Africa, the tsetse fly. At that time I happened to have a store in the district for purchasing rubber, beeswax, etc., from the natives; and, wrapping up the remains of my poor old friend in a roll of cloth, I buried him in a hole in the earthen floor of the store. So upset was I at losing my old chum that somehow or other that store became intensely obnoxious to me; so, putting a match to the place, I sent it with the stock of goods and chattels heavenwards in smoke and flame—a funeral pyre to as fine a dog as anyone could wish to meet. I left the district the same day, and have never returned."

None of the occupations to which Jim had turned his hand seemed to suit; so after the death of his dog Brandy, he decided then and there to become an elephant hunter—he had shot a few elephants before—and as he told me, it was not entirely a question of pecuniary gain. His intense passion for sport brought him to this decision far more than the love of lucre. After the burning of his trading-store, Jim set out straight for Portuguese East Africa to become, once and for all, an elephant hunter.

I know of no hunter who had followed the spoor of " My Lord, the Elephant " so continuously and for so long. He did so from 1899 to 1932, except for three flying visits to England and one to the United States, also participation in three wars.

In 1905-6 Jim fought as a volunteer with the German Forces against the Angoni and Watai tribes in the southern part of German East Africa during the Maji-Maji rebellion, of which the Germans made a very thorough job; but, give the devil his due, I do not think they used Hunnish methods to the same extent as in German South-West Africa against the Hereros between 1904 and 1908. In the Maji-Maji rebellion Jim was wounded by a spear and decorated with the Iron Cross by the Germans. Many were the times during the Great War (1914-18) when we used to pull his leg about this German decoration.

From 1914 to 1916 he was employed with the Nyasaland Field Force on Intelligence duties in the southern portion of German East Africa and along the Portuguese East Africa border. Whilst thus serving Jim was rather badly wounded when acting as scout to a small Force. When Brigadier-General Edward Northey arrived in Nyasaland in 1916 to take over the command of the Nyasaland-Rhodesian Field Force, he appointed Jim Sutherland as his Chief Intelligence Officer. He did most excellent work on the staff and was of very great help to General Northey because of his unique knowledge of German East Africa, more especially the southern portion (in which General Northey's column, designated " Norforce," operated) as it was in this region that Jim had done most of his hunting for ivory. Before the Great War there were very few Englishmen with any real knowledge of German East Africa, except in so far as a few of the coastal and inland towns were concerned. The southern portion of that country was a closed book, except to a few hunters. Jim, however, knew this territory very well indeed. At that time, as in most other parts of East and Central Africa, there were practically no roads and all transport work was done by native porters except in the north, where a good deal of ox-wagon transport was used. No such things as motor-cars or motor-lorries were ever seen, except a few in the larger towns—such as Dar es Salaam and Tabora. For his services as Chief Intelligence Officer of " Norforce " Jim was twice mentioned in despatches and awarded the French Legion of Honour.

From 1919 until his death (June 26th, 1932) at Yubo in the Southern Sudan, on the Sudan-French Equatorial Africa border, Jim was hunting practically all the time except for two short visits to Kenya, when he came down there and stayed with me. In this period from 1919 he hunted in Uganda (on a Government elephant licence), the Belgian Congo and, finally, in French Equatorial Africa. As to the number of elephants he had shot, I never could quite tell. I don't think he really knew himself. I did know, however, that at the end of 1911 he had killed 447 bulls and all big ivory; and I should say that he must have shot well over 1,000 elephants. When he started hunting for ivory in Portuguese East Africa Jim had shot a certain number of cows, being then hard pushed for cash; but he always had a great contempt for anyone shooting cows.

He did most of his hunting in Portuguese East Africa in the northern part of the territory: in Mataka's country, on the Lochiringo and Lugendo Rivers which both run into the Ruvuma River—the dividing line between German East Africa (now Tanganyika Territory) and Portuguese East Africa. In those early days this portion of the country was very little known to white men. Few had penetrated it, and certainly none of the Portuguese ever did; they seldom left their *boma* and the less said about the administration of the country by the Portuguese the better. That, of course, refers to many years ago but now the régime is greatly improved and changed.

At the time when Jim was doing his hunting in Portuguese East Africa there was very little administration outside the *bomas*. In Mataka's country there was none whatever. Sultan Mataka was a law unto himself and openly defied the Portuguese Government. After Jim had been hunting in this area and had accounted for a good many tuskers, he was resting and refitting at his main camp prior to going off on another safari, when news was received from the local natives that a patrol of Portuguese askari were en route for his camp. He at once jumped to the conclusion that they were going to arrest him for poaching elephant. When the patrol was near his camp he had two of his native trackers (they had full instructions beforehand) hidden in his tent both armed with rifles, whilst he himself had his automatic pistol, and was sitting in the veranda of his tent. Up comes the native askari Sergeant with about eight fully-armed men in front of him.

" *Jambo, bwana*! (Greetings, master!) " began the sergeant.

" Well," says Jim, " What d'you want? "

" Oh! We've come to arrest you for shooting elephant, and are going to take you to the *bwana,* Master."

" But," says Jim, " Where is your Master? "

" Oh! He is a long way away, waiting for us to take you to him."

On this Jim called out the armed boys from his tent, covered the sergeant with his pistol, and told him and his men to drop their rifles. This they did without a murmur. He then proceeded with the aid of his boys to smash up their rifles, also made the Portuguese askari take off their uniforms and put them on the camp-fire.

" Now," says Jim, " I'm going to move my camp and you're going to help carry my loads."

Then he gave orders to his headman to collect his porters and strike camp. He made straight for the Ruvuma River and crossed into German

East Africa, while the askari helped to carry his loads. That was the end of his hunting in Portuguese East Africa. On crossing into German territory he gave all the Portuguese askari a good present and, before they left, gave the sergeant a note with instructions to give it to his *Bwana*— the white Portuguese officer who was waiting for Jim to be brought back under arrest. The gist of Jim's note was as follows: " I do not object to you trying to arrest me for poaching elephant, but what I do object to is your trying to have me arrested by a native when no white man is with them in charge."

And *that* was the end of that! Some time afterwards the Portuguese officials reported him to the German Government, but by that time he was well known to the Germans there and they took no notice of it.

I do not know what year Jim started hunting in German East Africa, but I should say it was about 1902. After crossing the Ruvuma River he proceeded to Dar es Salaam (the chief port and the capital) and obtained a licence from the Government to shoot elephants *ad lib*. These elephant licences were only granted as a special privilege and with the sanction of the Governor. I have heard, and seen made, many statements to the effect that Jim received this privileged licence for his good work in the Maji-Maji rebellion. That is quite untrue. I do know, however, that when the new Game Laws were enforced in 1912, all licences for shooting elephants were stopped by the German Government. The German Governor, Baron Von Rotenburgh, told Jim personally that, if he went to the north of the territory and poached elephant in the Belgian Congo, the German Government would take no notice of the ivory which he obtained and would allow him to export it through German territory. As it was not much of an elephant country, Jim decided not to do so. He returned to England on a visit. It was then that I met him at Tanga.

There is no doubt that the years which he spent in German East Africa were the peak of his hunting days. Only at one time was he very ill with dysentery, having to pack up and go into hospital at Zanzibar. From that date onwards Jim was never free from it, and this was really the cause of his death.

After obtaining his elephant licence and roaming over different parts of the country (ending with the Mahenge district) Jim finally settled his main base camp close to Sultan Leanduka's village on the Lewagu River. It was a beautiful spot on the edge of a small cliff and looked down on the river, which was bordered with palm trees, but in the dry seasons it was just a very small stream trickling through a sandy bed. From this camp one could see, for miles and miles, nothing but the *pori* (or *porini*—bush-country); all elephant country and not a sign of any kind of civilisation. In those days, if one struck south, there was no sign of a white man and

33

no trace of civilisation for a distance of about 350 miles—and then only a Portuguese *boma*. At the time very few white men had been into that part of the country and, in fact, there were big areas which had never been penetrated at all.

That was Jim's main camp as pictured in 1914 when I was there. It was ideal as headquarters for elephant hunting; and it had also another important adjunct, plenty of food could be obtained in the way of eggs and chickens for the hunter and *posho* (maize meal) for the porters. Nearby lived old Sultan Leanduka, a jovial old character and a law unto himself; he led a carefree existence and his chief interest in life was *pombe* (Native beer) and women. But he would do anything for a white man— a type which in these days of rapidly advancing civilisation is fast disappearing in Africa. What more could the heart of an elephant hunter desire?

From this camp Jim would leave, with about 15 to 20 porters, for anything from seven to fourteen days' hunt. One cannot do much with a lesser number of porters. It must also be remembered that all *posho* for the porters had to be carried and extra porters taken along to bring back the ivory to the main camp, for one could never depend upon picking up spare porters from any of the villages. In the area where Jim hunted there were very few Natives. Old Sultan Leanduka was an old friend of Jim's and would send out some of his men to different parts of the country several days' journey distant in order to obtain news of the elephant.

Jim had a wonderful aptitude for getting all he wanted from foreign officials. The first time I heard Jim's name mentioned was at Iringa in 1911 whilst on safari in German East Africa, and this was from German officers, who all spoke well of him: " *Bwana* Sutherlandi," as they called him " very good man," " *Bwana* Sutherlandi a great hunter." I also heard his name later at one or two German Stations and think this was due chiefly to his work in the Maji-Maji rebellion in 1905-6. Very occasionally a German officer, or perhaps a German N.C.O. from Mahenge, would visit him at his main base camp near Sultan Leanduka's village. If any did, he would go out of his way to make himself polite; also look after them well in the way of food and drink during their stay. The conversations mostly took place in Swahili, if they did not speak English. Jim spoke no German or French, or very little. It did not matter if he had no use for his guests, he was most careful not to show it. He often told me he did this simply to keep in with the officials so that he could always get special licences or a renewal of an elephant licence.

Remember that if they disliked a Britisher or had anything against him, they would cancel his licence and turn him out of the country. It was a very simple matter for the *Benshinaman* (corresponding to a District

Commissioner in British territory) of the district to bar a man out of the territory, even if he had nothing against him. The *Benshinaman* had only to tell the sultan of the country not to supply porters and food to the hunter, and put other small difficulties in his way, and this would make it impossible to continue in that district. Once Jim overdid the polite business; at least, I thought so. But I was wrong.

On one or two occasions I have seen him go up to some Belgian or foreign official and welcome him as if he were his bosom friend, when I knew well enough that he had absolutely no time for him. After getting what he wanted out of the official, he would take his hat off and make a little bow before leaving. On one or two occasions when I was with him, I used to say, " Jim, you're nothing but a damned old hypocrite!" To which he replied on one occasion: " Politeness costs nothing, and it counts for a hell of a lot!"

I attribute one of Jim Sutherland's great successes as a hunter to the fact of his very great knowledge of the Natives. No white man knew them better.

On one occasion that jovial old reprobate Sultan Leanduka came to his camp and begged Jim to give him some *dawa* (medicine) to make him a strong man as he had just married a young wife.

Jim said " I'll soon fix you up, if only you wait until I write to *Ulaya* (Europe) and get the *dawa*." In due course it arrived and some was given to the old Sultan, who said it was most effective, and that it was *dawa mzuri sana* (very good medicine). Jim used this as a bribe whenever the Sultan came to his camp to get a dose, and told him that he must first send out some of his men, perhaps to some distant parts where Jim wanted to get news of elephant and the conditions (such as food, etc., for his men). Jim told me this medicine was worth any number of elephants to him. He also tried it out on several other big headmen, and the result always produced the information required. It was certainly a unique way of getting information, and one which I have never heard previously being used.

Whilst on the subject of medicine, a rather amusing incident occurred which I think is worth relating. Jim had a bull-terrier called Mosoko, which he adored and which (like his master) was quite a character. On one of his visits from the Belgian Congo, when he came to stay at our home (about six and a half miles outside Nairobi) Jim engaged a cook to take back with him to the Congo. The cook got very drunk one night, went into Jim's tent when he was out, and swallowed all Mosoko's worm pills which he had bought in Nairobi. The cook nearly died. I don't know what else he got from Jim, but I fancy he was a better cook afterwards and was a teetotaller for the remainder of the safari.

Poor Mosoko met the same fate as Jim's dog Brandy. Jim was away from his camp whilst hunting in the Belgian Congo, and left Mosoko with an Englishman, an ex-officer of the King's African Rifles, to look after. Mosoko was sleeping on the end of the Englishman's bed—as he always did on Jim's—in a tent. The fly of the tent was open and, about midnight, a leopard walked in and sprang on to Mosoko. A terrific fight took place, much to the discomfort of the occupant of the bed. It lasted only a very short time, for the leopard cleared and made off, pursued by Mosoko. The latter caught him up and another battle royal took place, about a quarter of a mile from the Englishman's tent. The next morning they found Mosoko dead on the site of the second battle and a few yards farther on was the leopard also dead. That was the end of Mosoko: a gallant fighter to the end! On his return to camp, Jim was very much upset by the loss of his beloved companion.

Jim used to come out with the most priceless remarks and one that he made at the time he was staying with us I think is worth repeating. I remember one night when several of us, my wife included, were sitting down having our sundowners, Jim squatting on his haunches like a Native (an attitude he often adopted) and talking about hunting. He suddenly turned to me and said in a very loud voice: " Andy, Andy, if I had a home like this and a charming wife like yours, go hunting? No, no.—old man! What's the good of your rifle? You can't go to bed with your rifle!" Of course, everyone roared with laughter and poor Jim was so overcome that he kept on saying: " Oh, forgive me, Mrs. 'Andy.' I'm so uncivilised!"

Jim was a bit of a martinet with his boys and expected a great deal from them, and made them work hard. A bad boy never stayed long with him. Kind-hearted to a fault, Jim always looked after them if ever they were sick; and I know on several occasions when hunting out of British territory, if he had to leave or send a boy to the nearest *boma* where there was a Native hospital, besides paying the hospital fees Jim would give the doctor in charge a good present to insure that his boy was well cared for and looked after until he recovered.

VI

JIM SUTHERLAND: THE LAST OF THE "OLD-TIME" PROFESSIONAL ELEPHANT HUNTERS (Continued)

DURING the many years of his hunting life Jim Sutherland had some very near calls. I cannot do better than quote from his book the following episodes:

" I had, in the autumn of 1908, a most exciting adventure with an elephant. All day long we had kept doggedly on the tracks of a herd of five bulls. Towards the evening we came up with our quarry in an open space where the sere grass had been levelled by winds and trampled by game. Here I managed, without any notable incident, to account for four of the herd. The fifth I wounded in the region of the heart as he was bolting full speed across a clearing (where the Natives had fired the grass), dotted here and there with a few stunted trees. Immediately on being hit, he pivoted round, lowered his enormous head and, screaming with rage, charged straight at me! Waiting until he was within about 20 paces, I gave him the contents of the second barrel full in the face. Though the bullet tore through his left eye and emerged on the same side of the head, it utterly failed, to my amazement, either to stop or turn him. The next moment he was upon me. A vicious blow from his tusk sent me hurtling against my tracker, Simba, who was a few paces away to my right, and together we came heavily to earth.

" Ere I had time to scramble to my feet, the elephant had turned, and seizing me by my khaki shirt underneath the right shoulder, flung me high above him in the air. Though rudely shaken, as I spun through the air the awful conviction flashed through my mind that I had seen the last of my hunting days. I landed on the elephant's back, rolled helplessly off and came with a thud to earth, where I had the presence of mind to lie absolutely motionless. I had fallen on my face and lay with my lower limbs beneath his towering bulky body, between his fore and hind legs, my left foot actually touching his left hind foot. The elephant then deliberately turned round and with his trunk caught me by the shoulder, and flung me violently into the branches of a small tree some 14 yards away, the impact knocking me senseless.

" I found myself lying on the ground, with Simba kneeling over me and vigorously shaking me with one hand while he pointed excitedly with the other to where the elephant stood trying to get my wind. I made a desperate effort to try and get on my feet but, owing to the injuries I had received, this was impossible. To my annoyance, I discovered my left thumb was dislocated and my shoulder so badly strained that I was unable to hold my rifle in position. In the melee I had dropped my .577 elephant rifle; so, bidding Simba sit beside me, I managed with great difficulty to place my .318 across his shoulder and fire for the elephant's ear. Owing to the shaking I had received, the bullet went wide and struck him on the right side of the head. At once he slewed round and advanced towards us, so telling Simba to hold my rifle barrel firmly, I drove another cartridge into the breech and waited until he was within 14 or 15 yards of us. Then I took aim, making an effort to steady my hand, and pressed the trigger. The bullet struck him right between the eyes, bringing him to his knees as if pole-axed; and then I finished him off with another shot.

"Early next morning, with the assistance of my boy Tumbo, I got my Natives to make a machilla (a species of portable hammock rigged up out of my blankets). I arrived back at my main camp just as night was falling. Liberal applications of an emulsion of whisky and olive oil, and fomentations supplemented by a course of massage at the hands of my Native servants, who are quite expert, soon restored me to my normal condition. Some of the Natives of the village adjoining my main camp, who had accompanied me on the hunt, on seeing me being flung into the tree by the elephant, felt certain that I had been killed, and spread the news as only Natives can, which in a very short time reached Lindi with the report that I had been killed. About a month later a somewhat garbled account appeared in the *Deutsch-Ostafrikenisde Gazette,* with the following account:

"'3rd October, 1908. From our correspondent. Sutherland, the elephant hunter, has been seriously injured between Songea and Sassawara. He had the good fortune to bag three elephants. A fourth animal, which he had wounded, pursued him furiously, seized him with his trunk and flung him upon his back. Sutherland, seizing a favourable opportunity, leaped off again and put another bullet into the ear of the enraged beast. Thereupon the elephant it seems, crushed some of the hunter's ribs with his trunk and killed two of his Native boys. The disaster occurred towards the end of August.'

"I have often had a good laugh over the ludicrous picture called up by the idea of my waiting for a favourable opportunity before leaping off an enraged elephant's back!"

Jim Sutherland's other adventure with Kom-Kim or the Mighty One, as known to the Natives, is worth relating. Many elephants, more especially ones which are bad *shamba* raiders or who have turned " rogue " elephants, are well-known to the Natives and very often receive a nickname.

Kom-Kim was a bad *shamba* raider and had accounted for several of the villagers and three Native hunters. As Jim Sutherland was hunting in that district, the Natives begged him to come and shoot Kom-Kim. At the break of dawn he started out in quest of Kom-Kom and towards eight o'clock had the fortune to come on his fresh spoor after returning from one of his nightly *shamba* raids. By noon, Jim and his trackers knew by the droppings (which were comparatively fresh) and the condition of the leaves and grass that Kom-Kim was at no great distance. Shortly afterwards the sharp snap of a breaking tree warned them that he could not be more than 50 yards ahead. Yet the bush was so dense that it was impossible to catch the slightest glimpse of him, but Jim advanced with his rifle in hand.

All at once there came to their ears the noise of an elephant crashing and smashing headlong through the bush. Kom-Kim, The Mighty One, had got a whiff of their wind and was off at a tremendous pace. At length, he entered some very dense bush, and began to double and redouble in his tracks. Shortly afterwards Kom-Kim made a wild impetuous rush at them from the rear and Jim fired both barrels into the bull's face at very short range, which sent him swerving aside. The bull came to a standstill a short distance away. Even at this short distance Jim could not see him clearly; but, judging the probable location of the brain, he fired once more but the bullet, instead of stopping him, only served to rouse his anger. He made a furious charge with lowered head and ears cocked and came thundering on. With his second rifle, handed to him by Simba (his tracker), Jim drove another bullet full into the bull's face. This failed to stop him, and Jim was hurled violently to the ground but slightly to the left and half buried beneath the debris of bush. He was nearly trampled upon.

Kom-Kim came to a standstill about seven yards beyond where Jim lay, and began to try with his trunk to get a whiff of his scent. Jim managed to find his rifle, which had been buried close by in the bush, re-loaded it and drove another bullet into Kom-Kim close to the ear-hole, which brought him down with a tremendous crash. Kom-Kim, The Mighty One was no more. The cry was raised: " *Socolai! Socolai!* (It is finished! It is finished!) " by his boys and was taken up by the Natives in the vicinity. Jim had been badly bruised and shaken, but lucky to get off so lightly, and in a few days he felt no ill-effects. I think this goes to show how, at times, a really vicious elephant, which is out to kill, will take a lot of stopping even with a rifle in the hands of an expert. To celebrate the occasion of Kom-Kim's death all the villagers of both sexes and every age arrived *en masse* at Jim's camp bringing food and *pombe*

39

for his men.

When hunting on the Mbarangandu River, while halting in the middle of the day for lunch and to await the arrival of his porters, Jim heard a succession of yells from his porters some distance in the rear. Seizing his rifle and running in that direction, he found one of his porters had been knocked over by a buffalo. It seems that this porter had been loitering some distance behind the others when, without warning, a buffalo, on seeing a human being, deliberately turned and tossed him. Fortunately, though badly bruised, the porter was not seriously injured. With his tracker, Jim followed the spoor and about half an hour later caught a brief glimpse of the buffalo moving swiftly through the long reedy grass. Hastily firing, he heard the bullet's dull thud strike — too far back. Following on with all caution he again came up suddenly with him, standing within 20 yards.

Like a flash, when the buffalo caught sight of Jim and the tracker, he was on to them in a headlong charge. Jim fired a bullet which ploughed through the shoulder but failed to stop or turn the buffalo. Catching Jim a sharp blow with his horn, he flung him headlong into the dense grass, then fell dead a few yards distant. Jim was lucky to get away with nothing worse than a very severe shaking and a rather badly bruised shoulder.

This, I think, again goes to show how difficult it is to stop or turn a dangerous beast once it has made up its mind to kill or be killed. This applies equally to elephant, lion and buffalo. These episodes with elephant and buffalo are only taken as exceptional experiences, not with the idea of making people believe that they are everyday occurrences or that the hunter is always being charged every time he hunts dangerous game. Any hunter who is continuously hunting will invariably be charged at some time in his career and, perhaps, a good many times; but the odds are always in favour of the hunter, and the beasts are nearly always either killed or turned. Yet the risk is always there and the best are liable to slip up sometimes, and that is what makes it so fascinating: more especially with elephant.

The late Major Hugh Chauncey Stigand, that very well-known and great hunter, had the unique experience of being mauled by a lioness, gored by a rhinoceros, and badly injured by an elephant. Mind you, Stigand was no amateur at the game but had been hunting for years. A man of exceptionally fine physique and very powerful, he had been a show pupil of Eugene Sandow in his younger days. Stigand met his death on Christmas Eve of 1919 in the Southern Sudan, on a small punitive expedition against the Dinka tribe, when he was Governor of the Mongalla Province. He had the reputation of being a very fine administrator, as well as a great hunter and naturalist. I never met Stigand personally, but

40

many of his friends spoke most highly of him.

All his life Jim Sutherland had hunted alone, as nearly all elephant hunters did. I was the only white man who had ever been with him for any length of time; and the only other occasion when Jim went out on safari with another white man was with the late Sir Pyers Mostyn, a very fine sportsman. Like the majority who have lived alone for any length of time, Jim rather avoided meeting other white men. The last time I saw him in French Equatorial Africa he trekked with me for about four days to near the Sudan post of Yubo, and I tried all I could to persuade him to come on to Yubo, and stay a few days to meet some of the officials at the station. They all knew him and were constantly asking him to come and see them for a change. But, no! After saying goodbye to each other, Jim went straight back to his main camp and started off on another hunt.

Jim Sutherland was by no means everyone's meat to live with and certainly took a bit of understanding. He was a man who never showed his true character before people, more especially before white men. If asked about his hunting exploits, Jim would always put them off with some joke and then try to switch the conversation on to what a good time he had when last visiting England or about all the "lovely ladies" he had seen. Jim always referred to the ladies as "lovely ladies." He had a great touch of romance in his character and, at one time, always carried a small copy of FitzGerald's *Rubaiyat of Omar Khayyam,* from which he constantly quoted.

He had no hobbies. Whilst in camp Jim devoted a great deal of his leisure to reading; and the last time when I was with him at a main camp, when we came back for two to three days' rest and a refit before going on another hunt, he spent his spare moments in reading or writing up his diaries. He always kept the latter up-to-date with the intention of writing another book. Messrs. Macmillan and Company, the publishers of his first book, had urged him several times to do so.

I do not know much about his taste in literature, but when with him in French Equatorial Africa he used to read the Bible a great deal. He was a great letter-writer to a few friends, but his writing was most difficult to read. Amongst them was my wife after he had met her, and in his letters he often quoted the Bible but never a word about his hunting, even when he wrote to me. Jim was a man with decided views on religion, but never once did I know him go to Church. His views were that the life and actions the person led on this planet would be carried on in the next world. Not a bad theory, either!

Jim often used to give me his views on the next world. I remember him on one occasion coming into my tent at about two in the morning and waking me up. I must say that, at this time in the morning, I was not feeling my best and asked him what the devil he meant by waking me up at such an unearthly hour, and what he wanted. " Oh," he said, "Andy, old fellow, let's talk about when we go to the Back of Beyond." Anyway, what happened was that we called the boys to get us some tea. Then, with some cigarettes, we discussed the pros and cons of the Hereafter—as Jim always used to say.

At the peak of his hunting days which, without a doubt, were when he was hunting in German East Africa and before I met him, Jim was sending out of the country £2,000 or more each year: all made with his rifle out of ivory, and after paying the overhead costs of his safaris, always a very heavy item as anyone who has done any hunting knows. During the latter part of his life he lost money through bad investments and he also gave a great deal of his capital to some of his relations.

If any one thing annoyed Jim Sutherland, then it was to hear people accuse him of using armed boys to help him in his hunting. I have heard such a suggestion made against him. I know the accusation to be quite untrue, for he only had his gun-bearer (whom he always called his tracker in his book) to carry his second rifle; and he often had, as all hunters have, a couple of local Natives to help with the spooring. Another statement I have seen was to the effect that, when trekking about the country in German East Africa, Jim had a very large retinue of servants—men and women. This mis-statement probably arose from the fact that he always let any of his men keep their women at the main camp; being away from their villages for so long it kept them happy and contented; and the women looking after them in the way of cooking, etc., when they were in camp resting.

Jim Sutherland was a heavy-bore man and he shot most of his elephants with a double-barrelled .577, firing a 700-grain bullet and 110 grains of cordite. He generally used a .318 as his second rifle. All these rifles were specially made for him by Westly Richards and Company. He was a first-class shot and very, very seldom did he lose an elephant after firing at it. He knew exactly where to place his bullet in a vital spot. In his will he left me all his rifles and their leather cases.

The last time that I saw Jim was in French Equatorial Africa during 1925 and 1926, when I visited him and we had a main camp together, going off for about seven to eight days' hunting separately in different directions, but foregathering for a few days at the main camp of that area. At the time he was far from fit, so I did my best to persuade him to come home for a rest and change, which he promised to do later on. But it never so happened.

The last few years of his life Jim was a sick man, nearly blind in his right eye and the left none too good. He was shooting from his left shoulder, which he could always do before almost completely losing the sight of the right eye. He was carried by his Native followers, a very sick man, into Yubo, in the Southern Sudan on the borders of French Equatorial Africa,and there everything possible was done for him. I know how kind the officials at that station can be, as I had experience of it when passing through. Jim was looked after by Bimbashi J. R. N. Warburton, of the Sudan Defence Force Medical Services, who was also Doctor to the Duke and Duchess of York when they were shooting in the Sudan, and who was in charge of the Sleeping Sickness Camp at Yubo. He was very popular with everyone and known throughout the Sudan as " Tich." Jim died shortly after his arrival at Yubo, aged 60 years. Thus passed away the last of the " Great Elephant Hunters," following the spoor of " My Lord, the Elephant " until within a few weeks of his death, as Jim always told us he would do. Bimbashi Warburton, whom I had met at Yubo in 1925 and 1926, and also at home, told me all about Jim's death.

Although in the later years of his life we seldom met, yet we were never out of touch with each other up to the time of his death. In Jim Sutherland I lost a very great friend: one of the finest characters, and the most generous and kind-hearted man I've ever met, whose word was his bond, and who was quite incapable of doing a mean action. With the kind help of Mr. F. S. Joelson, Founder and Editor of *East Africa and Rhodesia,* I had a bronze tablet erected over his grave depicting two elephants standing below a palm tree, with the following inscription:

To the Memory of
that
Great Elephant Hunter,
JIM SUTHERLAND,
who died at Yubo on
June 26, 1932.
Aged 60 years.

Erected by a few of his Friends
and Fellow-Hunters.

I have often been asked if Jim Sutherland was the greatest elephant hunter of all time. That question is quite impossible to answer as all the well-known elephant hunters were hunting under such different conditions. I defy anyone to say so-and-so was the greatest hunter. One thing I am certain of; it is that no hunter ever followed the spoor of elephant for so many years and so continuously as Jim Sutherland did. There are so many names of well-known professional hunters that come to my mind: Arthur H. Neumann, Frederick Courteney Selous, W. D. M. ("Karamoja") Bell, Major Philip J. Pretorius, "Pete" Pearson, "Deaf" Banks, M. J. ("Micky") Norton, Thomas Baines and, of course, many noted Dutch hunters in the early days of South Africa. They were all shooting under diverse conditions, so that it is impossible to compare them. If asked to pick out the two most successful hunters, I should name Jim Sutherland and W. D. M. ("Karamoja") Bell; but that is only a personal opinion.

Now there is one hunter, an old friend of mine, "Samarki" Salmon, who I am certain has shot far more elephants than any man living or dead. Up to date he has shot well over 4,000 elephants; a most astounding feat! "Samarki" was selected to conduct the safaris of Their Majesties the King and Queen when, as the Duke and Duchess of York, they were in East Africa in 1924 and 1925, and also that of the Prince of Wales (now the Duke of Windsor) in 1930. "Samarki" has been employed by the Government of Uganda to shoot elephants for the past 18 or 19 years, but he was shooting under quite different circumstances as he includes cows in his enormous bag. A good many years ago he was caught by an elephant, being badly injured and lucky not to be killed, but "Samarki" is about as hard as you make them. He is, of course, a wonderful shot and hunter.

Writing of "Samarki" Salmon reminds me that I met him some years back, when I was out with two clients after elephants in Uganda. The two clients were both young men: one very fat, and the other very lean. The thin one was a very hard fellow and a good sportsman; the fat one was the reverse, so soon chucked in his hand when after elephant. "Samarki," who has a great sense of humour, nicknamed the thin man "all heart and no belly" and the fat one "all belly and no heart." He hit the nail plumb on the head.

VII

AN APPRECIATION OF JIM SUTHERLAND
by
George RUSHBY

I MET George Rushby, a well-known elephant hunter and now serving with the Game Department of Tanganyika, when hunting in Central Africa some years ago. I recently met him again. He was kind enough to write for me the following appreciation of our mutual friend, the late Jim Sutherland, and has generously permitted me to include it in this book. He wrote:

"When I first arrived in Tanganyika during 1921, Jim Sutherland was a name to conjure with, at least, it was to me, a young man still in the hero-worship stage and determined to emulate some of the great elephant hunters. Today one seldom hears the name and, to the new generation the name Jim Sutherland conveys nothing.

"It was not until 1926 that I met Sutherland in French Equatorial Africa where my profession of elephant hunting had taken me, as it had taken him. This was the last territory left for the professional elephant hunter and where he could hunt an unlimited number of elephants on a licence; but the French authorities closed down on this unlimited elephant licence in 1930, and thus put an end to one of the select professions in the world. (The day of the professional elephant hunter has been finished now for the past 16 years and is unlikely ever to know a revival.)

"During the four years I knew Sutherland we became great friends and, as our base camps were never more than 60 miles apart, we always spent a few days together either at his or my camp every two months or so. As a man and true gentleman, Sutherland was even greater than as an elephant hunter; although as the latter he was supreme. In my estimation, and I have had considerably more experience of elephant hunting than many who pose as authorities, Sutherland was the greatest of all elephant hunters since the days of the old black-powder guns.

"The part of the Ubangi-Shari-Chad region in French Equatorial Africa, where Sutherland finished his elephant hunting, was sparsely populated. The methods used were to establish a base camp in which to store one's ivory, supplies, etc., and as a place in which to rest. One hunted out from these main base camps travelling extremely light, with say 20

45

porters carrying a few essentials and food, and returned to the camp either when the porters were laden with ivory or the food supplies had finished after three to four weeks.

"It was a most arduous life, but Sutherland, although well over 50 years, stood up to it as well as any. During the time I was in that area Sutherland headed the list of all seven elephant hunters in the territory in the weight of ivory obtained for three out of four years. There is a lot of luck in elephant hunting as far as the old elephant goes, but such luck does not apply over a period of months or years. Yet he headed these hunters because of his great skill, courage and audacity. It may be vain boasting on my part to say that, in the year he came second in the weight of ivory shot, I topped the list; but I was then 27 years old, extremely fit and tireless, whereas he was years older than any of us and nearly 60. Even so, it is no idle boast but gives a measure of his quality as an elephant hunter.

"Sutherland was one of the greatest characters and finest of men I have ever met. He was once served a most despicable trick by a fellow-hunter, who was in that area for about a year and is well known in Kenya Colony. The following extract from a letter to me from Sutherland on this subject gives one an idea of his character:—' I only hope that the Powers-that-be will give me guts enough to try and be big enough to play the man. Better to have tried to play the game of life decently, even if one feels a damned idiot in not having played it with more acumen! '

"Earlier in life, Sutherland always fired from the right shoulder, but when his right eye gave in, changed over to the left shoulder. Anyone who has had experience of hunting elephants or other dangerous game will fully appreciate how big a thing that was.

"The Natives in that part of Africa are Azande and a pretty wild lot. Some ten years previously they had revolted against the French authorities, who had suppressed the revolt with a fairly hard hand. Whatever the reason may have been, they had a definite grudge against Europeans. During January of 1929 Sutherland was poisoned through his tea but, fortunately, had just finished lunch before drinking the tea. On feeling his legs becoming paralysed, he was able to vomit his lunch together with most of the poison. The poison, locally known as *banga*, is made from the tips of buds from a type of flame tree. It is colourless and tasteless, paralyses the whole of the body starting with the extremities, creeps towards the heart, and takes about six hours to kill a person. There is a local antidote, known as *bakalanga*.

"Sutherland never *fully* recovered from this poisoning, and it left him with a partly paralysed left leg. Nevertheless he continued his elephant hunting on mules, riding up as near as possible and then dragging himself close in for his shot. At the official inquiry into this case it came out that arrangements had been made to poison another hunter, named Simpson, but he was killed by an elephant before full arrangements could be made.

"Sutherland always said he would die on an elephant spoor, and he very nearly did. He hunted elephants to the last, and it was whilst he was on the spoor of elephant that his final illness came on, brought about by the poisoning from which he really never recovered. He was carried out of the bush by his men to the British post at Yubo on the Sudan border. There he died and was buried. And there one day over his grave elephants may stand swaying their huge bodies, fan themselves with their great ears, rumble, and swish their tails."

VIII

UPS AND DOWNS AFTER ELEPHANTS IN THE BELGIAN
CONGO — 1912-13

A S I have said before, I met Jim Sutherland on board ship at Tanga
in German East Africa at the beginning of 1912. We became great
friends on board ship, and I told him that I had serious thoughts
of leaving the Army and going out to British East Africa, making my
headquarters there, and going in for big-game hunting and conducting
shooting parties. We had many a long talk together, generally in his cabin
over a whisky and soda.

"Well," he said to me one night, "why not join forces, get a small
farm near Nairobi and run shooting parties from it?"

On our arrival in London we parted, with promises to meet shortly
and come to a final decision. Jim stayed in London, and was at that time
getting his book *Adventures of an Elephant Hunter* published. I rejoined
my Regiment, stationed at Tidworth. On the first evening after Mess, I
had a message from my Commanding Officer (Lieut.-Colonel the Hon. H. S.
Davey, C.M.G.), who lived in the C.O.'s house nearby, to say that he wished
to see me. I went at once to his quarters. After asking me about my trip
(I had got six months' leave for a semi-official job in German East Africa),
he said: "There'll be no more travelling leave for you. I should like you to
become Adjutant."

That made me come to a final decision. It was very nice of him to
ask me to become Adjutant, but it was not much in my line as there was
too much office work attached to it. So I immediately sent in my resigna-
tion and went on the Special Reserve of my Regiment. It was not without
regret that I did so after 11 very happy years spent with such a good sporting lot of fellows. Alas, not many of them are left. So many met their death
in the Great War. The Regiment was far more like a happy family, from
the Commanding Officer to the last-joined private, and it was a great
wrench to part from them, but a consolation to know that being in the
Special Reserve, I should be required to do an annual training of ten days
and so would keep in touch with them.

On meeting Jim, I told him of my decision, and shortly afterwards,
all details with regard to his book (he had written the manuscript of this
before I had met him) having been fixed up, we decided to leave for British

48

THE AUTHOR ON SAFARI

CHARGING ELEPHANT, TAKEN AT ABOUT 25 YARDS

BLACK AND WHITE STORKS (LOCUST BIRDS)

A BULL GIRAFFE

FRINGE-EARED ORYX

AFRICAN PORTERS, CARRYING ELEPHANT TUSKS, CROSSING A STREAM

THE AUTHOR WITH A PAIR OF ELEPHANT TUSKS (134 LB. AND 136 LB.)

AN INQUISITIVE ELEPHANT, " A QUIET OLD GENT "

AN ANGRY BULL ELEPHANT

BLACK RHINOCEROS

A LION FAMILY COMING TO THE KILL

A LION FAMILY ON THE KILL

A COW ELEPHANT, STARTING TO CHARGE, TAKEN AT ABOUT 75 YARDS

THREE BULL ELEPHANTS

A TYPICAL CAMP ON SAFARI

FERAGI, THE AUTHOR'S GUN BEARER FOR 20 YEARS

AN UNUSUAL GROUP OF ELEPHANT AND RHINO

CAPTAIN JAMES SUTHERLAND WITH IVORY

THE AUTHOR'S LAST ELEPHANT

MAJOR ANDY ANDERSON (RIGHT) TOGETHER WITH HIS FRIEND JAMES
SUTHERLAND ABOARD A SHIP GOING FROM EAST AFRICA TO EUROPE IN 1912.

AFRICAN SAFARIS

by
MAJOR
G.H. ANDERSON
("ANDY")

THIS ILLUSTRATION WAS USED FOR THE ORIGINAL EDITION OF *AFRICAN SAFARIS*. THE POST IMPRESSIONIST DESIGN ON THE DUST JACKET SEEMED SO REFLECTIVE OF THE ERA IN WHICH ANDERSON HUNTED THAT WE DECIDED TO RETAIN IT FOR THIS REPRINT.

East Africa.

Before our departure we both went down to Tidworth and spent a night with the Regiment, on a Guest Night, when the band attends for Mess. What happy and cheerful memories those Guest Nights bring back; how some of us did not break an arm or leg on some occasions, I do not know, as, after Mess, it used to be a bit of a rough house. A pair of boxing gloves would probably be produced, but never was there a sign of ill-feeling displayed. Other very happy remembrances I have are of the Sergeants' dances, and what a splendid lot of fellows they were; the best of good feeling existed between us all.

On introducing Jim Sutherland to my brother officers they, like everyone else on first meeting him, could neither place him nor quite understand what he said. Anyhow, in a very short time he had them all listening to his various tales. Very seldom indeed would he open up except to people who were really interested. They always remembered Jim's visit, and for years afterwards, if I met any of them, about the first thing they said was: " Well, how's old Jim Sutherland?"

We left England in April, accompanied by Jim's boy Tumbo, whom he had brought with him from German East Africa. A few lines on Tumbo will not be out of place, as he figures so largely in our safari. Tumbo — (Swahili for stomach and nearly always applied to fat men, black or white)—had been with Jim for many years. He had redeemed him as a slave. One of the best " boys " I have ever known and Jack of all trades: a good gun-bearer, personal boy, and a first-rate cook. Tumbo was the sort of character one reads about, a happy-go-lucky nature, a huge smile always on his face, and a real tiger to work when he had to.

I met Tumbo on several occasions walking down Piccadilly when Jim was in London, and he always greeted me with that smile that stretched across his good-natured black face. He was always dressed in a khaki coat and trousers, white tennis shoes, and a red fez, and he always had Jim's address written on a label tied to the lapel of his coat (he could not speak English). Now here was a Native, who had never known a bigger station than Lindi on the coast of German East Africa and had spent all his life in the *pori,* walking down Piccadilly perfectly contented and not the slightest way upset by all his strange surroundings.

It was interesting to note the impressions that civilisation has on the mind of a Native. The three things which impressed Tumbo most were: first when Jim and I took him to see a circus which had some performing elephants. That got him beat altogether. Secondly, he could not understand how all the people in London lived. Where did they get their food from? As he said he saw neither *shambas* (gardens) nor *ngombe* (cattle). And the third thing which impressed him was the Underground

Railway. I have heard Tumbo, when on safari and sitting round the fire at night, talking to his pals about the wonders of London. " The *Wazungu* (White Men) go down a large hole in the ground, and then go into a *gari ya moshi* (train), and come out of the ground again as far from here (the camp) as Lindi,"—Lindi being about 160 miles distant. Nothing lacked in the telling of the story, like all Natives. This was followed by grunts of surprise from his pals. Tumbo was never in any way spoiled by civilisation, and it made not the least difference in his character.

We left England in April on a German East African Line steamer, taking with us most of our camp equipment and all our rifles and ammunition. Nothing much of interest occurred *en route;* the passengers were mostly German officials and a few planters bound for Dar es Salaam or Tanga.

On arrival at Mombasa we had to pass through the Customs. In those days it was mostly run by Goanese and Indian officials, and anyone who has ever had anything to do with these officials knows what a trial to the temper they can be. Tied with red tape, they never seemed able to do anything without the Book of Regulations. I remember I had a lot of loose ammunition. An Indian clerk made me count it all and then re-counted it himself; not good for the temper in the middle of the day, in an old tin shanty, as it was then, and more like a Turkish Bath. I did not like to express my opinion of what I thought about it, as this would have made matters worse.

I always think that the journey from Mombasa to Nairobi must be one of the most interesting train journeys in the world, winding upwards through the palms and coconut trees to Mazeras, and then looking back and down upon Mombasa harbour after a few miles climbing, lying in the sweltering heat, as it does during the hot seasons. It is a great relief to strike into a cooler climate. All through the night the train passes over the Taru Desert, which is not a sandy desert but miles and miles of water-less country covered with thick thorn-bush which stretches to the Tana River.

Very few sportsmen in those days realised that they were passing through one of the best countries in Africa for elephants, country where there was a better chance of getting a really big tusker than in most other parts of Africa, and it still is so.

In the early morning you come into a more open plain country, and on both sides of the railway you can see masses of game of every variety: giraffe, eland, kongoni, hartebeest, wildebeest, Grant and Thomson gazelles, zebra and, in those times, sometimes a lion or rhino. If luck favoured and the weather was clear, one could see the snow-capped peaks of Mount Kilimanjaro, 19,520 feet, and the highest mountain in Africa. I only wish that I could get the same thrill these days over that journey as I experienced then.

On arrival at Nairobi, we stayed at the Norfolk Hotel, and I found Nairobi greatly changed from when I had visited it in 1909. It was then a one-horse tin shanty sort of a place. During our short stay in Nairobi we made inquiries about a suitable farm in the vicinity, and went to look at several, but we both came to the conclusion that farming was not much in our line. As to White Hunting, that is conducting shooting parties, it meant hanging about Nairobi, maybe for months before getting a job, for remember Jim Sutherland was at that time little known as a hunter and for years had been out of touch with civilisation. As for my own chances, I could cut them down as just *nil*.

Whilst at Nairobi we heard, in a vague sort of way, that we might get a chance of doing some elephant hunting in the Congo; but most people we asked seemed very pessimistic and said all the Game Laws had been changed. As a matter of fact, and as we found out afterwards, not one of them knew anything about the conditions in the Congo. Anyhow, we decided to take a chance on it and immediately packed up and left for Uganda and, in due course, arrived at Kampala, where we bought our stores, recruited our porters, and set out for Butiaba, about 180 miles away. During our stay at Kampala we met Michael Moses, that genial and well-known " old-timer " character. He had first started life in the early days in the Government service; left that and started trading mostly for ivory, in the Belgian Congo; then took up rubber-planting and cotton, and is now a sort of Rothschild of Uganda.

After collecting our porters together we started off for Butiaba. The country *en route* is mostly Native *shambas,* and the uncultivated parts chiefly long elephant-grass or bush. The Natives of Uganda are much better educated than in most parts of Africa, owing to the good work of the missionaries, who have been the real pioneers of the country. On arrival at Hoima, we were kindly put up by the Government doctor. It so happened that a European policeman whom Jim had known in Nyasaland, was dangerously ill with pneumonia, and the doctor was very much over-worked and short of sleep, as he had been sitting up at night with him. We therefore volunteered to give him a hand for a couple or days in looking after his patient. Shortly afterwards he took a turn for the better and quite recovered.

On reaching Butiaba I was walking on ahead of the safari, when J met the engineer (a Cockney) of the *Samuel Baker,* a ship of the Uganda Marine Service on Lake Albert and the Nile. After passing the time of day, he asked me where we were bound for. I said " the Congo."

" Oh!" he said. "Are you honest?"

" I think so, more or less," said I.

"And what are you going to do in the Congo?" he asked.

" We are going after elephant," I answered.

" Well," says he, " I know you're bloody well dishonest!"

That was *that*! Nothing like a candid opinion.

Butiaba lies at the bottom of the escarpment on the edge of Lake Albert and, in those days, consisted of one or two tin shanties, and is scorchingly hot. Here we met Commander Ferris, Captain of the *Samuel Baker,* who had recently joined the Uganda Marine Service, from England, and in whose ship we were to make the trip up Lake Albert. Ferris was most helpful in every way in getting our kit on board. Whilst we were sitting on board ship, having our " sundowners " of whisky and soda, one of the ship's boys suddenly appeared, very excited, to speak to Commander Ferris. As he had only recently arrived from England he did not understand the language very well, so Jim asked the boy what he wanted. " Oh," he said, " the cook has been caught by a crocodile and eaten!" What happened was that the cook had gone down to the lake shore to wash his clothes, when a crocodile seized and took him off. Needless to say, that was the end of a perfectly good cook! And we could do nothing to help in the matter.

The next morning we left for Mahagi, a Belgian post situated at the north end of Lake Albert, where we hoped to obtain our licences and enter the Belgian Congo. To pave the way we arranged a very fine breakfast on the *Samuel Baker* for the *Chef de Poste,* who always came down to meet the boat at the port. After giving him the best in the way of breakfast that could be provided (which included wine), we broached the subject of entering the Congo at Mahagi. Nothing doing! And quite impossible, he said, as there was no port of entry. So, back we went to Butiaba.

Ferris then said he would take us across the Lake to Kasenyi, a small Belgian post to the south of Mahagi, land us there at break of dawn with all our stores, equipment, etc., and then steam back to Butiaba at once so that they could not send us back to the boat. Accordingly, the following morning he dumped us with all our kit on the lake shore and returned to Butiaba.

Much to our dismay, when it got light we discovered that the *boma* was about nine miles away on top of the escarpment. We started off immediately and eventually arrived at the *boma* only to be met by a very seedy-looking Belgian official, who did not welcome us with open arms, and did not seem pleased to see us. He told us that there was no port of entry there and that we would have to return to Kasenyi and go up the Semliki River until we cut the Kampala-Fort Portal-M'boga road, which was the only route for entering the Belgian Congo. He said we might get canoes at Kasenyi from the local Natives. So, back we went feeling fed-up at again being turned back. We were lucky on our return to Kasenyi to be able to hire about six large dug-out canoes from the local Natives; and after getting all our kit, boys, etc., aboard, we paddled down the southern part of Lake Albert until we struck the Semliki River which at that time of the year was in flood. Anyone who has had the experience of travelling for any length of time in dug-outs knows that it is no " joy-ride."

My only recollection of the journey is the great number of crocodiles in the river. In places it was teeming with them—all sunning themselves on the banks of the river, and there were also a good number of hippo. The scenery in the morning was quite beautiful, the sun shining on the snow-capped mountains of Ruwenzori, the " Mountains of the Moon," in the near distance. Whilst going up the Semliki we threw overboard two prospector's pans for panning gold. We had thought of doing a bit of prospecting. From what we heard, the mention of prospecting for gold was like a red rag to a bull; the Belgians being scared stiff of any Britishers coming into that part looking for gold. So, overboard went the pans, as we thought that they would only prejudice our chances of obtaining an elephant licence.

Both banks of the Semliki were covered with very long grass, and we had the devil's own job in selecting a suitable place for camping. One night a violent thunderstorm blew my tent down. We struck the Kampala-Fort Portal-M'boga road about the fourth day. We were lucky to be able to recruit porters almost immediately to take us to the Belgian post at M'boga.

On arrival at the first camp, which is halfway from the Semliki at M'boga, there was a certain number of *bandas* (grass huts) erected for the use of Europeans. Just as we arrived with our safari, another white man came in from another direction. We went up and made ourselves polite and asked him to come in to our hut for a cup of tea about four o'clock as we wished to get all the information we could regarding licences, etc. The white man was a Belgian doctor, employed on Sleeping Sickness work, and spoke English. I have forgotten his name. As he had not appeared by five o'clock, I told Jim I was going for a stroll. " Don't go far," said Jim, " as he may roll up at any moment."

When I got about 100 yards from the camp, I heard a shot and all the Natives started yelling. Jim dashed out of his hut and shouted to me to come back as he said the doctor had shot himself. So back I went. Jim and I went into the hut to find the doctor stone dead, sitting in a chair with a Browning pistol fallen to the ground by his side. He certainly had made a job of it, blowing his brains out and killing himself instantly. His Native woman was in the hut and half-demented, jumping up and snatching

53

grass from the roof of the hut. We bundled her outside and closed the door, allowing none to enter and touching nothing.

Immediately afterwards we sent off a runner with a note to the *Chef de Poste* at M'boga, telling him that the doctor had shot himself. After the doctor's Native woman had calmed down and become more or less normal, Jim cross-examined her to try and find out the reason for the doctor shooting himself. The gist of her story was that the doctor had been ordered to report himself to the *Chef de Zone* (corresponding to a Provincial Commissioner in British territory), who was then on tour in his District.

The doctor had been sending a few tusks of ivory over to Uganda and selling them there, which was quite illegal. I think this had so worked on the doctor's mind that he would not face the consequences and shot himself. There is no doubt, there was no love lost between the *Chef de Zone* and the doctor; and there was something more behind it than the running of ivory over to Uganda.

Jim and I, discussing all this over a drink later, began to see that we might get into trouble, and had visions of being sent to the West Coast as one of the Natives might easily say that we had shot the doctor, so we both got rather anxious at that time. Britishers were none too popular in that part of the Congo; more especially elephant hunters, as there had been one or two real " bad hats " in this area.

The next morning, about ten o'clock, three Belgians and about 25 askari (headed by an askari carrying a large Belgian flag) turned up at our camp. One of the Belgians was the *Chef de Zone*. We had arranged a sort of breakfast, the best we could provide, all ready for them, and upon which they soon got to work. We told them all we knew about the death of the doctor. They never even asked us any questions; and about the only remark, which I remember one of them made, was that the doctor was a " damned fool to shoot himself," or words to that effect. In the meantime the askari were told off to dig a grave nearby the camp, whilst we were all having breakfast. After breakfast, they buried the doctor and we attended the funeral. The *Chef de Zone* said a few words. No burial service was read and the whole affair was very hurried. I must say it struck me that they were all very callous about the whole show. The *Chef de Zone* was a great big man. He rather struck Jim and myself as one of the bullying, blustering type of characters. After the burial, the three Belgians and the askari left immediately for M'boga, we telling them that we should be there the next day.

On arriving at M'boga and after passing through the Customs, we saw the *Chef de Zone* at his office and asked him to grant us a licence to shoot elephant. He asked us how many we required to shoot, and we told him about 40 between us. Much to our surprise, he granted the licences without a murmur. As far as I can remember, we paid about ten francs an elephant; on the condition that if we did not get elephants, the money would not be returned. In addition to these special elephant licences we each had to take a general game licence which, I think, cost about £20. Having brought about £600 from Nairobi in sovereigns, we paid on the spot.

After a couple of days' delay at M'boga in collecting porters, we struck out north-west, passing through the Belgian *boma* at Irumu, on the edge of the great Ituri Forest (the home of the okapi, gorilla, Congo peacock, and the Pygmies).

On arrival at the small Belgian post of Arebi, one of the officials asked us to show our licences. On seeing the special licences for elephants, he said: " I don't understand this. These licences have been stopped by the Government three months ago." The Belgian Government were always changing the Game Laws at that time. Anyhow, he could not cancel them. Now comes the point. I am certain we got the special elephant licences from the *Chef de Zone* because he thought we knew too much about the cause of the doctor shooting himself. The latter's Native woman, at the time and in her own language, led us to believe that the *Chef de Zone* had been bullying the wretched man. Anyway, the poor doctor did us a real good turn, after he was dead.

After trekking about for nearly two weeks, to find the best area in which to hunt—sometimes in the Ituri Forest, and at others, on the edge of it—we finally settled down to hunt west of the Gombari district.

In one part of the country, whilst looking-round for a suitable hunting area, we were on the march about three o'clock in the afternoon, when suddenly about 60 Natives — all armed with spears, bows and arrows — started shouting at us. They seemed to be in truculent mood. Through one of our boys, who knew their language, we told them that we were not *Bulli Mataidi* (originated from Sir H. M. Stanley's name means " the stone-breaker ") officials, but were out to find elephant and would give them the meat. As our porters refused to go on and the Natives seemed so truculent, we returned by the path on which we had come. They followed us up until dark, creeping along the top of the ridge.

This was the only time I have ever experienced Natives to be in any way truculent. We had a few personal " boys," whom we had brought up from Uganda; but when trekking on occasions they would lag far behind the safari through being too frightened of getting a spear into them. Not that this was likely to happen.

As I said we settled down to hunt elephant in the Gombari district and I will just try and give a short picture of the type of country we were

55

mostly hunting in. Situated on the edge of the Ituri Forest—some parts covered with long elephant-grass, from 12 to 14 feet in height, or dense bush, other parts nothing but primeval forest—up and down, all hills with small streams at the bottom. The local Natives, if you asked them the distance to such and such a place, would say "Oh! You have so many streams to cross." I should say the streams were on the average about a mile apart.

Rain in that country, it can: rain like the devil! This is always the case in forest country, as it attracts the rain; also this particular part of the country was high up—about 3,000 feet—and fairly healthy.

IX

ELEPHANT HUNTING IN THE BELGIAN CONGO — 1912-13

I SHALL not bore the reader (if he ever gets so far) about all the various hunts we had after elephant. All said and done one hunt is very much like another, so I shall relate only a few outstanding instances. We had settled down to hunt in this area as the reports were good of elephant and we had seen many spoor of bulls.

One morning we had sent out two pairs of Natives in different directions to see if they could pick up any fresh spoor or see any elephants. About nine o'clock the two parties returned practically at the same time. One pair reported that they had seen three bulls; and the other had seen one solitary bull. The elephants were only about three miles from the camp. As, at that time, I had practically no experience of elephant hunting, Jim said to me, " You had better go after the single bull, and I'll try for the three." He suggested that I should take our friend Tumbo with me as he had had a lot of experience of elephant with Jim during the old days in German East Africa, which suggestion I jumped at.

After going with the guides for about an hour, we struck the very fresh spoor of the bull, which led us into long elephant-grass. Not more than ten minutes afterwards there was a scream and crash as the elephant got our wind, and passed within about 15 yards of us, but we could not see a sign of him owing to the density of the grass. It is not often that an elephant screams when charging; at least, that has been my experience. I followed on with Tumbo and the guides, the spoor leading us out of the grass into the forest. After following for about 90 minutes, by the signs of the spoor we knew the elephant was not far away; and so we halted in a very small clearing in the forest, which was surrounded by dense bush and creepers, while listening to hear the elephant. (I was not deaf in those days.)

I was standing at the edge of a small muddy stream when suddenly, without any warning, there was a terrific scream and crash; and the first thing that I saw was the enormous head of an elephant bursting through the bush, ears cocked, and coming straight for me more like a runaway engine. At that time he was not more than 20 yards away. I blazed off both barrels into his face, slipped up and fell on the flat of my back. Tumbo fired at the same moment. Down came the elephant with a crash on to his knees and then rolled over on his side at about 10 yards distance. The guides had disappeared into the bush. After putting another couple of bullets into him to make sure, Tumbo and I went up to examine the tusks. They looked enormous to my inexperienced eyes, in those days. After cutting out the ivory next day, we weighed them and they turned the scales at 109lbs. and 112lbs.

Jim had also killed one of the three bulls, about 65lbs. per tusk, but did not have an opportunity to get a shot at the other two, owing to the density of the bush.

That was my first and rather unique introduction to elephant hunting in the Congo. I don't mind saying I was damned frightened and thought to myself: "My God, if elephant are always like this, one gets more excitement than one bargains for and any money made at this job is well earned!" As a matter of fact, I think my nerves were badly shaken and not fully recovered from the mauling I had received from the lion in Somaliland a few years before. I had been on two shooting safaris since then and shot dangerous game, but had no trouble. Anyhow, after a short time I got my confidence back.

We had no further exciting episodes with elephant on that safari, except that Jim was badly charged on one occasion in very thick bush. The animal was nearly on top of him before he was able to fire, but he dropped it and the elephant nearly fell on top of him. After that I had to force myself to go near an elephant, but in the end all was well, although I returned to camp that night suffering badly from shock and had to have a couple of stiff whiskies to recover. Afterwards I felt more or less my normal self again.

When hunting in that part of the country we nearly always had to camp in a Native village as, owing to the country being either forest or thick bush, this was the only available place in which to pitch our tents. The one and only advantage of this was that the Natives would always go out to try and locate elephants for us, for they would sell their souls for the sake of the meat. If we shot an elephant near one of the villages, they would be on it like vultures, the village turning out men, women and children to cut up the spoil. We would not allow them to touch the elephant until they had brought us chickens, bananas, etc., for ourselves and food for our porters.

Whilst camped in one of these villages, Natives brought in a report that they had seen a big bull elephant quite close to the village. This was about four o'clock in the afternoon, so we rushed off, and about a mile from the camp we came on a large open space in the middle of the forest. There are quite a number of these open spaces on the edge of the Ituri forest, and covered in long coarse grass but not the *matete* (long elephant-grass). On reaching this place, the two guides said that the elephant was about a mile further on in the forest, and Jim said: "I'll go after him as quickly as I can. You stay out in the open space, as there's just a chance that he may come out of the forest." So off went Jim at the double, while I went out into the open and took up a position on an ant-hill from which I could get a good view.

About a quarter of an hour afterwards out walked an elephant, carrying a pair of lovely tusks, about 150 to 180 yards away, and moving slowly across my front. As I am rather lame and cannot make very good going, more especially in long grass, I could not run to cut him off and get a close shot, so I took my light rifle and put about five shots into him. At the first shot, he swerved round and doubled back on his tracks into the forest. Shortly afterwards, I heard the report of Jim's heavy rifle close to where the elephant, at which I had fired, had entered the forest, so I said to myself: "That's quite all right. Jim has got the ruddy elephant," and I returned to camp. Jim returned shortly afterwards and we both agreed that it must have been the same elephant, so thought no more about it.

The next day, after cutting out the tusks, we moved camp to another village. After being there about three days, in walked four Natives carrying a pair of very big tusks (two men to each tusk). They said they had found the elephant dead close to where Jim had shot his elephant. It was a very pleasant surprise to get another pair of very fine tusks. They measured 10ft. 2in. and each tusk was nearly straight but, like all forest ivory, was very thin and only touched the scales at just over 90lbs. each. This, of course, was the elephant at which I had shot. We were very lucky to get the tusks from the Natives, as usually they either keep them themselves or take them into the nearest Belgian *boma* for the reward which they get for "found ivory." We gave them a real good present at which they were very pleased; it always pays in cases like this.

There is very little in the way of other game in that part of the country, except a few small buck, pig, and a few dwarf buffalo. I only once had the chance to shoot one, and did so to supply meat for ourselves and boys. On several occasions we came upon the spoor of okapi in the forest, but did not do any hunting for them as we were after ivory. One very unusual thing I did see—a couple of lions right in the forest, but they did not give me a chance of a shot. What they lived on I don't know. Probably pig.

The Natives kill a few elephants with drop-spears, the shaft being inserted into a log of wood suspended from the branch of a tree over an elephant path. A trip-rope (made out of vines) is placed so that, when the elephant comes along and hits the rope, it releases the spear and log which generally falls on to his shoulders. I don't think many are killed in

59

this way. We shot one elephant, which had the shaft of a spear buried right in the top of his shoulder; but the old wound had quite healed up and he was in perfect condition. There was also a certain number of game-pits, mostly made for pig and small buck.

During our hunting in these parts we came across a good many Pygmies. They were known to the other Natives by the name of Tic-a-Tic; but in those days, they were very shy and, when met, would disappear into the forest. They live by hunting and trapping small buck; always living in the forest, and going about in small bands, with their women and children. They have no fixed villages, just a few primitive huts made from palm-leaves. They stay in one spot only for a short time, and then move on to another hunting-ground.

They did not in those days have any contact with the other Natives and kept themselves to themselves, nor would they come near a white man if they could avoid it. On several occasions after we had shot an elephant, they would come for the meat, and that bait was too much for them and overcame their shyness. We always gave them a table-spoonful of salt, which is very much appreciated by all Natives in those parts, as we had a certain amount of salt which we traded for food, etc. In these days, with the rapid advance of civilisation and the opening up of the country by motor-roads, they have on many occasions been filmed both by Royalty and by American cinema expeditions.

There is no doubt that, a few years previously, cannibalism was rampant in many parts of the Congo; but it has now been practically stamped out by the Government and also, to a greater extent, by the influence of the missionaries. When we were there it did go on in isolated cases, as the following shows. A big Sultan, who lived quite close to a Belgian port, was very ill and on the point of dying, and told his headman that, before he died, he would like to taste human flesh again. The headman and some other natives went out into the forest and murdered a Pygmy, the body being brought back and cooked for the benefit of the old Sultan. So before he died, he had his pound of human flesh. I think, in a case like this, it is more of a fetish than a craving for human flesh.

About every month we had to engage a fresh lot of porters, as they would not work longer than a month at a time. We obtained the porters from a big local chief named Allimasi, who aped the white man by having Natives dressed as askari walking up and down doing sentry duty outside the zariba which surrounded his huts containing his many wives. Allimasi was the type of Native who was full of his own importance and imbued with little respect for the white man. The only way we could obtain the porters was by bribing Allimasi. I always did the collecting of the fresh relay of porters, as this left Jim a free hand to go on with the hunting. As far as I can remember, we employed about 50 porters and all these were needed when we moved our camp for carrying our tents, stores and ivory, etc. We used generally to remain in one camp for about five to seven days, according to the hunting conditions, and then moved on to another.

On one occasion, when I was returning to our camp with a fresh lot of porters, I was being carried in a *machilla* (hammock), called in that country a *zig-a-zag*. I always made them carry me when going and coming, because it meant that I could travel very much quicker and as I had all these porters, why not make them do some work? Whilst I was in the *machilla* on my return journey to our camp, the Natives carried me along at a sort of jog-trot; as anyone knows who has experienced this form of travel, they often sing a monotonous chant. Much to my astonishment, at the end of every chant they finished up in a sing-song voice with: " Ho, bloody bastard! Ho, bloody bastard! " I could not make out where the devil they had picked up these English words, as all were raw savages.

A few days later, a white man came into our camp, by the name of Mullins. He was a typical old-time prospector and employed by the Belgians to prospect for gold in the Moto goldfields area north of Irumu. We soon found out where the porters had picked up the disgraceful language as old Mullins (he was about 50), if he required a boy, always shouted out: " Come here, you bloody bastard! " Any Native was a " bloody bastard " to him. Several of the porters had been working for Mullins, hence their language; but, of course, they had no idea what they were saying. Mullins, who was not too fit at that time, as he had an attack of fever on him, stayed with us for a couple of nights. With all his rough exterior, he was a good fellow and had a heart of gold, and would give one anything. Shortly afterwards, I visited him at his camp. At that time Jim and I were very short of stores, as we had practically none left from what had been brought up from Kampala, Uganda. At the moment our chief diet consisted of native chicken, eggs, sweet potatoes and bananas; while the one good thing we could nearly always get was pineapple, but it was a very monotonous diet. We used elephant fat for cooking, and very excellent it was. I have often read in books about the delicious meat one can get from elephants' trunks. I've tried it when very hard-up for food. All I can say is that they can have all the elephant's meat, as it struck me as being very strong and coarse.

I have rather digressed from Mullins. As I said, I visited him at his camp and he was very well off for stores and had a surplus. He was kept well supplied by the Moto Gold Mines, who really did look after the white men in their employ. Mullins insisted on loading me up with all sorts of luxuries—cheese, tinned fruits, and so on. He would not take a penny for it. Mullins was a typical prospector, and like all prospectors optimistic about making a fortune which never seems to come their way. If they do strike a good thing, it is not the prospector who makes the money but the company on which they off-load their knowledge.

After hunting in the Gombari area for about four months, we both got very tired of that country. It has a most depressing effect, and one always has the feeling of being so shut in by the eternal forest, bush and long grass. I have often discussed this with other men, and they all say the same thing. Forest country for a short time is all right, but afterwards they all complain of that definite feeling, of depression. We decided to strike to the district of Faradje, and away from the forest country.

One day, when on the march to Faradje, we met another white man, a Belgian official on safari with his porters, coming from the opposite direction. We stopped and passed the time of day, for he spoke quite good English. He then said that, on the previous day, he had passed four natives carrying a pair of very big tusks, two men to each tusk. They were on their way to Gombari *boma* to take them to the *Chef de Poste*. Then he said that they must belong to an elephant which we had shot. We explained that we had not been hunting in this district, and had never put a bullet into an elephant round this part of the country.

" Oh ! " he said, " I'm certain it must be your elephant, and I will give you a note to the *Chef de Poste* at Gombari."

As he was so insistent, we did not argue the point any more. He then gave us the note to the *Chef de Poste* at Gombari, saying that he had seen the Natives carrying a pair of big tusks that must belong to us, and would he (the *Chef de Poste*) give us the tusks. Now, mind you, this was a man whom neither Jim nor I had ever seen before and he was a minor official in the Government Service. We thanked him very much, taking off our hats and being most polite (it always pays to be polite, especially to foreign officials), said good-bye, and hit the road again for Faradje, never thinking anything more about the note.

After reaching Faradje we hunted around the district for about two weeks. For an elephant country it was comparatively open, with scattered bush and long grass, not the real elephant grass, where you could see an elephant a hundred yards or more away—very different from the Gombari district. After seeing nothing but cows or small herd bulls, and no spoor of big bulls, we decided to return again to Gombari. As a matter of fact, we heard much later and after the safari was ended, that in certain areas of the Faradje district there were several good places for big tuskers. Another thing which put us off this district was the report we got from some Greek traders in Faradje, who said there were no bulls carrying big tusks in that area. The truth was, that they did not want us there as they were trading illicit ivory with the Natives.

So back we went to the Gombari district and continued our elephant hunting there.

Jim and I once had occasion to go to Gombari to sell some ivory to Aladina Visram, a big Indian trading concern which had posts all over that part of the Congo for trading in ivory, rubber and beeswax. They had in charge of the store an Indian who spoke a little English, a tall long slab of a fellow, of unhappy disposition. After having sold some ivory, and poking about in the store to see if they had anything in the way of stores to sell, we returned to our camp, which had been pitched about a quarter of a mile from the store. That evening, about six o'clock, I heard Jim shouting: "Andy, come over here and see this note I've just got from that blinkin' Indian! " I went over to Jim's tent and read the note, which was as follows: —

" Dear Old Jam,

    " I got venal disese. Pleas send medicine for same."

I have read some funny notes, but this was certainly quite unique. He did not mean to be impertinent in any way by calling Jim " Dear Old Jam," but got a bit mixed up in his English, as I suppose he heard me calling him Jim. Anyway, it gave us both a good laugh.

By this time we had nearly completed our licences. It was decided that I should return to England as I was due to do my annual training with my Regiment, while Jim would follow shortly as soon as he had completed his elephant licence. He had shot, of course, by far the lion's share. When Jim had completed his licence, we had collected on this safari about two and a half tons of ivory.

So we recruited a fresh lot of porters from Chief Allimasi, which meant waiting about for a few days as I required about 90 porters to enable me to get the ivory I was taking to England out of the country. Having got all the loads fixed up at our camp, I said good-bye to Jim and started on my way to Rejaf on the Nile, in order to catch the river-steamer which would take me to Khartoum.

I had first to make for the Belgian port of Gombari to get all the ivory stamped for export and the necessary papers. On arriving at Gombari and after fixing up my camp I went to see the *Chef de Poste* about it. He had his office in his private house, so I went up and called on him to know if he could possibly stamp my ivory at once, as I hadn't left myself too much time to catch the Nile steamer at Rejaf. I think the distance was somewhere about 200 miles. He was none too polite. He said his office was closed for that day, and I must come back with the ivory on the next morning. It was no good arguing, as we knew him before— a poor type of official; I think he had been an N.C.O. in the Belgian Army.

So, most politely, I took off my hat and wished him good morning, said nothing, but thought a lot, as he had absolutely nothing to do all day.

The next morning I turned up at his house with all the ivory and also the note which the Belgian *en route* to Faradje had given us, saying the natives had a part of our tusks. After the ivory had been stamped, I gave him the note and asked to be given the two tusks brought in by the natives which belonged to us. Immediately he sent a couple of boys into the store where all ivory found by natives was kept. The boys returned with a tusk each. I should say about 20lb. per tusk. " No," I said, " those are not our tusks. The ones which belong to us are very big. " He sent the boys back again. Presently, out came the boys carrying a couple of lovely tusks, two boys to each. " Those are the ones," I said. He then stamped them without a murmur, and off I went with all the ivory.

I don't mind saying I had no qualms whatever taking the two tusks (they were just over 100lb. each, and their total value at that time about £112). My conscience did not prick me, as I was not doing any individual down, but only the Belgian Government; and, also, the *Chef de Poste* had been most uncivil and disobliging to Jim and myself on more than one occasion. If he had known anything about ivory, he had only to look at the tusks to see that they had been kept in a native hut for a very long time, as they were discoloured by smoke and, probably had been buried, though the ivory was in perfect condition. So next morning, well pleased with myself, I hit the road.

I must say, I know of no more pleasant sight than seeing a safari of porters loaded up with ivory; knowing one has finished a successful hunt and is now hitting the trail for the delights of civilisation. About the second day from Gombari I passed a small temporary Belgian post, where there were a few Greek traders and a *Chef de Poste*. The latter official met me, about the first thing he said was " You no see Mr. Pickering? " I said, " No." " Oh! Pickering *very* bad man! "

Apparently what had happened, as I found out afterwards, was that Pickering when elephant hunting had come into the station with some ivory. In the evening they started to play cards, the *Chef de Poste,* Pickering, and the Greeks. I suppose they all got merry and bright, so, to liven up things Pickering pulled out his revolver and started loosing off in the hut, much to the consternation of the *Chef de Poste* and the Greeks, who promptly disappeared out of the hut. The *Chef de Poste* then got some askari, and promptly arrested Pickering, locking him up for the night in the native jail. Pickering bribed the *Chef de Poste* by giving him some tusks and was let out. He promptly made for British territory. The *Chef de Zone* heard the story and had the *Chef de Poste* arrested. That's the story I heard.

I knew Pickering well, having once travelled out in the same boat. He was a former N.C.O. in the Royal Artillery and had served in South Africa; came up to British East Africa in 1906; was barman at the Norfolk Hotel for a spell; drifted up to Uganda and worked for the Public Works Department; and then went ivory poaching in the Lado Enclave. Poor Pickering was killed by an elephant shortly afterwards.

The only other incident before reaching Aba was that I had considerable trouble with my porters. On one occasion they threw all my loads and ivory down and cleared. I could do nothing but sit down and wait as this happened miles away from any village, but eventually they turned up again, picked up their loads, and continued the march. The bottom of the trouble was that they did not like going so far away from their homes. After paying them off at Aba, they departed quite contentedly.

Waiting a few days at Aba, which is the frontier post between Belgian and Sudan territories, I changed to ox-cart transport, which was organised by the Sudan Government. I think the transport convoy ran about once a week, but only travelling in the early morning and evening. After about four days' trek, I arrived about 7.30 p.m. at the Sudan post of Yei. I was directed by some Sudanese askari to the house of (I think) the District Commissioner. He was Bimbashi P. M. Dove, seconded to the Egyptian Army from The Sherwood Foresters. Dove, at that time, was doing work in the Yei district as well as commanding a detachment of Sudan Army askari, and was the only white man at Yei. On meeting him, I asked him where I could camp, but he would not hear of my doing that and insisted that I should stay with him.

I spent two or three most enjoyable days with him; good food, plenty of drink, and reading the English papers. He could not possibly have been kinder. Here was a man who took me in and did everything possible, knowing nothing about his guest and more especially as I came in with a lot of ivory. The latter was not the best of introductions, as elephant hunters were not too popular in those parts because of one or two " bad hats."

I have had the luck to travel and hunt over very many parts of Africa, both in British and foreign territories, and, in later years, I passed through the Sudan several times and also did two safaris there. I have always met with every kindness as well as help from all the officials who are, in my own opinion, about the finest and most efficient anywhere in Africa. At that time they were nearly all soldiers, ex-Blues and several ex-Rugby internationals. It has always appeared to me, too, that the natives in the Sudan are far more respectful than in any other territory.

In writing about the kindness of the Sudan officials, a certain person a few years ago had the impertinence to write a book after a few months' stay in the Sudan and depicted the officials as if they were a drunken and immoral lot; he also brought a friend of mine into his book. This man, mark you, accepted all the help and hospitality for which the Sudan officials are noted. I hope by chance he may read this or hear of it (if he is still above ground) and take note.

After about three days' stay at Yei, I trekked on to Rejaf on the Nile, Bimbashi Dove coming with me as far as the small station of Loka. One evening Dove told me the story of the elephant hunter, James Ward Rogers, who came from California, and Bimbashi Charles V. Fox, of the Egyptian Army, now the Sudan Defence Force. The episode, at the time, caused a lot of excitement both in the Sudan and at Home, where questions were asked in the House of Commons. I think this incident happened about 1911.

Rogers, who was a pretty hard case, came into the Southern Sudan and was shooting elephants somewhere in the Yei district. This was illegal, so Fox, who was also a pretty tough proposition, was sent with some Sudanese askari to arrest him. Rogers, learning that Fox was after him, cleared for the Belgian frontier. After crossing over the frontier, he camped and naturally thought he was perfectly safe from arrest, which he legally was. This was after both parties had done some very hard trekking. When Rogers was in his camp, sitting in front of the tent, one of Fox's askaris came up to his camp. Rogers pulled out a revolver and the askari, thinking he was going to shoot him, fired his rifle and hit Rogers in the stomach. I do not know why the askari had come on alone, as Fox would be the last man who would not take the risk of arresting Rogers.

The askari returned to Fox who shortly afterwards came into Rogers' camp. Rogers was in his tent in bed a very sick man; on Fox coming into his tent, he pulled out his revolver and covered Fox, saying: —" I'm going to die, and so are you." Anyhow, Fox explained things and they made it up, Fox staying and nursing Rogers until he died a few days later. It was indeed a most unfortunate affair, with mistakes on both sides. Remember, Fox did not know at the time that Rogers was over the frontier as there was nothing to mark the frontier—nothing but eternal bush. I think that is pretty well the truth of the story.

After saying good-bye to Dove at Loka, I proceeded to Rejaf on the Nile and there got on board the steamer *Omdurman*. Dove rejoined The Sherwood Foresters in 1914 and was killed at the beginning of the Great War. He was another of those fine characters to pay the penalty of the Great War.

After a very monotonous journey of nine days, I arrived at Khartoum. The only bright spot on the journey was at Mongalla where I met Craigie

Halket (who was in Sister Agnes's Hospital at the same time as I was in 1909) again, now attached to the Egyptian Army. I went ashore and we had a most cheery dinner. I got back on board late at night, feeling very merry and bright.

On arriving at Khartoum I handed all the ivory over to agents to be shipped to England for sale, and continued my journey Home.

X

CINEMATOGRAPH EXPEDITION TO GERMAN EAST AFRICA — 1914

TOWARDS the close of 1913, after our return from the Belgian Congo, Jim Sutherland and I paid a visit to America with the idea of combining business with pleasure, that is Jim was to give some lectures on big game hunting, more especially on elephant hunting in Africa.

We first visited New York City, and afterwards Chicago. I am afraid that, from a financial point of view, it was not a success owing to lack of business acumen on our part.

The people were most kind and hospitable, so we had a most delightful time in both great places, and were continually entertained at lunches and dinners. Whilst in Chicago we were made life Honorary Members of the Adventurers' Club of Chicago at St. Hubert's Old English Grill in Federal Street, an honour then limited to a total of ten.

After one of Jim's lectures we were approached by a Cinematograph Company with a view to taking pictures of big game and native life in Africa. Whilst arranging the contract with the Company at their office, we had the pleasure of meeting Colonel Cody (" Buffalo Bill "). He was at that time a man aged about 70 years, and with his long hair and fine figure, he certainly looked the part. We had a long and interesting chat with him; he was most charming and unassuming. At that time, he was fixing up a contract with the Company to take pictures of the Indians in the last fight with General Custer.

Shortly after making all arrangements with the Company, we left for England. On arriving back from our trip to America we started to make arrangements for our Cinematograph Safari to German East Africa. It had to be done most carefully, going into every detail of all stores, tents, camp equipment, medical supplies and so on. By the end of March, 1914, we were ready to start. A real good outfit we had, with enough stores to last us for over a year.

Jim had bought a very nice young bull-terrier, which he called Whisky. Before this, I had gone down to Tidworth, where my old Regiment was stationed, for a couple of nights. Sergeant-Major Vesey, D.C.M., of my Regiment, very kindly offered to give me his bull-terrier,

Jock, who was more the type — an old prize-fighter in the dog world, and lorded it over all the dogs in barracks. Vesey was a very fine type of British Cavalry non-commissioned officer, having won the Distinguished Conduct Medal in the South African War for a very gallant action in the field. He was also a fine horseman, and the best man-at-arms at the Royal Naval and Military Tournament at Olympia in 1911.

I had met the late Captain Frederick Courteney Selous, D.S.O., to give him his full title, once before, when he kindly asked me to lunch at his home at Worplesdon; and I spent a most interesting time being shown his fine collection of African trophies. Jim often told me how much he would like to meet Selous, so I wrote to him, and he, with his usual kindness, invited us both to lunch just before we were due to leave for German East Africa. This was early in 1914.

I cannot do better than give a very short sketch of Selous, taken from Lord Cranworth's most interesting book, *Kenya Chronicles* (1940). He wrote: " Selous was justly famous as a great hunter and naturalist, and was the original of Rider Haggard's ' Alan Quartermaine,' and joined up in the Great War, at the age of 62, and fell as a Captain, early in January of 1917, at the head of his Company, leading the attack on Beho-Beho in the War in German East Africa. It was an end after his own heart and among the men he loved so well." He was awarded the D.S.O. for gallantry in the East African Campaign, when he served with the 25th Battalion of the Royal Fusiliers (Legion of Frontiersmen).

After lunch, Selous and Jim never stopped talking for nearly two hours; and it was most interesting to hear these two great hunters of Africa. Selous the hunter and naturalist; Jim purely the elephant hunter. A great deal of the talk was about the " old-time " hunters, whom both had known in Rhodesia and Portuguese East Africa; I can't now recall their names, except one called Bill Mahoney. I remember Selous telling Jim that, when he was elephant hunting in his early days (I think in Mashonaland of Southern Rhodesia), he really could not make much money at it.

I put this down to (a) there were very few elephants carrying big ivory in that part of the country, a 60-lb. tusk being an exception; and, (b) in those days Selous was very badly armed, using a muzzle-loading 8-bore rifle as one of his rifles.

It was indeed a very interesting visit. I have often heard people ask Jim if he knew Selous, and his answer was invariable: " Yes. A most charming personality (two words he always used with regard to people he liked) and the ' Father of all good Hunters.' " This, I think, was a very good summing up on Jim's part.

We had booked our passages on the D.O.A.L. *Tabora*. Just before she called at Southampton, I went down to Tidworth for the night to say goodbye to my old Regiment and collect Jock, also taking with me Jim's dog, Whisky. The next day I took both down to Southampton and put them aboard the *Tabora*, handing them over to the ship's butcher to look after until we joined the ship at Marseilles about eight or nine days later. One incident I recall was that when driving from the Mess to Tidworth station on an Irish sidecar belonging to the Regiment, Jock and Whisky had a slight difference of opinion. They started a real dog fight and both fell off the car. Luckily, they did not come to grips, otherwise I would never have got them separated.

Eight days later, Jim and I joined the *Tabora* at Marseilles. The ship was full of German officers and officials, with a sprinkling of German planters all returning to German East Africa. There were practically no British on board. At Genoa, we were joined by Luperte and Hargon, the two cinema-photographers, with all their outfit of cameras, two up-to-date cinema-cameras and several others for taking still-pictures. Luperte and Hargon were both German by birth but naturalised Americans. Luperte, who was fat and good-natured but not over-energetic had, at one time, served his time in the German Army. Hargon was thin and of a quieter disposition. Both men certainly knew their jobs well. It was a dull voyage, with no interesting personalities on board.

After sailing from Kilindini, our next port of call was Tanga in German East Africa, which is about 77 miles due south of Mombasa. On arriving at Tanga the Governor of German East Africa, Herr Heinrich Schnee, and his staff came on board, having just paid a visit to Tanga. From what I remember of Herr Schnee, he was rather an insignificant-looking little man. He was also accompanied by his wife, who was a New Zealand lady. On the arrival of the Governor on board there was no end of a show: the ship's band playing, all the " Square-Heads " saluting and much bowing and clicking of heels; they all seem to love that sort of a show!

A few days later we arrived at Dar es Salaam. It was very well laid-out, with many excellent stone buildings and an excellent hotel, the Kaiserhof, at which Jim and I and also the two cameramen stayed for a couple of nights before embarking on the *Somali*, a small coasting boat which took us to Lindi. That was the last I saw of the *Tabora* afloat. The next time I set eyes upon her was in 1919, when *en route* to Kenya from South Africa with my wife shortly after we were married; then the *Tabora* was nearly submerged in the harbour of Dar es Salaam. She had been sunk by Germans at the beginning of the Great War, and there were also one or two other ships sunk in the harbour.

As Jim Sutherland was very well known to many German officials, we thought it only polite to go and pay our respects to the Governor. We called on him at Government House and were shown by the A.D.C. into his private office. As we entered the office the Governor got out of his chair, clicked his heels, bowed, and immediately sat down, not even attempting to shake hands. He then turned to his A.D.C., and spoke to him in German. We told him through the A.D.C., who acted as interpreter, that we had come out to take cinema-pictures of game, native life, and the country. I knew damned well that the blighter could speak English, for he was married to a New Zealand lady, so it was simply pure rudeness on his part. You can imagine the conversation was not very lively. After a few minutes Jim and I left the room. On leaving, the Governor bobbed up out of his chair, bowed and sat down again immediately, not even attempting to shake hands. As a matter of fact, I did get a bit of my own back on the Governor.

After seeing all our stores and equipment transhipped to the *Somali*, we embarked after two days' stay in Dar es Salaam, for Lindi, which is about three to four days by steamer due south of Dar es Salaam. The only incident on the passage I remember was that I was sleeping on deck and it was a bright moonlit night. I was suddenly awakened by one of the German ship's officers, who was very excited and said I would get moonstruck. I've heard of this, but never known of anyone affected by the rays of the moon. Anyhow, I did not feel best pleased at being disturbed, although it was intended as a friendly act on the part of the ship's officer.

After about three days we arrived at Lindi, which is situated on the estuary of the Lukuledi River and was a small station, with a few German officials and officers of a half company of askari, stationed there. The first person to meet us was Jim's old " boy " Tumbo, and another of his former boys named Kijiko (spoon). Kijiko was the greatest mimic amongst natives whom I have ever seen. He could impersonate half-baked *washenzi* (which means an uncivilised native from the back blocks) to perfection, and could make one roar with laughter. Kijiko would have made his fortune on the stage. He was also a most excellent personal boy.

We made our camp just outside the station, close to the sea shore. A lovely spot it was, with palm trees all along the foreshore. We had a very busy time sorting out our stores and equipment, and making them all up into porters' loads of not more than 60 lb. in weight to each load; also passing through the Customs; getting the game licences; and last, but not least, recruiting porters, over which the Germans were very helpful. Some of the porters we signed on just to take us to Jim's old hunting camp near M'ponda's village on the Lewagu River—about 190 miles inland. We signed on about 140 porters for the safari to the main camp, 40 of them to remain with us for the duration of the safari, as we should require them when reaching the main camp in order to carry our loads when beginning work on the pictures.

A few lines about the tribes in German East Africa will not be amiss. The Germans were particularly lucky in having such fine tribes to recruit their Askari from, about the best and largest being the Wanyamwezi, around Tabora, the Yao and Walahi, and the Angoni, who came from near the border of Portuguese East Africa. The Angoni have a little Zulu blood in them, the remains of an impi which broke away from the rule of Chaka in the old days. They crossed the Zambesi River and some found their way to German East Africa. They settled there, assimilating the local tribes. Of course, in those days German East Africa was not on the map. As they always do in peacetime, and to save money, a few years before the Great War our Government disbanded a battalion of the King's African Rifles. A great many of the N.C.O.s and men promptly crossed over into German East Africa, enlisting in the German Forces, and many of them fought against us in the East African Campaign; damned well they fought, too! It did not seem to worry them on whose side they fought.

Having recruited about 140 porters, many of whom had been with Jim in his old hunting days, we set off.

Now, I forgot to mention about Jock and Whisky. They both stood the sea voyage well and were delighted to get on shore again. They never really became friends since their difference of opinion on the sidecar, but always looked sideways at each other. In order to keep the dreaded tsetse fly from biting them, we had them put into separate boxes and carried these on the porters heads, and they seemed thoroughly to enjoy it.

The country after leaving Lindi is covered in bush, and some of it very thick, there being a sameness about the terrain right up to our main camp. Like all coast stations, Lindi can be terribly hot, but it becomes much cooler after the first three to four days' trek inland. Our main base camp on the Lewagu River was about 3,000 feet up. In those days there were no roads, only native paths, and all transport had to be done by porters. Now, for the benefit of those who have no knowledge of a porter safari, I will give a general idea of the routine.

On this safari we did rather short marches, nothing over 15 miles a day. For the first three or four days after leaving Lindi we used to leave camp and be on the march by 4.30 in the morning—just before dawn was breaking, with about four porters who were carrying the films. I did this so that they would not be exposed to the great heat in the middle of the day. Jim and the two operators took the road about 6 o'clock, with the remaining kit. It was generally pitch dark and I had a boy carrying a lantern. One morning the *kiongozi* (guide) took the wrong path and,

72

after wandering about for an hour and a half, we found ourselves nearly back again at the place where we had camped.

Going by easy stages and camping *en route* near some village, we arrived at the main camp at M'ponda on the Ledagu River, after about 13 days' trek.

Now, when camping at, or near, a village, the *Jumbe* (headman) would always come out and meet you on the road, as he was certain to hear that a safari with white men was approaching. You would then tell him what you required in the way of *posho* (Matama meal) for your porters and boys, also chickens and eggs for yourselves. He would then show you a suitable place for a camp, and have wood, water, *posho,* chickens, eggs and milk brought in by his men and women. All of these things were put down for your inspection. A regular tariff had been laid down by the Germans as to the price one paid. If a white man did not pay the right price for the food, etc., he would be reported and the Germans dealt with him; and in the same way, if one reported a headman for some mis-demeanour, he also would promptly be dealt with by the Germans, which I think was quite a fair deal.

I also travelled over a considerable lot of country in German East Africa during 1911 and 1912, always finding the natives most respectful and helpful in every way. They also seemed to be quite content and in no way servile. Personally I have no use for the " Square-Heads " (Germans) but do think that, in some ways, they governed the natives well. The trouble with our officials, I think, is that they are frightened to govern in a great many cases. The advantage the German had was that if, for instance, you had to run a native in before the local D.C. he was promptly dealt with on the spot; if serious, getting so many lashes with a *kiboko* (hippo or rhino hide whip); but, if not guilty let off. There was no hanging about. The native understands this system, whereas with some of our local authorities (not by any means all) the native would hang about for evidence and there would be too much red tape, then if guilty, getting off with some very light sentence, which the native simply laughs at, and goes away with the impression that all white men are fools.

People seem to forget that it is only a comparatively short time ago that the greater part of Africa was taken over and administered by the European Powers. Before that time savagery reigned supreme. The Chiefs and Sultans were absolute autocrats, having the power of life or death, and, in a case of stealing, they thought nothing of lopping off the culprit's hand. To a certain extent, this is still engrained in the native mind. They appreciate physical force and think nothing of it, if they know they are being justly dealt with. Educate the Africans, yes, but don't overdo the educational business which I think we are now doing. We

73

are trying to make the native run before he can walk.

The only place of note which we passed en route to the main camp was the very small station of Liwali, about 100 miles from Lindi. We stayed there the night. All four of us had dinner with a German planter and his French wife, both of whom Jim had known well during his old hunting days.

On arrival at Jim's old hunting camp (our main camp), we got busy building grass huts for stores and equipment, also a couple of kennels for Jock and Whisky. A day or two after our arrival that jovial old reprobate, Sultan Leanduke, turned up with his retinue of headmen, also a lot of men, women and children all carrying food required for ourselves and porters; this was a present for Jim, as they were old friends. Though all this food is brought as a present yet one always pays the full value of it, and they know this.

Another very welcome addition to our native staff was Simba, Jim's old gun-bearer whom he had had for many years past. He was living about 100 miles south, down towards the Portuguese East African frontier. He had got the news in the uncanny way all news travels with the natives, that his old master, *Bwana Cherimchoo* (Jim's name amongst the natives), had returned to his old hunting camp.

Simba was an Angoni; he stood about 5 feet 10 inches, thin and wiry, absolutely tireless, and loved the game of hunting (more especially elephants) for hunting's sake. A quiet, reserved African, quite a different type of man from our friend Tumbo. He was a hunter, pure and simple; and one of the few natives I have ever met, who seemed to love hunting more than anything else. He was, of course, invaluable to Jim as they had hunted together for so many years over this part of the country, and between them they knew it like the backs of their hands — from the Ruvuma River (the boundary between Portuguese and German territory) to the coast. On more than one occasion he had saved Jim from being smashed up by elephants; he was also a wonderful tracker and what he did not know about elephant hunting was not worth knowing.

We got everything shipshape at the camp in the way of stores and huts, and discharged all the porters, except about 40 whom we kept permanently. A good many of these men had their women with them, who built their own grass huts and lived in camp.

XI

CINEMATOGRAPH EXPEDITION TO GERMAN EAST AFRICA
— 1914 (Continued)

A S I have mentioned before, the pictures we were out to obtain were mostly of game and native life.

Our main object was to get a picture of a charging elephant — no easy matter, as any old hunter knows. The two chief reasons why it is so difficult to get such a picture are (1) one has to get an elephant to charge; and (2) the elephant must be in comparatively open country to obtain a picture, as it is not the slightest good going into any thick stuff after them on the chance of getting a good photograph.

Mind you, we had two advantages: it did not matter if the elephant were a bull or a cow, as nearly a hundred per cent. of the general public would not know the difference between a bull and a cow; also a herd of elephants, which are practically all cows with a few young herd bulls, are more likely to be encountered in open country than the big bulls, who more often keep to themselves in the thick bush, and cows are much more likely to charge unprovoked.

The terrain round our main camp was all elephant country, covered with light forest or bush, and intersected by small streams mostly running into the two main rivers — the Lewagu and M'barangandu, all these streams being covered on both banks by dense bush and *matele* (elephant grass) which reaches to a height of from 11 to 14 feet. There is a certain amount of open country, which the natives called *dembo*. This was the type of country which stretched for miles and miles round the main camp.

The way in which we used to try to obtain pictures was for Jim, Luperti, Hargon and myself to go out on safari from our main camp for about a week to ten days, taking rations for ourselves and the porters for that period. As it was the beginning of the dry season, we seldom took tents, just our beds and mosquito nets.

I'll try to give a picture of the way we set to work to try and obtain a picture of a charging elephant.

Supposing we got on to the fresh spoor of elephant early in the morning, we would follow it up and, with luck, come up to the elephant in open country before they had gone back into the thick bush. Jim

75

would be leading with his gun-bearer, Simba, and about 30 to 40 yards ahead of the two operators with a cinema camera each, and myself. The porters followed on a hundred yards behind. Now, say we have come up to some elephants in country suitable for a picture; getting the wind right, Jim and Simba would work up towards the elephant, myself following about 30 or 40 yards behind with the cameramen all ready with the cameras. What generally happened was that when Jim and Simba got within anything from 40 to 80 yards of the elephants, the latter would just turn round and slink off quietly into the bush. On a few occasions they would get up-winded and all go off, crashing through the bush, which was very disappointing.

On one occasion, we came up to three or four cows, and one of the cows deliberately beat the ground with her trunk in order, I suppose, to shoo us off. Pure bluff! Then she turned round and disappeared into the bush. Another time we came on some elephants in the bed of the M'barangandu River, which then happened to be practically dry and covered with a sandy bed. In the middle of the river was a small sort of island, covered with long elephant grass, in which six elephants were lying up for the day. We got the camera in position, and out came the elephants in single file. One just turned and saw us, cocked his ears and started to charge; but another elephant came out of the long grass and with its forehead gave this elephant a bang behind which completely put the other off his charge. I tell you we blessed that damned elephant!

After we had been at work for about three to four months, we obtained a charge of a rhino, which we were lucky to get, as there are not too many about in that part of the country. It was not really a bad charge, as the old rhino did not come on " all out " but more as a bluff. Anyhow, that would not matter when put on the screen.

We also got some very good pictures of elephants feeding; and one of a big solitary bull, with tusks round about 100 lb. each, digging with the forefeet for water in the sandy bed of the Lewagu River. We also got some pictures of buck, and a certain amount of native life, but not until we had been at work for nearly four months did we get a chance of an elephant.

One day we came upon some elephants in open country. Jim and Simba went forward as usual, while the two cameramen and I took up our usual positions. Out came a cow, ears cocked, in a full charge. Jim let her come within about eight or nine yards, when he dropped her with a frontal brain shot as if she had been pole-axed. What is more, the cameramen got a good picture! As you may imagine, we were all well pleased and had visions of making a lot of money out of it. This was about the hardest of the pictures we were trying to get.

A few days after this, when I was not present (as I think I had gone off to buy *posho* from some nearby village), Jim and company had come up to another lot of elephants in good country for a picture. Jim told the cameramen to put the cameras in position, and went forward towards the elephants. Out came a cow full out in the charge, followed by another one about ten yards behind. Jim dropped them both stone dead within about eight to ten yards of him. This was too much for the cameramen, who were about 40 yards behind him with the cameras. They elected, as the Americans would say, " to beat it."

Many people when I have told them this story, have remarked: " Well, I don't blame the cameramen for offing it!" As a matter of fact the men at the cameras take little risk; it is the man in front of them with the gun who takes nearly all the risk. Anyhow, one could not blame Luperti and Hargon for offing it when they saw two elephants bearing down on Jim, for they were quite unaccustomed to that sort of life. When I rejoined Jim, he said: "Andy, old fellow, we've lost a ruddy fortune!" And then he told me all about it.

When we were away from the main camp on these safaris, we always left Jock and Whisky behind with one of the boys to look after them. We did this on account of the tsetse fly, which were very bad in some parts when after elephant. As our main camp stood high up, overlooking the Lewagu River, and was clear of all bush for some distance round it, we thought there was little chance of the dogs being bitten by the tsetse fly. After about two months at the main camp, however, they succumbed to the dreaded fly which simply wipes out all cattle, horses, mules, etc. This does not apply to human beings, except where the fly has been infected with the sleeping sickness germ, but it's the same fly. The tsetse is very much like a large house-fly, and the wings are crossed when the fly is settled. We were both very much upset at losing Jock and Whisky, as they had been great companions when back at the main camp. We buried them near the camp, making the boys dig quite deep graves for them and pile stones up on top of them purposely to prevent hyena digging them up. These precautions were of no avail, as after a few days we found that hyena, those damnable scavengers of Africa, had dug up their bodies and taken them.

The only other episode which happened at the main camp whilst we were away was that several lions were always coming round it at night; so one of our followers whom we had left at the camp had a brain-wave and got hold of a lion-trap from old Sultan Leanduke. He placed and set the trap on one of the paths which led up to the camp one night. That night the boys at the camp heard a native yelling blue murder. What had happened was that some village native was coming up to the camp, put his foot in the trap and sprung it. The most remarkable thing was that it caught the boy just above the ankle, and never broke or injured his leg, the spikes of the mouth of the trap not even touching his leg. How the devil he escaped, I don't know! Anyway, they released him and he was none the worse, only suffering from severe fright.

Some time in the beginning of August, before leaving our camp to go off on a safari for pictures, Jim had written a note and sent it off by one of the boys to the German planter at Liwali, asking him if he could send us some vegetables. The boy returned on August 20th, having followed our spoor when we were away on safari about two and a half days' march from our camp. In his note to Jim the German planter said that things looked very black in Europe; that Germany, Austria and Italy on one side were mobilising; and that Russia and France on the other side were doing the same. He thought that war was quite probable between these nations. He also said that England might be drawn into the trouble. (He was a bit out about Italy.)

This was somewhat of a bombshell to all of us; we decided there and then to get back to the main camp. I left by another route, to get the natives from a village to bring us some *posho* to the main camp as soon as possible, in case we required it for our porters in the event of war and having to clear out of German East Africa immediately. The next day, when crossing the sandy bed of a dry river, I saw the spoor of a white man (no natives ever wore boots in those parts), and I wondered whatever brought a white man down to that part of the country. Shortly afterwards I passed a great many natives carrying *posho*. I asked where they were taking it, they said that a white man had come from Mahenge to give orders that all *posho* had to be brought in to the *boma*. I must say that news did not look too good, so I hit the trail as rapidly as possible for our main camp.

I reached there about noon on the next day (August 23rd), practically at the same time as Jim and the rest of the party arrived. Shortly afterwards, when we were having lunch, a native in uniform from Mahenge Station (about 35 miles distant) walked into our camp, with a letter. On opening the letter, which was addressed to Messrs. Sutherland, Anderson, Luperti and Hargon, we read:—

"As the colony is in a state of war, you are hereby ordered to report yourselves at Mahenge Station as soon as possible." (Sgd.) Von Gravotte.

That put the finishing touch on it. We realised that Germany and England were at war, which confirmed the contents of the other letter we had received from the German planter at Liwali. We knew it was war. Never a word in Von Gravotte's letter about England being mixed up in it or even what war was taking place.

We then wrote a reply and addressed it to Von Gravotte in which it was stated that we hoped to have the pleasure of seeing him in the course of a few days but should be delayed as there were insufficient porters to lift all our loads from the camp. But, as soon as we had obtained some more porters from Sultan Leanduke, we would come to Mahenge Station as quickly as possible. We then gave the native from Von Gravotte the note, and told him to give our salaams to the *Bwana mkubwa* (the Great Master) and say that we should be at Mahenge shortly, just as soon as more porters had been collected.

Jim and I had decided beforehand, in the event of war, to make a bolt for Portuguese East Africa—a distance of about 280 miles from the main camp, but roughly 300 miles by the route which we eventually took. We asked Luperti and Hargon what they wished to do, and also pointed out to them that being American citizens they could go to Mahenge *boma* and leave the country without any difficulty. But if they decided to come with us, they would probably have a rough trip and must be implicitly under our orders. They decided at once to accompany us.

For some unknown reason, the jovial old Sultan Leanduke with all his headmen turned up at our camp whilst we were in the middle of making up our loads for an early start the next morning. We then had about 40 porters and told them we were going off the next day on another safari to take more pictures. As we happened to have more whisky than we required, and in order to get rid of old Sultan Leanduke, we filled him and his headmen up with whisky. They were supposed to be Mohamedans, who by the Islamic religious tenets were forbidden to touch strong drink; anyhow, it did not seem to stop them from putting away a lot of real good whisky. In a short space of time, the old Sultan and his headmen left in a most hilarious state. Sultan Leanduke was half-carried out of camp by his headmen. Another reason why we did this was that in case any native from Mahenge Station asked them what we were doing, the Sultan and his headmen would be past knowing or caring about any of our activities. They also took away several bottles of whisky — Fortnum and Mason's best, too. But what a waste of good whisky!

Having made up all our most important loads, cutting down the weight to about 40 or 45 lb. per load, we had them all laid out ready for an early start next morning. We told all our boys that we were going off on another safari for pictures to a new part of the country, much farther away, so were not taking our usual few days' rest in camp but leaving very early the next morning.

Our personal boys called us with the usual cup of tea at three o'clock next morning, it being then bright moonlight. On getting up and calling the porters, we found that the majority of them had bolted during the night, and only six to eight remained. The reason for this desertion was that they had got news from the coast, in the uncanny way in which, as I have said before, news travels rapidly among natives, that the *Wazungu* (Europeans) were fighting among themselves; that is to say, the *Germani* and *Ingalasa* (as the natives called the Germans and ourselves)! Their point of view was that, if the Germans caught them helping us to escape, they would be punished, so that's what decided them to clear out, nor can one blame them. A great many of them were owed several months' wages, for some preferred not to draw any of their wages until the conclusion of the safari.

As can be imagined, this was what Tommy calls a " fair box-up "; he also has another name which more aptly expresses it. It meant that we had to chuck away most of our loads of food, etc., as we had to take the cameras, rifles, and a certain amount of ammunition with us. This left us with only sufficient porters to carry the bare necessities, such as blankets (no valises) and food, but little enough, too, of that. All this was done in an awful rush, as we were so afraid that a German patrol might have come on its way to our camp with the intention of arresting us. Our personal boys, with the exception of two, had not run away, so at about four o'clock in the morning we hit the long trail for Portuguese East Africa, leaving all the lamps burning in our tents.

XII

OUR ESCAPE FROM GERMAN EAST AFRICA — 1914

IT was a bright moonlight night, so we had no difficulty in following the native paths. For the first two or three miles we followed the Lewagu River, walking in water which at times was only about one or two feet in depth, and just a small stream down the sandy bed of the river. The formation we went in was, Jim and Simba guiding, the safari in single file, whilst I did a rearguard to the porters in order to see that they kept well closed up and on no account would I allow them to fall out. Luperti and Hargon generally walked in the rear. We used to do about one and a quarter hours, and then halted for a ten-minute rest.

After about three or four miles down the Lewagu River, we cut across the *pori* and, as at this time the grass was very dry, we fired it so that any patrol following us could not find our spoor. At about 6.30 p.m. we camped, which just meant lying down in our blankets after having our food. I think for the first three days we must have touched 40 miles a day, as we were lucky enough to have a moon to help us in the early morning.

The second or third day out Jim heard the porters talking among themselves, and saying: "Tonight, when we put down the white man's loads, and when it gets dark, we will run away to our homes. The *Germani* will punish us for helping them to escape." Now, as luck would have it, we had some thin porters' rope in one of the boxes, used for lashing up the loads. Why we had it, I don't know.

So when the porters put down their loads that night to make camp, we got the rope and tied them neck to neck (like ringing horses), so as to prevent them from bolting. They all took it in very good part, and seemed much amused, not resenting our action in any way. From that time onwards, and until we crossed into Portuguese East Africa, we roped them up every night; whilst Jim and I took it in turns to do a guard warning our natives that if they tried to clear we would shoot them. Luperti and Hargon were not in a fit state to do their turn. I must say Jim and I felt this was about the worst part of the trip.

The fifth day on the trek we had to put into a big village to get *posho* for our porters and chickens for ourselves. I don't suppose we stayed more than three-quarters of an hour. We got all the food required and paid its full value to the *Jumbe*. After about the fifth day out practically all our

81

stores were finished, also the one bottle of whisky, which was a calamity. We had made rather a mix-up with our stores on the morning when leaving the base camp, as everything was in such a rush and confusion owing to all the porters having bolted. We might have brought a little more, but not nearly sufficient to last for our journey. Anyhow, we had to make the best of it and lived mostly on *ugali*—a sort of native porridge made out of *posho*. One thing that did last us was tea, and never did it taste so good! As we avoided all native paths and villages, travelling practically all the time on elephant paths, the distance (so Jim and I reckoned) to the Portuguese border was about 300 miles.

The country we travelled through was mostly what is called light forest; sometimes fairly flat, but, at others, up and down. Our one difficulty was the trouble to obtain water when making camp; but we got it at most places, sometimes having to dig down for a few feet into the sandy bed of a stream. There was one landmark which could be seen for miles— Itungwe Hill. It is a solitary hill situated, I should say, about 80 miles from the frontier of Portuguese East Africa. That damned hill! One used to see it for days and the hill never seemed to get any closer; this was just the same after we had passed it, as the hill always seemed to be sitting on top of one.

On the early morning of the tenth day out from the main camp we crossed the Ruvuma River into Portuguese territory, at one of the drifts, the name of which I cannot now remember. The Ruvuma, where we crossed, was about 100 yards in width, and the drift about three to four feet in depth, and right glad we were to get over it into Portuguese East Africa, out of the land of the Hun!

We had covered about 300 miles in ten days which was not bad going with porters. Of course, they all carried light loads. We had very little trouble with them, but I am afraid on two occasions one had to be rather harsh as they refused to pick up their loads. Poor devils, I felt rather sorry for them as they had had a hard trip! But it was imperative to force them on the trail, as any delay might mean that some of the German patrols might come up with us.

Probably the reader will want to know if the Germans made any effort to arrest us. We did not hear anything at the time, but later, during the war, we heard news from German prisoners, and Jim also got a certain amount of information from the natives when doing intelligence work in Portuguese East Africa. It was as follows: —

A patrol of two Germans and about 20 askari waited on the Mahenge road for us to come to the *boma*, having been despatched by Von Gravotte. Why on earth they never came to our camp, I can't think. The story I heard was that Von Gravotte got properly told off by General Von Lettow-

Vorbeck, the German Commander-in-Chief, for allowing us to escape. The patrol on the Mahenge road, after waiting for some time to arrest us and finding we did not turn up, came down to our camp and then tried to follow our spoor. They were unable to do so as we had followed the water in the Lewagu River. Another patrol was sent out from Songea *boma,* about 50 to 60 miles west from the village where we went to collect food, and just missed us by a day. Two other patrols were sent to the Ruvuma River to watch all the drifts but, by the greatest good luck, we crossed at one which was not guarded.

Now, having crossed into Portuguese East Africa, we were in neutral territory. We pushed on for about another 15 miles before camping, and did so for two reasons. One was, we heard rumours from some natives, met after crossing the Ruvuma, that a patrol of Germans and askari had shot up a small station down the Ruvuma River and killed a Portuguese. If this was true or not I do not know. Anyhow we were taking no risks. So we pushed on. The other reason was that we wanted to recruit fresh porters and allow our porters to return to their homes. So we camped near to a large village in order to get relief porters. This we did with practically no delay, leaving again at noon on the following day.

As we had very little cash on us, each of the porters was given a " chit " to the manager of the German East African Bank at Lindi, where we had credit, to ask him kindly to pay every man all that was owed to him. We heard afterwards that the bank paid in full. The porters left us in a most cheery mood, not bearing us the slightest grudge. Whilst at Mahenge Station in 1923 when I was hunting elephants on a Government licence, and was recruiting porters for my safari, a native came up and saluted me with a smile all over his face, " *Jambo, bwana!* " (Greetings, master!) he said in Swahili, " You don't remember me? " Nor did I immediately. Then he went on to say: " You and *ndugu yako* (your brother, meaning Jim, and a name often given by natives to white men who are always travelling together or are friends), tied me up by the neck when on safari with you." I then remembered him and he joined my safari as a porter; and well he did his job.

Just about this time we heard rumours from the natives that a white man had been wounded by the German askari in German East territory, and not far from where we had crossed the Ruvuma River, but had escaped into Portuguese East Africa and made his way towards Nyasaland. This rumour, I shall explain later, proved to be true, as it turned out to be Major Philip J. Pretorius, the famous scout and hunter.

We still had another 200 miles' trek after crossing the Ruvuma River before we reached Fort Johnston in Nyasaland, situated on the southern shores of Lake Nyasa. So, after collecting porters and a short delay, we

83

hit the road again, and about the fourth day we passed through the Mission Station at Mtonia. There we were most hospitably received by Archdeacon Eyre, who gave us what he could in the way of stores and also a very good lunch.

Archdeacon Eyre was a charming old gentleman and a well-known character in those parts. In his younger days he had spent all his life at sea, then retired to become a missionary. Prior to retirement he was a captain in the Merchant Service. Jim had met him before, in his early days when hunting in Portuguese East Africa. At the time we met him the Archdeacon must have been well over 70, but as tough as you make 'em and thought nothing of covering a 20-mile trek a day. He dressed and looked more like a sailor than a missionary. He was respected by all who knew him, both whites and natives. I met him again, about three years later, in Portuguese East Africa during the war; he was just the same, as cheery and charming as ever.

A few days later we passed through a small Portuguese Station and were hospitably received by the Portuguese official in charge. The country through which we were then passing seemed very similar to the country in German East Africa—light forest and bush. The going was good, fairly flat, and all on native paths.

On or about the twelfth day's trek after crossing the Ruvuma River, and just before crossing the frontier of Portuguese East Africa into Nyasaland, we noticed that several villages we passed were completely deserted, only perhaps a few old and decrepit women being left behind. I discussed this with Jim. Neither of us could understand it, nor could we get anything out of the women who were left in the villages, but on the following day, however, we were to find out the reason for it all.

About ten o'clock in the morning, when on the march, I was ahead with Jim as it was no longer necessary for me to be always behind to keep the porters up. We suddenly encountered a white man, followed by a native, carrying a pick, spade and prospector's pan, and coming from the opposite direction. He seemed very surprised to see us, and we said, " Good morning." " Good God! " he said, " I thought you were Germans." He seemed quite relieved and even pleased to see us. He turned out to be Mr. Martin, who ran the local hotel at Fort Johnston.

He gave us the latest news of the war, as at that time we had heard nothing. The story he told was as follows: —

The night before they were giving a farewell concert to some troops who were proceeding to Karonga, which is quite close to the frontier of German East Africa on the eastern shore of Lake Nyasa. Some natives rushed in with news of the approach of a large German patrol, with machine-guns. The "machine-guns" were the cinema-cameras, being

84

carried on their tripods, as we had thrown away the boxes on account of weight. This all accounted for the villages being deserted. It was these people who had brought the news into Fort Johnston. The troops had also started digging trenches at Fort Johnston, so Martin said. We all had a real good laugh over it. When the news arrived at Fort Johnston, Martin volunteered to go out and get some authentic news and went disguised as a prospector, hence the boy carrying the pick.

Shortly after meeting Martin we struck the shore of Lake Nyasa, and we were lucky to get several native dug-out canoes to put ourselves and kit into, which saved us another 12 to 14 miles march to Fort Johnston. We were right glad to finish with this foot-slogging business, as our feet were pretty well done in, having covered 500 miles from our main camp to Fort Johnston in 23 days! We arrived at Fort Johnston about five o'clock in the evening, and stayed at Martin's hotel. Whilst in the canoes, Martin told us all the local war news.

He told us about the fight at Karonga three weeks earlier, of which we had heard vague rumours from the natives in Portuguese East Africa. At the outbreak of the war, Nyasaland had only one battalion of the King's African Rifles and a small Volunteer Corps, the Nyasaland Volunteer Rifles, which was composed mostly of planters in Nyasaland. This force was rushed up to Karonga, a very small station, as soon as possible on the outbreak of war. Meanwhile, the Germans had concentrated a great many troops at New Langenber (now Tukuyu), about 50 miles north of Lake Nyasa; but, shortly afterwards, a strong German force came down south, mostly composed of regular native askari and a certain number of Rugaruga (armed local natives chiefly used for scouting). Their intention was to attack Karonga, and then march on south to Zomba, the capital of Nyasaland; and at one time, it looked as if there was a very good chance of them doing this as they had a very much stronger force than we could get together.

Our troops at Karonga were commanded by Colonel Barton, King's African Rifles, an officer who knew no fear and was wounded on five different occasions during the campaign in German East Africa. On getting news of the German troops marching on Karonga, Colonel Barton's force moved out to attack them. A few troops, mostly sick men, and two very antiquated guns—I am not certain that they were not muzzle-loaders —were left behind at Karonga. The country to the north of Karonga is covered with a great deal of bush. What happened was that the opposing forces, Germans and ourselves, passed quite close to each other, neither being aware of the fact. Anyone who knows this type of country will know how easily this may occur. This happened very early in the morning.

One of the white men at the rear of the British column suddenly heard the distant boom of guns at Karonga, and immediately reported the fact to the Column Commander. He, at once, re-formed his troops and marched them back to Karonga, attacking strongly from the rear. The Huns, taken completely by surprise, were all put to flight, but the British had a very stiff fight as the Germans greatly outnumbered our troops. I forget what the casualties were, but I think we lost about a dozen white men killed and about 50 African askari, while the wounded numbered probably about 90. The Germans had a great many more casualties than we had; also they lost several machine-guns.

The amusing part was that the Germans had brought several big Sultans from German East Africa, to see them knock hell out of the *Ingalasa,* instead of that they got a real good doing and retreated over the frontier. It was one of the luckiest things that ever happened in this part of the world, otherwise the Germans would have been right into Nyasaland.

The other episode was a naval battle on Lake Nyasa. The latter is a long, narrow lake, about 350 miles miles in length and with an average width of about 50 to 60 miles, and with a maximum known depth of 2,316 feet. Its overflow is discharged into the Zambesi River by way of the Shire River. The north-western shore was German territory. We had a stern-wheeler, the s.s. *Gwendolin,* used for taking passengers and cargo up and down the lake. The Germans also had a steamer used for the same purpose, the *Von Weismann.* Our captain's name, I am almost certain, was Commander Rhodes. The German's name I do not know. Anyhow, they were well known to each other and on very friendly terms.

On the outbreak of war, the *Gwendolin* had orders to put out of action the *Von Weismann,* and steamed off immediately, as they knew the *Von Weismann* was in port at a small harbour called Wiedhafen but now re-named Manda, in German territory. Up comes the *Gwendolin,* armed only with one very antiquated gun, to find the *Von Weismann* there and undergoing some repairs. Captain Rhodes let drive about a dozen shots from his gun, a good many taking effect. On the commencement of the firing, the German skipper got into a rowing-boat, pulled for all he was worth to the *Gwendolin,* came aboard and said to Rhodes: " What the hell are you doing? I suppose you are drunk again? "

" No," answered Rhodes. " There's a war on and you are my prisoner. And that's that! "

After this, I believe, they both retired to Rhodes' cabin and had a drink together. During 1918 I got possession of the *Von Weismann's* flag with the German Coat-of-Arms upon it, under rather peculiar circumstances; but that is another story, which is not for publication. I also got three other German flags during the war in the East African Campaign, but they were only the ordinary red, white and black flags which the Germans had dyed on a sort of *amerikani* cloth. But I did not get those under the circumstances in which the other was secured.

The first thing we did after arrival at Fort Johnston was to pay off Simba, Tumbo and our Portuguese porters. For this we had to borrow money as we had no cash with us. I forget who the kind person was, but believe no other than Martin. Then we heard that Major Pretorius was in the local hospital with a bullet wound in his leg, and had arrived only 10 days before. Jim had known Philip Pretorius in the old days, as they had been elephant hunting in German East Africa and in very much the same part of the country. So, the same afternoon, we both went to the hospital and called upon him. I remember it so well. Pretorius was half-sitting up in bed and looked a pretty sick man, but it did not seem to make much difference to what he thought about the Germans. His opinion of them was an education!

Pretorius had done a great deal of elephant hunting in German East Africa during earlier years: disliked most Huns: had often fallen foul of their authorities; and had never forgiven them for imprisoning him at Dar es Salaam under conditions of indignity for the trifling offence (as he regarded it) of having shot too many elephants. He was 400 miles or more from the nearest frontier when, in August of 1914, he received a note from a German *boma* ordering him to come at once. That was exactly the same trick they had tried on Jim and myself. Instead, Pretorius and his safari decided to shoot their way out if necessary. They managed to get within easy distance of the Ruvuma River before meeting trouble. Then they found their path barred by parties estimated at about 25 Germans and three or four times that number of askari.

A characteristic ruse got them out of the trap. Just before sunset they erected their tents and started camp fires, but the moment it was dark crept off into the bush. An hour or two later the main German force attacked the camp, firing wildly into the tents. But Pretorius and his safari were marching hard for the Ruvuma River. As they reached the bank they ran into a German askari patrol. They opened fire and Pretorius was hit. He dived into the crocodile-infested river, hid in the reeds for hours while a search went on just above him, expecting the blood from his wound to attract crocodiles, but at length swam safely across the river to the Portuguese bank.

His boys, who had disappeared when his camp was rushed, managed to locate him and turned up on the Portuguese side the following day. They carried him, with the help of some locally recruited porters, in a *machilla* (a sort of hammock slung on poles) all the way to Fort Johnston.

Pretorius had a most remarkable and adventurous career, and died at

87

Pretoria towards the end of November, 1945. He was the famous Scout during the East African Campaign and for his services was awarded the C.M.G. and the D.S.O. He was a wonderful marksman, a master of bush-craft, imperturbably modest, and claimed only one gift: a " hunch " for knowing when approaching an enemy outpost, patrol or other danger. I am indebted to Mr. F. S. Joelson, the Editor of *East Africa and Rhodesia,* for permission to quote from his obituary notice of Major Philip Jacobus Pretorius:

" When General J. C. Smuts assumed command in East Africa during 1916, Major Pretorius was appointed Chief Scout and performed a great deal of fine work behind the German lines in many parts of the country. In particular, he set himself to locate the exact position of the German cruiser *Koenigsberg,* which was heavily camouflaged with vegetation some 12 miles up the Rufiji River. The Germans got to know that, during moonless nights, he was landed by the Royal Navy either to the north or south of the river, and accompanied by a few trusted native trackers. and then picked up again at a prearranged rendezvous a few nights later. They did all in their power to capture him, and even placed a high price on his head, dead or alive; but he repeated this performance for several months without being captured.

" After the *Koenigsberg* had been sunk by the fire of British cruisers and monitors, Pretorius often went behind the German lines, and scarcely ever returned without a party of captured enemy, usually three or four times as numerous as his own small party. Almost without exception, his prisoners became so impressed with the power and skill of Pretorius that they eagerly volunteered to serve under him. Within a few weeks many of his erstwhile prisoners were in British uniform and assisting him to destroy German supply depots wreck their communications, capture patrols, and learn the secrets of the enemy's military operations. He used to assert emphatically that not one of these men had ever tried to trick or betray him to the Germans. His communications to British Head-quarters, written from behind the German lines, were always laconic in the extreme. Pretorius and his men held invaluable knowledge, but that was not discernible from his infrequent, uninformative, and sometimes scarcely decipherable scribblings on odd bits of paper. The late Lord Tweedsmuir (John Buchan) made Pretorius the hero of his famous novel, *Greenmantle.*"

Pretorius was credited with having shot more than 500 elephants including five with five successive bullets. During 1920 he was invited by the Government of South Africa to reduce the herd of elephants in the Addo Bush, when about 120 more animals were added to his bag. The old warrior joined up again in World War II, and did much valuable work against the Italians in Ethiopia and Somaliland. One of his exploits was the single-handed capture of a loaded lorry and the Italian occupants in the centre of Ethiopia. Pretorius brought back to our lines the lorry and its crew.

XIII

NYASALAND TO FLANDERS — 1914

THE next day I got the very kind offer of a lift to Zomba, on the back of a motor-cycle, from a missionary who was in the Nyasaland Volunteer Rifles. Zomba, the capital of the Protectorate, is about 100 miles from Fort Johnston, and the road, in those days, was full of ruts and sand and it was no joy-ride!

I remember that, when about half-way, we skidded in some sand and took a toss, the bike and my friend partly falling on me. I thought I had broken one of my legs, but it really was nothing much. Just before arriving at Zomba, we pulled up at a small stream to have a wash as we were both covered in dust, and I was going straight to see the Governor of Nyasaland in order to obtain his permission to continue the journey home to rejoin my Regiment.

On arrival at Zomba in the afternoon, my friend dropped me at Government House. I am afraid that I was not very suitably dressed for calling on a Governor: khaki shorts, no puttees, khaki shirt, while all the kit I had was tied up in a towel. I met Sir George Smith, who was then Governor of Nyasaland and explained what had happened to me on the outbreak of war. He immediately told me to come and stay at Government House during the time I was at Zomba. Both Sir George and Lady Smith could not have been kinder to me and his A.D.C. fixed me up with clothes.

Jim Sutherland turned up the next day, and stayed with Captain Charles Thorburn, a well-known settler who was growing tobacco. Jim took up Intelligence work on the Portuguese frontier, having two other white men and several natives under him. I am afraid he did not always stay in Portuguese territory (as he was supposed to do) but on several occasions crossed over into German East Africa. On one of these trips he was followed by a patrol of about four German askari, but got to know they were following him, and so doubled back on his tracks and lay up for them. He blotted out one askari and wounded another, the other two bolting. I said goodbye to Jim, little thinking that we should meet again at Zomba in a little over a year's time, when we were both appointed to the staff of Brigadier-General (later Major-General Sir) Edward Northey.

The first thing I did at Zomba was to cable home for some money to continue my journey. Before leaving Zomba, Sir George Smith very kindly gave me an open letter explaining what had happened to me and that I was en route homewards to rejoin my Regiment—the 18th Hussars. After a few days' thoroughly enjoyable stay at Zomba, that very lovely and semi-tropical station, I said goodbye to my very kind host and hostess. I shall always remember Sir George and Lady Smith's great kindness as they took me without any sort of introduction.

I made my way by sidecar to Blantyre, then by train and river-steamer down the Zambesi River, about five days' journey, to Chinde—a God-forsaken spot at the mouth of the river. From what I remember of it, the total population was only about eight to ten Europeans, mostly traders. There was also a British Consul upon whom I called, and he also gave me another open letter to help me home.

After about three days' stay at Chinde I caught a Portuguese steamer for Beira; stayed there for one night, and then boarded a train for Cape Town, about five days' journey, which I found very monotonous.

Bishop Bevan of Southern Rhodesia got on the train at Salisbury, and I was introduced to him. He was about the most popular man in the Colony and known to everyone; his special pets seemed to be all the old "hard cases." I remember that we halted at some wayside station and a pretty tough-looking bloke, who had done himself pretty well, boarded the train. Immediately he spotted the Bishop, he made a bee-line straight for him and greeted him as an old friend with: "Hullo, Bish, how the bloody hell are you?" At the same time he slapped him on the back. This did not in the least upset the Bishop, who answered, "Quite all right, my man," and they chatted together for some time.

It was interesting to me to pass through Mafeking, for it brought back memories of the Boer War, as I had been with both General Carrington's and Lord Methuen's columns which operated in this part of the country. After Mafeking there is nothing but rolling veldt until one gets into the Cape Province, where one travels through some lovely scenery, especially the Hex River Mountains.

After arrival at Cape Town I was delayed for about ten days before getting a passage on the Union-Castle liner *Norman Castle*. I spent most of my time at Muizenberg, a seaside resort just outside Cape Town, and greatly enjoyed the bathing there. I made several trips to Cape Town from Muizenberg, and bought myself a complete uniform. The reason for this was that I intended to get off the boat at Madeira and cross to Lisbon; go by train from there to Paris and make my way to the Front and rejoin my Regiment. Like everyone else, I thought the war would be over before very long and if I were sent to the Depôt of my Regiment in England, I should be kept there owing to my lameness.

On one of the train journeys into Cape Town I got into a carriage with a soldier. In the course of conversation I asked him if he knew that part of the world. He replied: " Know it! I bloody well think I do know it, for I was working on the Breakwater at Cape Town as a prisoner." He had fought with the Boers against us during the South African War, but he bore the British no grudge and seemed a real good fellow and full of enthusiasm, as he was off shortly, with the South African troops to German South-West Africa, to serve under that great leader, the late General Louis Botha, to whom the British Empire owes so much. General Botha was taking over the command of the Expeditionary Force then being organised to fight the Germans in German South-West Africa.

On getting on board the *Norman Castle*, I found her to be packed full of volunteers all going to England to enlist. A great proportion of them were Rhodesians who nearly all joined the 60th Rifles (King's Royal Rifle Corps), and what a splendid lot of men they were, all terribly keen. They spent a great deal of their time in drilling on deck every morning. About the third day out from Cape Town the captain of the *Norman Castle* asked for volunteers to go down to the stokehole as they were very short-handed owing to many of the firemen taking French leave at Cape Town and enlisting in one of the many units going to German South-West Africa. Many of us volunteered but we did only very short shifts. Of all the rotten, dirty jobs that I've ever done, this was about the worst. As a matter of fact, we did not all do the stoking but what is called trimming— wheeling out the cinders and tipping them into a bunker.

I left the boat at Madeira, with my uniform. Some very kind fellow-passenger (whose name I've forgotten) presented me with a valise, which I had been unable to obtain in Cape Town. I spent five very delightful days at Madeira, which was full of Germans, and an infernal noise they made, with their singing at night in the German Club there. After leaving Madeira I was very short of money, and had not enough to take me from Lisbon to Paris. I had already cabled for some from Madeira but had got no reply up to the time of leaving.

On boarding a Portuguese steamer for Lisbon, I found myself in the same cabin as a Hun. All diplomatic relations seemed to have been broken off, and we never spoke a word to each other—just looked at one another sideways.

On arrival at Lisbon I went straight to the British Consul, explained my case and told him that I was short of money to continue my journey. He, like a real good fellow, handed me £25. It was most kind and trusting of him. I am glad to say I was able to pay him back on the following day as, just when leaving by train for Paris, one of Messrs. Cook's men turned up with the money for which I had cabled from Madeira.

On arrival in Paris on the following day, I put on my uniform and reported to British Headquarters, showed all my papers and was instructed to proceed to St. Nazaire, which was then the British base. That night I went out to dine and have a last fling. At dinner I met a friend of mine in the Royal Horse Artillery, who was on a few days' leave from the Front. I asked him which was the best way for me to rejoin my Regiment. He advised: "Don't go to St. Nazaire, but take a train straight to Haze-brouck."

The next day I acted upon this sound advice, getting into the train and not even buying a ticket and, after a slow journey, arrived at Calais about seven p.m. to find the town was chock-a-block with Belgian troops. After some difficulty I found myself a billet in a private house.

The next morning I caught a train for Hazebrouck, which left at about 8.30 a.m. On the platform I saw a British soldier asleep, about the first I had seen since leaving Paris. All the information I had been able to obtain was that the 18th Hussars belonged to the 2nd Cavalry Brigade, 1st Cavalry Division, but where they were, or how best to reach them after arrival at Hazebrouck, I did not know. I woke up the sleeping British soldier and he turned out to be a despatch-rider attached to the 1st Cavalry Division. He gave me a deal of useful information. He was a nice young lad, and told me that since the beginning of the war he had been with the 1st Cavalry Division, having come down from the 'Varsity, but was now on his way to England to get a commission. What a lot of fine work a number of these lads did as despatch-riders, more especially at the beginning of the War; indeed, they were invaluable.

On arriving at Hazebrouck I was asked by a Staff Officer where I was going. I replied: "To rejoin my Regiment, the 18th Hussars." He told me to put my kit and self on the transport which was at the station and going up to the 2nd Cavalry Brigade. This was the first, and *only,* time anyone ever asked me where I was going.

The lorry-driver, who took me to where my Regiment had been in billets at St. Jean Cappel, near Bailieu, entertained me with all sorts of lurid stories about the war. He had been attached to the 2nd Cavalry Brigade since the start. He knew a certain number of my brother officers, and when I asked " How's so-and-so?" he would promptly reply, "Oh, he was killed several days ago." In fact, he had all the Regiment killed. I thought to myself that this is a nice bit of trouble to tumble into; I can't say he cheered me up but I found out later nearly all his reports were untrue; but the Regiment did suffer very heavy casualties later on.

When I arrived at the billets, I found that the Regiment was up in the trenches in the first battle of Ypres. This was about November 10th, 1914, but I was not officially reported as rejoining my Regiment until the 20th. About the first person I met at the billets was our dear old Quartermaster,

Captain and Quartermaster W. H. Parsons, an old friend of mine. He said: "Don't you worry about being in time for the blinkin' war; you'll soon find out there's a war on!" Which shortly, I did. Parsons told me all the news of the Regiment. He said that, as they expected to be relieved shortly I had better wait at the billets and make myself comfortable with him. This I did.

The following evening at about 8 o'clock, an urgent message came from Brigade Headquarters, to the effect that all available men of the Brigade left behind in billets were to go up to Ypres immediately and report at a certain kilometre stone this side of Ypres and wait there for a mounted orderly who would take them to Brigade Headquarters. I went up with about 60 men of the Brigade (mostly composed of shoeing-smiths, farriers), all of them belonging to our Brigade — the 4th Dragoons, 9th Lancers and 18th Hussars.

It was a black November night and there was about a seven-mile ride to Ypres. I've had many more enjoyable rides than that one. On meeting the mounted orderly just outside Ypres, he took us through the town to Brigade Headquarters, and I handed over all the men with me. When passing through Ypres, the Germans were dropping a few shells into the town, and one knocked out some Frenchmen, and that was my first introduction to the war.

On staying the night at Brigade Headquarters, I was told to take the horses of the Regiment (which at that time were at some chateau just outside Ypres, the name of which I have forgotten) to meet them the next night when they were relieved from the trenches. On going up the following night with all the Regiment's horses about midnight I ran into the relief going up and other troops coming back. I fairly got hung up, with French gunners going one way and the mounted troops the other. I had led horses strung out all along the road.

About two a.m., after leaving the led horses at a place behind, and haltered, I rode forward to make inquiries from all the troops coming out of the trenches. I asked: "Are you the 18th Hussars?" and was answered mostly with a sort of grunt "No." Some of the poor fellows were about "all in," and in many cases had had a devil of a doing, so it was unfair to blame them for not being very cheery at that time in the morning. After about half an hour, and having asked all troops that passed the same old inquiries: "Are you the 18th Hussars?" I got an answer from an officer who was leading another regiment.

"By God!" he exclaimed, "I believe it's that blighter Andy turned up!" It was my old friend and Squadron Leader, Major C. H. Corbett. He was killed shortly afterwards, and he died, beloved by everyone in the Regiment.

94

The first thing they all asked me was: " Have you got the led horses?" When answering in the affirmative, I became quite popular. The horses saved them about a five-mile march. As one can imagine, it was grand to be back with one's old brother officers once more and to meet again all the old N.C.O.s and men one knew. But, alas, there were many familiar faces missing and never to return.

I reported myself to Colonel C. K. Burnett, who was one of the finest Commanding Officers, never upset by anything, and one of the coolest of men under any circumstances. If he had any fault, it was that of being too great a gentleman. He was afterwards wounded and gassed during the second battle of Ypres, never again being fit for active service. He is now a Brigadier-General, a C.B. and a C.M.G., and always takes a great interest in anything connected with the Regiment.

Later, I put in a claim through the Commanding Officer for my travelling expenses from the Lewagu River (German East Africa) to England; also a claim for all our camp equipment and stores which had been lost. I was paid the travelling expenses in full, even down to my porters, without a query. For the camp equipment I put in endless claims and had given up all hope until one day in Nairobi, just after I had returned from a safari in 1930, I met a Government official who said that he had a cheque for just over £600 for me. That was a most pleasant surprise! I sent Jim Sutherland half of it. The money deposited in the German East African Bank at Dar es Salaam for the expedition in German East Africa went down the drain, for the bank went into liquidation.

I remained with my Regiment in France until the August of 1915, when I was wounded in the leg. Later I was sent out with General Northey to Africa.

XIV

WITH "NORFORCE" IN EAST AFRICAN CAMPAIGN — 1916-18

E ARLY in 1916, when in London on sick leave after being wounded in France, I ran into Major Jack Riddell, a well-known character in Kenya, who had done a lot of hunting and trading in the early days on the northern frontier and in Abyssinia. " Oh! " says Jack. " You're wanted by the War Office. You have to report yourself immediately to General Northey."

This conveyed nothing to me. I had never heard of General Northey before and wondered what the devil the General wanted to see me about. He was formerly in the 60th Rifles and had commanded the 1st Battalion of the K.R.R.C. in France, being twice badly wounded, and then had commanded the 15th Infantry Brigade. He had now been chosen to take over the command of the Nyasaland-Rhodesia Field Force. For his services he was promoted Major-General, awarded the G.C.M.G. and C.B., and appointed Governor of Kenya Colony in 1918, serving in that capacity until 1922.

I reported as soon as possible to General Northey at the War Office, and he told me that he was going shortly to Africa to take command of the Nyasaland-Rhodesia Field Force, and would I come on his Staff as a Staff Captain. I told him that I had had no experience of Staff work and hated office work. " Oh," said the General, " that doesn't matter." I then told the General I should like to go but, before making a definite decision, I must see my Commanding Officer and get his views about it. I saw Colonel A. E. W. Harman, D.S.O., who was then commanding my Regiment, and who happened to be on leave. He advised me to take the job in view of my experience of that part of Africa; and, if not, to come back to the Regiment immediately. Colonel (now Sir Wentworth, and a K.C.B.) Harman, better known as " Jakes " Harman, was a great character; an Irishman with all the fiery temperament of his race, a master in the use of the English language, a fine soldier and a great sportsman.

Anyhow, I was duly appointed to General Northey's Staff. As a Staff Captain I was a bad bargain, being mostly away on some patrol or job with one of the columns. General Northey had only himself to blame, as I had already told him in England when he asked me to go on his Staff that I hated office work. On one occasion he told me that I was the biggest damned fool he had ever seen as a Staff Officer. Probably he was right. Anyhow he has always remained a true and old friend of mine.

I know that on General Northey's arrival at Zomba in Nyasaland he was rather undecided as to whom to appoint as his Chief Intelligence Officer. He knew that I had been with Jim Sutherland for a long time and that he was a great friend of mine, but he never mentioned to me that he thought of giving him the appointment as his Chief Intelligence Officer. Jim was recalled from up-country to interview the General, and after the interview the General came to me and said: "I can't place that man. What nationality is he? I can't quite understand what he says." I expect Jim got a bit of Swahili mixed up in his conversation with the General. Anyhow, I told him he was pure Scotch, and Jim was shortly afterwards appointed Chief Intelligence Officer. He did most excellent work on the Staff and was a very great help to General Northey, with his unique knowledge of German East Africa, more especially the southern portion (in which General Northey's column operated) as it was in this region that he had done most of his hunting. For his services Jim was twice mentioned in Despatches and awarded the Legion of Honour.

He always kept himself very fit, and was exceptionally so during his younger days, until he suffered very badly from dysentery and repeated attacks of malaria. Never missing a morning, Jim always did exercises with a very light pair of dumb-bells. One morning at New Langenburg (now Tukuyu), in the highlands of German East Africa, he was engaged in his morning exercises outside his tent when Charlie Grey, the late Earl Grey of Fallodon's younger brother, passed by. Grey and Jim were great friends.

"Well, Jim!" says Charlie Grey, "I suppose you're doing that to keep fit? Well, anyhow, I will bet you £100 that I live longer than you."

"Right!" says Jim; and they both put it down in their wills.

Poor Charlie Grey died about 1930 as the result of being knocked over and gored by a buffalo, which he had wounded and followed up. Jim received the £100, but lost a good friend.

Charlie and his brother George were both well-known characters and pioneers in that part of Africa; they both loved Africa and the life of hunting and prospecting. Charlie Grey had lost his left arm at the beginning of the War, near Kisii, when with the King's African Rifles, and after recovery he was attached as an Intelligence Officer to General Northey's Force. I knew him well. A very fine character and great sportsman he was. No one who was not would have followed a wounded buffalo into bush with only one arm. He had a rifle specially built for him by Rigby's, and a first-class shot he was with it. His brother George, I only knew by reputation. He was also a great sportsman and was badly mauled in 1908 by a lion on the Athi Plains, dying a few days later from gangrene poisoning in the European hospital in Nairobi, from the result of the mauling.

When General Northey's Force, known as Norforce, first made their advance into German East Africa from Nyasaland and Rhodesia, General Northey made his Headquarters at New Langenburg, an old German *boma* situated about 25 miles north of Lake Nyasa on the slopes of the Livingstone Mountains, a beautiful district known to the Germans as the "Switzerland of German East Africa." At that time Jim Sutherland, being at Headquarters, had a great deal of office work to do, which he hated. Every day, after finishing with the office in the evening, he would go for a walk, which he always called a "constitutional," accompanied by his beloved bull-terrier Mosoko. One evening, on his way back to the *boma,* two chatty Natives followed close behind.

One Native said to his pal: "You see that *mzungu* (white man) in front. He must be a very old man. His hair is white and his dog is white." Jim's hair was very slightly grey; Natives always exaggerate everything.

Much to the Native's astonishment, the "old man" suddenly about-turned, and hit him with the open palm of his hand, sending him flying. His pal, the second Native, took to his heels and fled, pursued by Mosoko, who kept jumping up and trying to get the man's cap—a trick he would always do if told to do so, never biting them, just pure devilment and play. After that, I think the two Natives learned that they must be more careful in their remarks about a white man. They had no idea, of course, that Jim understood Swahili as well as themselves.

I met Bishop Bevan of Southern Rhodesia again in 1919, when he came on a visit to the Rhodesian troops under General Northey and stayed for some time at Headquarters. Jim Sutherland and I became great friends with him. There was nothing he loved more than telling the most amusing stories about some of the "hard cases" in Rhodesia during the early days. What a great pity there are not more men of his type in the Church, for Bishop Bevan was the most understanding of men and beloved by everyone with whom he came into contact. I remember on one occasion he said to Jim and myself: "If either of you ever get married, I'll come and marry you anywhere south of the Zambesi." As Jim did not marry, and I was married in England we did not have that honour. As a matter of fact, when about to get married, I wrote to Bishop Bevan and asked him to marry us but, as he was in Africa at the time, this was impossible.

At one time during the East African Campaign (1914-1918), General Northey's Headquarters occupied the old German *boma* at Njombe, 158 miles south of Iringa. Like all German *bomas,* this was built in a sort of square with a wall all round, loopholed and with a parapet inside the wall, so that the askari could man it and get a good field of fire. Always situated on the top of some hill, these *bomas* were simply forts, built for defence in case of trouble with the Natives. In all German administrative policy, the military came first and the Civil administration second. Inside these forts were about a dozen rooms, which were used by the Germans for living-quarters for their officers and white N.C.O.s; one large room being set aside as the Officers' Mess. The living-rooms for the officers and their mess were up one flight of stairs. The *bomas* were well-built with stone, being solid and quite comfortable.

In one of these rooms upstairs Jim had his sleeping-quarters, with a flight of stone steps leading down. At that time he had a boy called Matola, a first-class personal servant, but with a very high-pitched and squeaky voice. He was always a great source of amusement to us all on account of his voice. Every night Matola filled his master's tin bath with hot water, leaving another bucket of hot water ready to be poured over Jim when he said the word.

One night when Jim was having his usual bath he told Matola to pour the bucket of hot water over him. By mistake poor Matola emptied a bucket of cold water over his master, who leaped out of the bath with a shout, picked up the bath and hurled it at Matola. By this time the latter was well on his way down stairs at a terrific pace. Down came the bath, Matola and the bath finishing on a dead heat, all mixed up together at the bottom of the stairs.

The sequel of the dead heat of Matola and the bath was that when Matola had recovered from his fright, he had a perfectly normal voice, the same as any other native. The next morning Jim and I took Matola to the doctor and told him the story. The doctor said that Matola had recovered his voice owing to shock (he had had this high-pitched voice all his life). So Matola had some compensation for having a bath hurled at him and doing record time down the stairs.

Earlier I mentioned our experiences with the German Governor, Herr Schnee, at Dar es Salaam, when arriving with our cinematograph expedition. I also said that later I managed to get even with him at Government House. This is the story.

In the beginning of 1918 I was with a column in Portuguese East Africa, and on ahead with one or two white men. One of them was a very old friend of mine, Charlie Mills, an Australian who had come over with the Australians in the South African War. I first met Mills in 1916, when with General Sir Edward Northey on the Northern Rhodesia-German East Africa border during the war. At that time he was doing splendid work as a Scout, and had the nickname of " Dead-End Dick." Whilst on the subject of nicknames, I cannot refrain from mentioning two nurses in General Northey's force who were known by the names of " Hell Fire Kate " and " Dynamite Jane." Both these nurses were always up at the most advanced Field Hospitals, as near the firing-line as it was possible to get. Nothing daunted them and they did the most splendid work during the War.

We were then passing through rather thick bush when suddenly we heard some Natives talking, went on a few yards further and came on most of the German transport, with a great many loads of personal kit. Most of the porters were chained together, to prevent them running away. Just at that moment we saw two Germans standing on the edge of some thick bush and about 100 yards distant. We covered them with our rifles, and they surrendered immediately. On coming up to them they said: " You no zee the Governor, *Bwana* Schnee? He just go this minute." Unfortunately we just missed him.

As suddenly heavy firing started all around us, we took back the two prisoners to where the German native porters had been left with our troops. Later, on opening some of the boxes, we found all Schnee's personal kit, including his white official uniform and several of his orders. I took the orders and handed them to General Northey on getting back to Headquarters. I believe these orders were sent to Schnee when the war was finished. I only wish now that I had kept them!

Schnee and General Von Lettow-Vorbeck, the Commander-in-Chief of the German Forces in East Africa, never hit it off. Von Lettow-Vorbeck had no use for him and he was simply taken round the country with the transport, never having any say in anything of importance.

Shortly after this I had to go into hospital with typhoid and malaria and when I recovered I was invalided home. Our troops chased Von Lettow into Portuguese East Africa and out again, and he finally surrendered at Fyfe in Northern Rhodesia.

XV

ELEPHANT CONTROL ON A GOVERNMENT LICENCE: UGANDA, 1921-2; TANGANYIKA, 1923-4

DURING 1908, owing to the great amount of damage caused by elephants to Natives' *shambas*, the Government of Uganda granted licences to authentic elephant-hunters to shoot these animals in parts of the Protectorate where they were especially destructive. A hunter could take out a Government licence for 10 or 20 elephants at a very nominal fee. Anyhow, it proved quite a profitable proposition. The result was, naturally enough, that all the old elephant-hunters of Kenya and Uganda came out from their retirement and were swiftly on to this opportunity like a swarm of bees around a honey-pot.

Hearing about this Government elephant licence some time in 1921, I packed up immediately and left for Entebbe, where I was at once granted the necessary licence to get busy on the marauding herds. I had been advised to go to the Mubende district (Mubende is 104 miles north-west of Kampala, and about midway between Kampala and Fort Portal), and hunt elephants along the Katonga River. On arrival at Mubende *boma* I called upon the District Commissioner, Mr. J. R. P. Postlethwaite, and he most kindly gave me every possible assistance in the manner of recruiting porters and purchasing *posho* for my safari. I was also lucky enough to be able to hire a good riding-mule, about the only one in the Mubende district.

One morning very early, whilst camped near the Katonga River, I saw a single elephant about 300 yards distant and going over the rise. The animal disappeared from sight down the slope on the far side. The countryside thereabouts was exceptionally open, with rolling plain and scattered bush, so not the type of terrain in which you might expect to find elephants. On sighting this beast I set off on the mule as fast as possible, the gun-bearer running alongside the mule and carrying my heavy rifle, while the Native syce followed closely with the light rifle. On gaining the crest of the rise over which I had seen the elephant disappear, I gazed down on a kind of broad valley and witnessed the most amazing spectacle—an enormous herd of elephants. I estimated that there must have been about 500 animals in the herd. On telling Mr. Postlethwaite about this on my return to Mubende *boma*, he stated that I had probably seen two well-known large herds which had joined up temporarily.

The valley looked like a seething mass of elephants. All the animals were packed fairly close together. I saw one single bull standing about 30 yards outside the fringe of the great herd, under a tree, and managed to get up to within about 100 yards of it. I drove into this bull a couple of bullets in the region of the heart. At the first shot it headed straight back into the herd but, before reaching the other elephants, toppled over. Much to my astonishment I saw two other elephants close round the fallen giant. The latter was striving to struggle erect and get on its feet again and, with the aid of the two others, this was accomplished. Then with an elephant supporting it on each flank, the wounded bull made off with the herd. Once they started moving, as it was the dry season of the year, nothing could be seen but a huge cloud of dust.

Another lot of elephants, about 30 in number, broke away from the main herd and went off in a left-handed direction. I hastily remounted the mule. With the syce carrying my light rifle and the gun-bearer the heavy one whilst hanging on to my stirrup leathers, I stirred the mule into an unaccustomed burst of speed. The elephants travelled in a half-circle but, after covering about half a mile, halted again and allowed me to come up with them. I dismounted at a range of about 100 yards and dropped one of the animals with the light rifle. The others, strangely enough, did not stampede immediately at sound of the shot. One of them deliberately went up to the fallen elephant and gave it a prod with the tusks, and I then dropped another bull. Then they all stampeded once more and, remounting the mule, I followed up at the best speed possible.

After travelling about another mile they stopped again, and I dropped another couple of bulls. This went on for a distance of about five miles. I managed to shoot 10 beasts out of that herd—seven bulls and three cows—but all of them carried very small ivory. I found that none of the elephants in this particular area carried big ivory, and a 40-lb. tusk was the exception. After that, the remainder of the elephants stampeded and went straight away without again halting.

I should think that this is what elephant hunting was like during the earliest days in southern Africa, about which one reads in old-time books of travel and sport. Why these elephants kept on halting after covering only a short distance, I cannot imagine. After returning to the spot where the first bull had been wounded, I followed up its spoor but never saw a sign of my quarry. My own experience has been that if an elephant falls to a body shot it will rarely get up again, but not so with the brain shot, as this may only have stunned the animal. I employed my .318 rifle all the time in open country and for all long-range shots at an elephant.

102

A few days after this episode, and whilst camped, the headman of a nearby Native village came to implore me to shoot some elephants that had been raiding the *shambas* and playing terrible havoc with growing crops. So I instructed this headman to send out about 50 of the villagers to the valley, in order that their wind would blow over to the herd, to shout lustily and beat drums all the time, and then advance towards the elephants. Meanwhile I took up a position in an open space at the end of the wooded valley and about three-quarters of a mile up-wind of the herd.

About half-an-hour later the entire herd emerged into full view, coming slowly and straight in my direction. I dropped the leading bull of the herd. Then the other animals got bunched up together as if undecided what they should do for the best. I did not waste any time. For a few minutes things became pretty lively, as shooting was rapid and at short range, not more, I imagine, than 15 to 30 yards. The heavy rifle, which I used all the time, became so hot that it was scarcely possible to hold it in my hands. As I was standing on a very steep slope of the valley when the elephants came out of the forest, they were still coming on even after the first few shots had been fired. My gun-bearer—a Native whom I had only just recently employed, for Feragi was not with me in those days—said to me in English: "Time to go upstairs, *bwana*!" What he meant was that I should ascend the hillside so as to get out of the path of the steadily advancing herd of elephants. I dropped seven animals before the entire herd stampeded.

Shortly afterwards Sir Geoffrey Archer, the newly-appointed Governor of Uganda and previously Commissioner of Somaliland, arrived at Entebbe. That was in 1922. He immediately stopped all new issues of these Government elephant licences. The work of Elephant Control was taken over by the Government, especially selected hunters being appointed to the new branch of the Game Department to carry out this important task. Without any doubt, this was the correct policy to pursue. Many of the hunters, naturally enough, had been out only after the bulls carrying big tusks and ignoring the genuine *shamba* raiding elephants. As usual, the big tuskers were solitary bulls or, perhaps, two or three keeping company, and these animals kept well away in the forest, never approaching the Natives' *shambas* as devastating raiders of the growing crops.

In relating these two personal experiences when shooting the *shamba* raiders, I realise that it may give an entirely false impression to the average person who knows nothing, or very little, about elephant hunting. They would say there seems to be nothing to it. But it should be remembered that those two episodes were quite exceptional: firstly,

103

because of finding an elephant herd in such open country; and, secondly, on account of the conditions governing the shooting, as it did not matter whether bulls or cows were killed. That is still another good reason why I believe it is not possible to compare the prowess of individual hunters, or to determine which man is, or was, the greatest elephant-hunter. It does not follow that the man who has shot the greatest number of elephants is necessarily the greatest of all elephant-hunters. Elephant hunting is a hard and strenuous life, crammed full to the brim with many bitter disappointments.

I was shooting on a Government Control licence in Tanganyika in 1923-1924, and my most unpleasant memories of that safari was the trip on a small dhow from Mombasa to Dar es Salaam. I did this as otherwise it would have meant waiting at Mombasa ten days for a steamer. Dhow journeys are for short journeys, with a good breeze, but when one has to spend two days with the bow of the dhow all packed with dried shark and a scorching hot sun beating down on one, it is quite enough to put you off fish for the remainder of your life. There is quite a big trade in this shark business carried on by Arab and Coast Natives, the sharks being caught off the coast, cut up and sun-dried, and sold to the local Natives.

It was an exceptionally wet season during 1923 to 1924, the long rains running with very little break into the short rains. At that time I was hunting on the upper reaches of the Rufiji Valley. That is not the district I should have chosen to hunt in, but it was allotted to me by the Game Department of Tanganyika, owing to the damage done to Native *shambas* by elephants. This meant travelling from village to village according to the reports one had of elephants raiding the *shambas*, and a great deal of the country was under water, owing to the exceptionally heavy rains.

What a country some of it was to hunt in! There were large areas of *matete* grass, from 12 to 14 feet in height. To compete with this long grass I made a folding step-ladder out of a palm tree, rather similar to a garden ladder. This was quite light and could be carried by two porters. I gave them a bit of ladder-drill, and they became very good at putting it up without any noise. On getting near to elephants in this type of country I set the ladder up, and made the two porters hold the base of it, to support it and prevent it wobbling. From the top of the ladder I could get an excellent view of elephants and I shot several in this way, using a .318 magazine rifle.

I found this method most useful, not only for shooting but also for spotting elephants in long-grass country. I never put the ladder up much closer than 60 yards as, in the case of a charge, one could be fairly certain of stopping them with a magazine rifle, and it would give one the chance of several shots.

Just before finishing the safari I met Rex Fawcus, an old hunter and friend of mine, who also was on the same job for the Game Department, and I handed over the ladder to him. Later on I received a letter from him saying that he had met a double charge from elephants, and that one had smashed the ladder to pieces, killed the local guide, and knocked him and his gun-bearer over. I don't know the details of it all, but I expect he came down the ladder much quicker than he went up. He said the elephants in that area were getting most truculent, owing to being so much hunted.

I had with me, at that time, a most excellent lot of porters, a great many of them Wanyamwezi, and they are the finest porters in Africa. What a joy it is to be on safari with good porters! There is no more fascinating way of travelling. You come into your camping-ground, up goes your tent like clockwork, your loads are all tucked away under the fly of it, every man knows exactly where to place his load. A porter leads a strenuous life, carrying a 60-lb. load on his head for an average of six hours a day and sometimes a great deal more, over all sorts of country, into camp only to go out to collect firewood and water.

No wonder at times they get fed-up! But they are a happy-go-lucky lot and have a great sense of humour. Visit them in the evenings when they have finished their food, and they are sitting round their fires, and they are all split up into small messes. One finds them chattering away like monkeys and as happy as sand-boys. Feed them well and get them to laugh, and then they will do anything in the way of work.

On several occasions I had to visit the Mahenge *boma* to see Mr. Hickson-Mahoney, the District Officer, to find out the exact locality I was to hunt in. He was always most kind and hospitable, and did anything he could in the way of helping me if I required any more porters.

I had an ex-German askari, by the name of Musa, a most excellent man and a bit of a wag. I made him the *mnyapara* (headman) of my safari and well he did his job in looking after the porters. On the second day out from Mahenge *boma* I noticed three women, all dressed up in bright-coloured clothes, and I asked Musa who they were.

"Oh!" said the gallant Musa. "Those are *blankity yangu watatu* (my three blankets)."

I said, "What d'you do with three blankets?"

"Well," he said, "one sleeps on my right, the other on my left, and the fat one I use as my pillow."

About a month later I noticed that one of the fair "blankets" had disappeared, so I asked Musa what he had done with her. "Oh!" says Musa, "she has broken down and I've sent her away; the other was no good, so I gave her to your boy Feragi. That fat one I have kept as she keeps me warm."

I had also another ex-German askari, whom I used as a guide and tracker. As he had fought all through the German East African Campaign under General Von Lettow-Vorbeck, I nicknamed him "Von Lettow," and he was known as such by all the other boys in the safari. He was an excellent boy, quite a character and a great actor. Often when in camp he would get hold of some porters and drill them, strutting up and down with a stick and giving a very good imitation of a German N.C.O., all the time making ribald remarks to the porters in a mixture of German and Swahili words, all of which they treated as a huge joke. All these incidents go to keep everyone amused and add to the charm of safari life.

It has often been stated that elephants never lie down, and it is the exception for them to do so, but I have often seen impressions where they have been lying down. When hunting in Tanganyika Territory on the upper reaches of the Kilombero River, I was following up the spoor of a bull that had been raiding the Natives' *shambas* where I was camped. This elephant was a bad *shamba* raider and had killed the wife of the *Jumbo* of the village.

After following the spoor for about two hours my trackers suddenly said, " *Tembo, bwana, karibu, sana!* (Elephant, master, quite close!)" At the time we were passing through some flats covered in grass about 5 feet high. Suddenly I caught sight of something black in the grass and there, to my astonishment, was an elephant lying on his side with his head resting on an ant-heap as a pillow, 40 yards distant.

As the wind was right, I walked up to within 20 yards and put a bullet into the back of its head so as to get the brain but, owing to the grass, I could not get a good view. When I fired, the elephant was on to his legs and into his stride like a rabbit, and I was astounded that such an enormous animal could be on his legs so quickly. I dropped him with a heart shot with my second barrel.

On my return to camp, there was rejoicing, all the men, women and children turning out to welcome me. To show their thankfulness for being delivered from the marauder and killer, they brought food for my men, and eggs and chickens for myself.

On another occasion I came up to a small herd of elephants and on the windward side of them. I could just see the back of an elephant moving slowly at right angles to where I was then standing on an elephant path in bush and long grass, and as I thought this was probably a cow, the gun-bearer and I kept ourselves well hidden in the bush. When it came to the junction of the path I was standing on, it deliberately stopped,

106

turned and looked up the path, and without a moment's hesitation came bald-headed for us from about 60 to 70 yards away. I fired a shot high to turn her, but it had no effect and she came straight on and I had to shoot her. She had a quarter-grown calf with her, which probably accounted for her vicious charge.

The upper reaches of the Rufiji Valley, more especially in the wet season, are no health resort and a bad place for fever. After returning I went down with a real bad attack, one of the worst I have ever had.

XVI

FRENCH EQUATORIAL AFRICA — 1925-6

THE Ubangi-Shari district of French Equatorial Africa during the years 1925 and 1926 can aptly be called the last frontier of the professional elephant-hunters. Practically no hunters knew that, after the War of 1914-1918, the " old-time " elephant hunters could carry on elephant hunting under a legitimate licence and could shoot elephants *ad lib* with a few restrictions as to weight of tusks. Those who did know it, kept it very quiet. This licence could only be obtained from the Governor-General of French Equatorial Africa, at his own discretion.

My old friend Jim Sutherland had drifted up there from the Belgian Congo, but from his letters I could never gather full details of this licence. Through occasional letters from Jim and also having read that most excellent book of W. D. M. (Karamoja) Bell, *Wanderings of an Elephant Hunter* (1923), who had done a safari in French Equatorial Africa after the War of 1914-18, I knew very well that hunters like them would not go to a country like that just to shoot two elephants.

I was most anxious to go to that country. It was well off the beaten track, away from the ordinary safari in Eastern Africa, and apart from the hunting, there is always the charm of going into a country that has been little touched by civilisation, which was the case in French Equatorial Africa. It is an enormous country, bounded on the south by the Congo and Mboma Rivers, which divide it from the Belgian Congo; on the north, by Lake Chad, Nigeria and the Sahara; on the east, by the Sudan; and on the west, by the Atlantic Ocean.

The country in which Jim was hunting was an area in the Ubangi Shari district at the south-east of French Equatorial Africa, wedged in between the Belgian Congo and the Sudan. After having decided to go and join up with my old friend I could not get into touch with him, as letters took nearly three months to reach him. The other stumbling block was the licence. I got a letter of introduction to a high official in the French Colonial Office and went over to Paris to see him. He was most polite but told me I could only shoot two elephants on any licence that was issued. I don't think he knew any more about the Game Licences than I did.

On my return to England—I was home on leave from Kenya at the time—I happened one day to be walking down the Haymarket and went into a sort of French " Thomas Cook and Son " office and asked the clerk if, by any chance, he knew anything about the shooting licences in French Equatorial Africa. Much to my surprise, he said: " I can give you all the latest information about elephant licences in F.E.A. as, about two months ago an Englishman asked me the same question, and I've got all the information."

This he showed to me, and that is how I discovered it possible to get an elephant licence from the Governor of F.E.A. to shoot elephant *ad lib*. Who the Englishman was I never found out. Naturally, on this information it did not take me long to make all preparations for my safari.

I happened to meet about this time His Majesty the King, whom I had the honour of accompanying on safari as a hunter when he visited Kenya in 1924-5. He was then the Duke of York. He asked me all about the proposed trip and was most kind. He took all the trouble to go personally to see the French Consul at the French Embassy, who gave him a letter of introduction on my behalf. This, of course, was a tremendous help to me, as I found out later when entering the French territory.

I was accompanied by Dr. G. H. L. Fitzwilliams, a good sportsman, on the understanding that we should be quite independent of one another and that I could join up with Jim Sutherland. Fitzwilliams remained in French Equatorial Africa after I left and did quite well. The last time I met him was during the recent war, when we had a long talk about elephants and hunters. He was badly crippled with arthritis but had done splendid work during the " Blitz " on London.

We travelled by sea to Port Sudan in the Red Sea, then on to Khartoum by the Sudan Railways, and down the Nile by steamer to Terrekuta near Malakal. There we hired two rather dilapidated lorries and made our way to Yubo, a British post near the border of French territory. We had the devil's own job with the lorries at times as, owing to the rains only just finishing, they were continually sticking and sinking right up to the axles in mud. We would never have got through but for the aid of the local Natives, pushing and hauling. At that time the road was only about halfway through to Yubo, so we did the remainder of the journey with porters. One or two of the rivers were also in flood, and we had to swim across them.

On arrival at Yubo, officials were most kind and put us up, but the best news of all was that the French authorities at Zemio had sent porters and that they were waiting for us on the border. The porter question is always a difficult one, and it generally means hanging about for several days until one can collect them. Bimbashi J. R. N. Warburton and Bimbashi Burgers Watson were most kind and helpful to us during our stay. Warburton (better known throughout the Sudan as " Little Tich ") had accompanied the King and Queen (when Duke and Duchess of York) as Medical Officer on their safari in the Sudan.

He was in charge of a large Sleeping Sickness camp at Yubo and doing splendid work. He showed me round this camp, which was most interesting. If taken in the early stages, Sleeping Sickness (trypanosomiasis) can always be cured, and many Natives were doing work, and you would think nothing could be wrong with them. I met several Frenchmen up there who had had the disease, and after treatment were cured. I believe that Charlie Grey was one of the first white men to be cured.

After a stay of a few days at Yubo fixing up our loads, we left for Zemio. We were lucky to buy a couple of Abyssinian mules, not much bigger than a donkey; and now a few words on the much maligned mule will not be out of place. He is a good asset in elephant hunting; hardy as you make them; will live on next to nothing; sure-footed as a goat; and seldom ever goes sick; can be pulled and hauled across any sort of river or swamp; and, what is more, when going through very thick bush country where you cannot ride, will dodge and crouch under overhanging boughs just like a dog. He is a great saving when following elephant, if they cut out into the open bush and won't stop for miles until reaching some real thick bush again. When near the elephants one dismounts and the syce falls back with the mule for a couple of hundred yards or so.

But the trouble with the mule is that he is always unreliable, a bit too free and handy with his heels, and he will shy at almost anything. For instance, after leaving Zemio I was sitting on my mule, trekking along peacefully with the porters, musing about different things in general, when I dropped my cigarette case. The mule gave a terrific buck, and I turned a complete somersault, landing on the flat of my back. But with all his faults, give me the old mule to ride when after elephants. Being an old cavalryman with a lame leg, I think a bad ride is better than a good walk; and when after elephants you do have some gruelling tramps.

On arrival at Zemio we were entertained and put up by the French officials and received every courtesy from them. After a stay of two days, fixing up Customs, licences, loads and porters, Fitzwilliams left to make a main camp to the east of Zemio, and I made my way to Jim Sutherland's camp.

We used our main camp as a base of operations, and would go off for about seven to eight days' hunting in different directions and taking about 17 to 20 porters each. With this number of porters the loads were very light, and it had the advantage of allowing us spare men to bring back the ivory.

The country was rolling hills, covered with light bush and long grass, intersected by many streams and a few rivers all running into the Mboma River, which is a continuation of the Congo. On both banks of these rivers were thick bush and long grass, and that was the sort of country in which one generally found elephant.

What a glorious feeling it was in the morning to start off on safari thinking you were practically king of all you surveyed, roaming about where one liked and with no restrictions, and then, perhaps, coming across the fresh spoor of a big bull, or bulls on their way back into the " thick stuff " to lie up for the day. And what a thrill it gave, to know that, with luck, provided they did not get your wind you would be up with them within three hours or so!

There was little other game in this part of the country; a certain number of buffalo, a few roan antelope, reed buck and pig, and only on one occasion did I catch a glimpse of a lion disappearing into the bush. There is not much I can relate on this safari in the way of actual hunting, apart from the experience of five elephants charging or stampeding nearly over me.

Having been out for about seven days, I was just returning to my main camp when I came quite unexpectedly on to a single bull in fairly open forest country. I dropped it with the first barrel of my heavy rifle and put a second shot in to finish it off. Then, without any warning, I suddenly saw four elephants in line, close up to each other, through a thick belt of bush about 20 yards from me in the opposite direction from the elephant I had shot. They were coming for all they were worth straight for me. I only had time to seize my second rifle from Feragi, the gun-bearer, and blaze off straight into the face of the one nearly on to me. Luckily, this made it swerve aside, as I had no time to aim. In the meantime Feragi had slipped a cartridge into my heavy rifle and sent a shot into another half-grown elephant, which was following just in the rear of the four, which he luckily turned as it was also bearing straight down upon me. If it had not been for Feragi, I am certain one of us would have been in for a rough time and probably been smashed up, as I had no time to reload for a second shot, and the elephant was only about five to six yards distant when Feragi fired.

My porters were following on behind, about 70 yards away, and I thought that some of them might have been caught, but they had thrown down their loads and disappeared in the way only Natives have, and greeted it as a great joke.

In a case like this, one can't say it was a deliberate charge; it might just have been a stampede, but personally, I think it was a young herd bull, which was slightly in front that was really charging, and carried the

111

cows along with him.

The day before this episode I had been following a big herd of about 150 elephants for six days. I had got one bull out of this herd on the first day I had come up with them, carrying ivory of about 85 lbs. a tusk, and after that, they were moving fairly fast. On one occasion the herd split up into two, joining up again a day later, and it almost seemed as if they had a pre-arranged meeting place. I came up with them again on the fifth day, when they were resting in a large patch of long grass, about two miles long by a mile broad, and from a small hill I could look down and see the whole herd, which was scattered and broken up into small groups. I spent about three hours inspecting all the herd, looking out for a good tusker. I was at that time riding a mule and the grass was broken down by the wind. I could, by standing up in my stirrups, ride up to within about 60 yards of them and so was able to get a good view, always testing the wind, but there was nothing worth shooting.

Following the spoor on the next day, in the evening and just as I was about to make camp, I saw a great deal of smoke going up, obviously from a grass-fire, and at the same time heard a number of shots, so I pushed on for all I was worth. The herd had gone into another big patch of long grass and the Natives had fired the grass all round, making a ring of fire, with the intention of burning the elephants to death.

When I arrived the grass was nearly all burned out, and I saw about a dozen Natives disappearing into the bush on seeing me arrive on the scene. I sent a couple of bullets over their heads to hurry them on their way. I found two elephants had been burned to death and suffocated, also several with wounds from their rifles.

What happens in a case like this is that the elephants become so panic-stricken with the fire that they get burned and suffocated by the smoke. This is indeed a most cruel way of killing elephants and, of course, is illegal and firmly stopped by all European Governments in Africa, so that it seldom happens in these days.

Fire seems to upset elephants more than anything else, and on another occasion I saw a large herd driven out by a great grass-fire into open country. I tried to get a shot at a couple of bulls, which were right in the centre of the herd, but it was impossible, as every time that I got within about 80 yards of the herd, a cow would come rushing out making a half-hearted charge which really was all bluff, and the whole herd was in a thoroughly truculent and restless mood. This, I think, may account for the incident I have just related.

Once elephants have left the thick stuff, and gone into more open country, it often means a long and hard trek to come up with them. One rather amusing incident happened to Jim Sutherland at that time. He was following on the spoor of a single bull, with his porters about 200 to 300 yards behind him, when out rushed an elephant and charged the porters. The latter, of course, downed loads and fled in every direction. The elephant smashed to pieces Jim's load of chair and table, put its tusk through several of his cooking pots, and then cleared off.

One great advantage when hunting in this part of the country was that you did not have to bother about *posho* for the porters. When on a hunting safari, the porters just dug up a sort of sarvo root, which was to be found in all parts of that country, and boiled it; and as they were well supplied with dried elephant meat, they did themselves quite well.

Previously, I mentioned Jim's habit of being exceedingly polite to foreign officials. I'll quote one instance. Whilst with him at our main camp in French Equatorial Africa during 1925-1926 we had a lot of trouble with our porters. Most of them deserted one night, which put an end to all hunting. They were engaged on a month's contract, the reliefs being sent along every month by the local Chief. On this occasion, the reliefs did not turn up and our porters were about 10 days overdue, hence the desertions. The only thing was to go and see the *Chef de Poste* at the *boma* and get him to give us his help, so that we could make the Chief carry out his contract.

We left our camp one morning early, Jim riding his pony, Tumbo and myself on a mule—my mule was nicknamed Klondyke. Jim had his pony which had been brought down from the northern territories by Natives, and which he had used for hunting for nearly two years. The most extra-ordinary thing was that the pony, though in a tsetse fly country, had lasted so long; if going into some areas where the fly was really bad, he would leave the pony in camp. It eventually succumbed to the dreaded tsetse fly. Mules do better than ponies on safari. They can be kept alive for some time, even in a tsetse fly country, by giving them a very small dose of arsenic for about three days and then missing a day.

We arrived at the French *boma* about 11.30 a.m., were met by the *Chef de Poste*, and sat down at 12 o'clock and started on drinks. At 12.30 two missionaries turned up for lunch. Lunch started, and we never left the table until four o'clock. I must say I was thoroughly fed-up with the party, and all the wine that I was bound to drink did not have any hilarious effect. When the *Chef de Poste* had got into a good humour after a certain number of drinks, Jim got him to arrange with the Chief about our porters. In fact, by that time the *Chef de Poste* would promise anything that Jim asked him. The party broke up after four o'clock, and we hit the road for our camp and reached there about nine o'clock. I am afraid I told Jim what I thought of the lunch party and his overdoing of the diplomatic business.

113

One rather interesting thing happened at our main camp. The Natives brought in a leopard which had been caught by a python and crushed to death; they said that they had seen signs of the fight, but no trace could be found of the python. On another occasion, when we were back at camp, one of Jim's porters who had been absent a few days, turned up at the camp with an awful face, all bandaged up with dirty old cloth. When asked what had happened, he said that his wife had bitten him. He had evidently been having a "night out" to which his wife took exception. She certainly had made a real nasty mess of his face. European ladies take note of a novel way to deal with erring husbands!

Whilst sitting around the camp-fire one night, after being away on a hunt, yarning about our different experiences and making plans as to the part of the country in which to hunt so as not to interfere with each other, Jim related to me the following story. It was told him by a well-known missionary named Studd, who had taken up missionary work in the Belgian Congo in his early youth and spent the best years of his life there. I saw in the papers quite recently that he had died, doing missionary work up to the time of his death. Studd was the brother of the famous cricketer in the seventies and eighties of the last century, the late C. T. Studd, who played for Cambridge University and Middlesex; also for England at home and in Australia from 1882 to 1883. C. T. Studd died in his 71st year, on July 16th, 1931.

Here is the story. Studd was on safari somewhere near the Belgian Congo-French Equatorial border, but a good deal to the west of the country in which we were then hunting. Whilst passing through a village he went into a Native hut to shelter from the rain, and await his porters' arrival. Sitting on a stool, with food in front of her, was a rather ancient native woman. A man was in the hut and, as the woman took no notice of Studd and never moved, he asked the man who she was. The man replied: " Oh! That's my mother. She has been dead for years." This woman had been embalmed and it was perfectly done, but from where the Natives got the secret is a mystery. Perhaps from the Arabs, who had drifted down from Egypt in the old slave-raiding days. Personally, I don't put much faith in third-hand stories, but as this one had come from two absolutely reliable men, I leave it to others to judge.

There were, at that time, one or two French hunters. One could hardly call them hunters, as about all the " hunting " they did was to send out their armed boys to shoot elephant. The result was that they practically got none but wounded a great many.

Shortly after I left French Equatorial Africa, several of the old elephant-hunters went up there. Amongst them were Major Philip Jacobus Pretorius, Bill Buckley, a namesake of mine, Anderson and George Rushby, who is now in the Game Department in Tanganyika. Another English hunter, whose name I have now forgotten, was killed by an elephant in that part. One well-known hunter and character fell foul of the French authorities, who made no bones about it, but sent a patrol of askari out to his camp to arrest him. They tied him up and rushed him back to the French *boma*, and confiscated all his ivory and rifles —a rather drastic measure! I believe he took legal action against them, but got little satisfaction.

On the conclusion of my safari in 1925 I had to pass through Zemio in order to get my ivory stamped and the necessary papers for export. I also had Jim's ivory and we had made an agreement to go half shares on all ivory shot during my stay with him. Whilst at Zemio I saw two Natives brought into the *boma* by some police askari. The askari were taking no risks of their escape, as they were marched with their necks fixed between the fork of a bough of a tree, exactly like the slaves in the old slave-raiding days; they also had their arms lashed tightly behind them. As they had been marched for several days like this, I felt quite sorry for them.

These were the Leopard men, who had killed a Native. It is, I believe, a secret society which kills Natives, probably by a jab of a spear, and then claws them like a leopard, for they have a sort of claw fixed on their fingers. It was quite common on the West Coast and may go on in a quiet way at places off the beaten track even in these days. It is all a sort of fetish, to which uncivilised Natives are so prone.

The French officials told me that 60 per cent. of the population in that district had been wiped out by Sleeping Sickness, but now it had died out to a great extent, though there still remained a certain amount of it in the district. I must say I did not see the French taking much trouble to combat the disease, so different from just across the border in the Sudan, where some years ago it was rampant, but is now to a great extent stamped out, owing to the good work performed by the medical officers and Civil Officials. During my stay at Zemio the French officials were again most hospitable and helpful.

After getting all my papers for the export of the ivory, I left for the Sudan frontier, and there I met Jim as we had arranged. We spent a couple of nights together, yarning over old times and I finally parted from Jim. That was the last time I was ever to see my dear old friend, as he died in 1932, seven years later, still following the spoor of elephant. Like the good fellow he was, Jim had done everything to see that I had a good safari, always giving me the pick of the country to hunt and also the best local guides. What more could he have done for me?

XVII

ELEPHANT HUNTING: A CLASSIC SPORT

ONCE an elephant-hunter, always an elephant-hunter; never was there a truer saying. All other game seems little and insignificant in comparison with the hunting of the African bull elephant. What monsters they are, some of them standing nearly 12 feet at the shoulder and weighing over six tons.

The sportsman may have a surfeit of hunting other game. But for those who have had the luck to hunt elephant, legitimately or otherwise, continuously for years, it gets into their blood and becomes almost an obsession. It is a sport one will never tire of and one is always learning something new. The more one hunts elephants the less one seems to understand what they will do next. Very little of the romance, sport and adventure is left with the modern big game hunting; it has been killed, by the use of the motor car, but it still remains with hunting the elephant.

The motor cannot be used owing to the dense bush, but it has the great advantage of getting the sportsman quickly on to his hunting ground, where he can make his base camp to hunt from. After that, he has to do a real old-time safari with porters.

Any true sportsman who likes the actual hunting, the free and roaming life, and who is prepared to work hard and go light in the way of loads and few porters, and put up with disappointments, will enjoy a sport that is second to none, and will be provided with as much excitement as the average sportsman requires; and in the case of a charge in thick bush, or long grass, perhaps even a little more than he wants.

Even with the most modern rifle the killing of a big bull elephant in thick bush is not such a simple matter as most people imagine. Even at 20 yards one often cannot see him or, at most, only patches of him through the bush. It is extraordinary how such an enormous animal camouflages himself with the surrounding bush; and it is often most difficult to get a vital shot; and if he is not hit in a vital spot, owing to his enormous size and strength, his vitality is perfectly astounding.

There is, of course, a great element of luck attached to the hunting. I have known a safari go out for only about ten days' hunting and come back with two pairs of really big tusks, but that is the exception in these days when big tuskers are hard to come by. All this goes to make elephant

116

hunting the most exciting and fascinating of all big-game hunting.

And what a dance he will lead you! Sometimes through swamps where, if you step into his footmarks, you find yourself nearly up to your waist in mud and water; through long *matete* grass standing from 12 to 14 feet in height, forest country, bush country, up hill and down dale and more often in these days in a low-lying country with a pitiless sun beating down upon the hunter. No type of country seems to stop him. It is indeed a strenuous game, but what a thrill.

The days of the professional elephant-hunter are now finished as there are no countries left in Africa where you can get a licence to shoot elephants *ad lib*. Practically not more than two elephants are allowed to be shot on a licence for the year, and a hunter would be lucky to have anything left after paying for his licence and safari expenses. In these days the lot of the elephant-hunter is a hard one and full of disappointments. Perhaps he has the luck to strike a fresh spoor early in the morning and should be up with the animal after about three hours' spooring, and then, when he gets close up, the elephant gets a whiff of his wind and off he goes again. This may mean following all day and perhaps sleeping on the spoor before one comes up with him again, only perhaps to find that the elephant carries small tusks and that he is not worth shooting.

Very few sportsmen on their way up from Mombasa, on the Kenya and Uganda Railway, realise that they are passing one of the most untouched and finest elephant countries left in Africa. There are big stretches of country north of the railway, to the Tana River and beyond, that no white man has been into. (I am writing now of the year 1930.) It is an arid and waterless country, covered in most parts by dense bush, with practically no roads and a very little Native population, a hard country for both man and beast. All this goes to make it a natural sanctuary for the elephant, and here in this vast area roams " My Lord, the Elephant." Some of the biggest tuskers left in Africa are still to be found here.

I know of no country in Africa where the sportsman may stand so good a chance of getting a tusker carrying 100 lbs. or over on each tusk. There is a saying that the hunter walks a hundred miles for every elephant he shoots; personally, I should say that on an average he walks well over 200 miles in the above country to get a big tusker. He may, of course, have the luck to get one in the course of two or three days!

Different types of country require different methods for hunting elephants. The one I always followed, and which most hunters employ, is first to settle on the area in which to hunt over and make a base camp. Before selecting a base, there are two most important things to consider:

117

(1) it must be near some village or *duka* (Indian or African trader's store) where *posho* can be obtained for the porters; and (2) it must be a really good centre in elephant country to radiate from.

I cannot do better than describe a safari after elephants in the country east of Kitui, in the Ukamba country, and about 200 miles by car from Nairobi. This is all part of that good elephant country I have just mentioned lying between the Kenya-Uganda Railway and the Tana River. I have been hunting in that country on many occasions, sometimes on my own and at other times as a professional hunter to a party. First one takes over personal "boys," cook, gun-bearers, stores and equipment by lorry to a small village at Kanzigo, and there one recruits the porters. If one is by oneself there is generally not much difficulty, as one does not require many, but if taking a party a large number are required, and what's more, the Natives know that you must have porters and stick on the price of hire per month accordingly.

For hunting in that country it is absolutely necessary that one should get a really good guide who knows the country and all the waterholes. Otherwise, in the dry season one is absolutely jiggered and, what is more, the porters will not go for any great distance from the main base camp unless they have faith in the guide.

There are a few old Native elephant-hunters left who did a good deal of ivory-poaching before the Colony was properly controlled by the Game Department. Even up to recent years some of them have done a bit on the quiet, selling the ivory to Indians who cut the tusks up and smuggle them to the coast. One of the best known is M'kula, whom I have had several times with me on safari. He generally turned up after being engaged full of *pombe* (Native beer), from which it took him a day or two to recover. M'kula was an old man as Natives go and, like all Wakamba, slight of build but very wiry, always dressed in a loin-cloth and with a blanket or sheepskin slung round his shoulders, always carrying a bow and quiver full of poisoned arrows.

M'kula certainly knows the country for miles round and every waterhole in the district, and has nothing to be taught in the way of elephants. Although a first-class tracker, he is unreliable and is apt to get fed-up for no rhyme or reason. It's a devil of a job to keep him in good humour and, at times, he would make a saint use bad language. Like all Africans, he is full of superstition.

Every time I have engaged him as a guide, he would come to me before starting off on a hunt, for a cigarette, matches, some *posho* and a little whisky, which he would place on the grave of a pal of his who, some years before, had been killed by an elephant and was buried on the side of Itumba Hill, where I always made my base camp. If one did not

118

do this it would put M'kula in a bad humour, and all the boys would say a spell had been cast on the safari and that we would never have any luck.

One night, when I was questioning M'kula in my tent as to the particular area we should hunt, he being in a good humour under the influence of a cigarette and quite confidential, I asked him about the number of elephants he had shot, and he admitted that he had shot a good number. I know this to be true as the old rascal was constantly wanted by the Game Department, having spent a considerable time in jail at different periods for poaching elephants.

When asked about the effect of the poison, he said that if an arrow struck an elephant in the vicinity of the heart, that elephant would be dead within an hour; if in a less vital spot, it would take as much as 24 hours, but they seldom lost an elephant once it had been wounded, of course spooring it up afterwards. The poison, he said, was made from the bark of some tree (the name of which I have forgotten), boiled in a little water for many hours and mixed with goat's fat, which he insisted must be from a he-goat. Why a he-goat I don't know, nor did M'kula give any explanation when I asked him. This poison must be of terrific strength to finish off an elephant in such a short time. That is M'kula's version of it which I should say is true. The poison is formed into a thick paste, something like beeswax, and smeared over the base of the arrow head.

After collecting all the porters required I would start off from the base camp with about 12 to 15 porters, with rations for everybody, including myself, for about seven to ten days, all made up into light loads, sometimes in the dry season carrying water. One would then cut down, perhaps towards the Tiva River, a sandy river which in the dry season has only a trickle of water flowing, to see if we could pick up a fresh spoor.

All along the Tiva River are date-palm trees and fairly thick bush on either bank, but once one gets away from the river, one is into an arid and waterless country covered with patches of thick thorn-bush, some of it very dense. All this is a favourite haunt of the elephant, and one stands a good chance of picking up fresh spoor. Very often, however, one goes several days without seeing any spoor, and I've been as much as two weeks or more in that country before finding the fresh spoor of a bull to follow up. If not finding a fresh trail, I have often followed a day-old spoor as I found it quite often led me to a fresh one.

There is no mistaking the spoor of bulls as, in comparison with the cows, they are much larger. The circumference of the forefeet of a bull is anything from 50 to 60 inches, which means a big elephant, but one cannot lay down any hard and fast rule that the very big elephants always carry the biggest ivory, although it is the only thing to go on.

If not coming on to any fresh spoor by about one o'clock, I make

119

for some suitable place to make camp as, if by any chance one comes on to fresh spoor in the afternoon, it's 20 to 1 you won't come up to the elephant the same day, which means extra work for the porters with no results. One has to save them as much as possible as Wakamba in that part of the country, at the best of times, are a difficult lot to handle, and think nothing of going on strike and refusing to work.

From what I have seen and heard from Native hunters, the old bulls go to the Tiva River at night and drink and then they get away back into waterless bush-country, 15 to 20 miles from the river, and remain there for two to three days without drinking. They get a certain amount of moisture from sansaveria, a wild sisal plant, of which they are very fond. All this makes the country very difficult. To follow up a herd of elephants in this country is practically useless as the big bulls nearly always keep to themselves, either singly or, perhaps, two to five together. The Natives say they are like old men; they don't like to be worried with a lot of women about them. It is my experience that the bulls carrying big ivory are nearly always by themselves. The exception to this I have found to be in the Western Nile district of Uganda and in the Ubangi-Shari district of French Equatorial Africa. There I have seen the big bulls in large herds. up to 300, and when alarmed they get right into the middle of the herd surrounded by cows. This has been in comparatively open country for elephants, and I am certain they do this for protection, knowing they are safe in the middle of the women.

The great charm of hunting elephants is in the tracking and following the spoor. In soft ground a man who is nearly blind can follow the tracks, but when it comes to hard or gravelly soil it is most difficult to follow. To follow the spoor of a bull, which perhaps a herd of elephant has passed over, requires a real artist at the game, and there are very few Natives who can do so, and certainly no white man can compete with a really first-class tracker. The best tracker I've seen was an African who came from the Voi district of Kenya, and I had him on several safaris. He was a past-master at the game, never once did I know him to lose the spoor for any length of time; he would follow the spoor of a bull over which a herd had passed, and never faltering. At other times, if the bull we were following took a turn down-wind, he would leave the spoor, and make a half-circle round so as to prevent the elephant from getting our wind. cutting the spoor again a half-mile or more distant and that, mark you, on hard ground.

Hunting in this country when the leaf is falling, one can often follow the elephant by the leaves he has brushed off when passing through the bush, and this, at times, is most useful when passing over very hard ground. If one strikes the fresh spoor of a big bull, what a thrill it gives one and what a difference it makes to one's feelings! One can then keep going all day, and this also applies to porters. Wandering around the country looking for fresh spoor is a heart-breaking job and, when one camps one cannot go and shoot any meat for one's porters as the sound of a shot in that country scares the elephant away at once. Personally, I always take a .22 rifle when hunting in that district, and in the evenings stroll out and shoot guinea-fowl or dik-dik, the smallest buck in Africa, with a height of only about 15 inches, of which there are a great number and first-rate eating they are. The advantage of the .22 rifle is that it makes very little noise.

If I strike a fresh spoor, I make the porters, who are following myself and Feragi (my old gun-bearer) and a local guide, fall back about 200 to 300 yards; I always have a good tracker at the head of the porters who follow us. Very often one loses the spoor and then one casts round in circles until one picks it up again. It is always a good plan to mark where the spoor was last seen. Nothing is more disappointing than going all day on the spoor of an elephant and then entirely losing it. This often happens in a country where the going is hard and one has no really expert tracker. One can always tell when one is close on the elephant by the droppings and the chewed sansaveria; and when you get to steaming hot dung, you know that you are really close. One must move absolutely silently, testing the wind all the time. This I do with an empty film-tin, punctured with holes like a pepper pot, and filled with flour.

Supposing one has come up with an old bull; he will nearly always lie up for the day in the very densest bush he can find, very often turning and twisting in his tracks before doing so. This is done so that he can get the wind of the hunter who is following him. He may do the following: slink off without a sound, and how such an enormous animal can move so silently is almost uncanny; or he may go off with a rush, crashing through the bush and making a terrific noise. Then, occasionally, when an elephant knows he is being hunted, he will lie up in dense cover and wait for the hunter, often coming back on his own tracks and trying conclusions with a charge. This is not often the case, but more so in a country where elephants have been hunted by Europeans or Natives.

There are charges *and charges*! Some are merely bluff and only half hearted; others carry the charge right home and are out to kill. An elephant does not often start a charge from a distance of more than 60 yards, and for such a big animal he comes at a great pace, about 20 to 25 miles an hour.

I have, on several occasions, been charged by a cow or a bull carrying small ivory and, not wanting to kill, have put a bullet high up in the forehead, which will nearly always turn the elephant, and will do no more

121

harm than give it a bad headache, as the bullet just passes through porous bone without touching the brain. But it is a shot that I would not advise anyone to take in the case of a real bad charge when the elephant is at close distance, and when one cannot get in a second shot.

Often, in the case of a bad charge in thick bush, what makes matters so difficult is that one cannot see the elephant until he is only a few yards off, and what a sight he presents! Ears cocked, like two enormous sails, something between a runaway engine and a sailing-vessel as he comes bearing down on one. Sometimes with a scream but more often silently, he crashes through the jungle. There is only one thing to do. Stand and drive a bullet between the eyes at the base of the trunk. If the brain is reached the elephant will collapse on its knees as if pole-axed; if the brain is not reached it will nearly always slew him aside and give one a chance of putting a second shot into his heart, or its vicinity, as he passes. Sometimes I have seen elephants reel back into a sitting position on their haunches.

I have often heard of a herd of elephants charging on the sound of a shot in a country where they have been much hunted but, if that is the case, I think it must be very exceptional, otherwise there would be very few elephant-hunters. In most cases I think it is a case of the herd stampeding in the direction of the hunter. There is no doubt that, if one is firing at a bull which is mixed up in the herd, one stands a very good chance of being charged by a cow, and I have known of several accidents which have occurred in this way. In the previous chapter, dealing with the safari in French Equatorial Africa, I mentioned an experience of this nature which happened to me at that time.

XVIII

ELEPHANT HUNTING: SOME NOTES ON THE QUARRY

THERE is no doubt that the most important thing in hunting elephant is to work up against the wind. The slightest taint of a human being, and they are off. They rely on their sense of smell more than anything.

Nothing is more annoying than after following up an elephant all day, he gets a whiff of your wind in a country where they have been much hunted, and goes off for miles before stopping. Often, when I have been near elephants and the wind has been changeable, I have just gone back some distance, sat down and waited until the wind has been more settled before taking up the spoor again. As everyone knows, the wind is much more changeable in hilly country.

The elephant's sense of smell is very acute, and I have watched a herd of elephants from a hill when they were resting in the middle of the day about half a mile away, and the wind has changed suddenly, when up would go their trunks and off they would go.

Just above the eyes of an elephant there is a small gland, which gives out the most pronounced smell of elephant, more especially is it strong with old bulls. In this gland one often finds a small piece of wood, and the only way I can account for it is that the elephant is continuously brushing through the bush, and small bits of stick get broken off in the gland. I have found these bits of wood more often in old bulls — why I don't know. When cut out they simply stink.

Once I cut out one of these pieces and put it in a corked bottle, and gave it to a chemist. He made up some ointment with the same smell, as I thought this might defeat the elephants from getting wind of me. I tried this dope on two occasions when after elephant and the wind was changeable, smearing my arms and neck with the ointment, and making Feragi, my gun-bearer, do the same. It did not seem to have the desired effect, as they were off like the devil when they got our wind. Feragi said it was bad *dawa* (medicine), to which I agreed, and did not try the dope again.

The elephant's hearing for the enormous size of his ears does not seem to be anything like so acute as other animals; more so, when he is feeding or resting, but an unusual sound, such as the click of a camera,

123

seems to attract his attention. I don't think it is a question that they cannot hear, it's because they don't seem to bother, but once an elephant knows that he is being hunted, his sense of hearing is quite acute and even a broken twig is enough to make him bolt.

On one occasion whilst on the march with my porters following close behind, we ran straight into a herd of elephants in thick bush. The porters all threw down their loads and were up the trees like so many monkeys. You never heard such a clatter and noise. The elephants simply walked slowly away and started feeding again only about 100 yards away.

On another occasion, when following the spoor of a bull, I was suddenly caught in a heavy shower of rain. I shouted for my boy, who was some distance behind, to bring me my mackintosh. I put it on, gave the boy my blessings for being so far behind, and had only walked a few yards when I ran straight on to quite a good tusker standing in an open glade, about 20 yards away. He was not taking the slightest notice of all the noise we had been making, so I promptly dropped him.

Many hunters say that the elephant's sight is very bad. Personally I don't think it is nearly as bad as most people imagine and, it is like their hearing, they just don't bother, but when they know that they are hunted, I have known their sight can be quite good. I have previously quoted one particular instance of this. There are many other instances when I have seen elephants make quite good use of their sight, but then again one can approach quite close, and with little cover, and they will take no notice of one, always provided the wind is right. This goes to prove that one cannot lay down any hard and fast rules as to the elephant's eyesight and hearing.

There are many arguments and discussions as to the height of elephants. A 12-foot elephant has often been put down as a myth. I personally measured one shot by Mr. Lawrence C. Thaw, of New York, and it was 12 feet 2 inches at the shoulder, and as this elephant was shot under rather exceptional circumstances, I will relate the incident.

Whilst on safari with Mr. Thaw and his wife, in the Kondoa Irangi district of Tanganyika, early one morning we came upon the fresh spoor of three bulls. The spoor of one was enormous. We followed up all day, but I think they must have got a slight taint of our wind and it was not until about 5 o'clock in the afternoon, while following the spoor through a patch of bush, that we suddenly saw an elephant coming at right-angles all out, and bearing straight for us. Mr. Thaw and I fired practically together, as he was only about 12 yards away. I fired my second barrel as the elephant fell. Mr. and Mrs. Thaw were a little distance to my right. Without the slightest warning, another elephant burst through the bush on our left, nearest to me. I had only just time to jump aside and if he had stretched out his trunk he could have caught me. At the same time the faithful Feragi blazed off with my light rifle into his face, sending the animal reeling back and at the same time slewing him round.

As I was up against some very thick bush I could not get back any further, and had to do a sort of cake-walk to dodge the elephant's hind feet. The only thought that passed through my mind at the time was that I wondered if elephants kicked or not. He then went straight away and disappeared in the bush. Mr. Thaw had tripped up and fallen in the bush, so could not get a second shot off. Here, again, Feragi saved an awkward situation. Whether the second elephant was charging, or only stampeding to the shot, one cannot say, but it is the only experience I have had of two elephants charging from different directions. All this goes to show how the unexpected suddenly happens when after elephants, making it such a grand and thrilling sport.

The first elephant fell on to his knees and rolled over on his side with both forelegs fully extended straight out, and we both remarked on the unusual size of it. Old Feragi, who had had a lot of experience with elephants, said, " *Bwana,* that is the Sultan of *all* the elephants! "

I took a careful measurement from the shoulder to the feet, with an upright spear and straight stick stuck into the ground, and with a porter's rope stretched between. When we returned to the main camp I measured this rope and it turned out to be 12 feet 2 inches. As a matter of fact, I made it to be 12 feet 3½ inches, but knocked 1½ inches off to be on the safe side. The elephant had only one tusk of 81 lbs. If his size and height were any criterion, he should have been carrying tusks of over 200 lbs. each.

It is seldom that one can get a correct measurement of an elephant, as it is not often that they fall with the forelegs straight out and it is quite impossible to straighten them.

One reads of " elephant cemeteries " — a place where all elephants go to die. This statement probably originated from some white man coming across the bones and skeletons of elephants—but they never say they found ivory—that had been burned and suffocated by smoke caused by Natives firing the long grass.

It is not often one finds a dead elephant, but I have found them, with tusks intact, on several occasions. The only explanation I can offer is that elephants, if sick or wounded, make their way into the densest bush and then hyena and vultures clear up the mess. Many hunters say that a sick or wounded elephant, about to die, makes for the nearest water. The elephants I mentioned were a great distance from any water.

Whilst on safari with Captain T. Colville and his friend, Major Abell, both first-rate sportsmen, we found a dead elephant, with tusks of 81 lbs.

125

and 83 lbs. respectively, in the Ukamba country. The peculiar thing about this dead elephant was that the upper tusk was about 20 yards away from the remains of the body. Now how did it get there? Major Abell wrote to *The Field* at the time and stated the facts. There were many solutions, some saying that hyena had pulled it out of the socket in the skull, others that Natives had taken it out, had become alarmed, and dropped it. Personally, I think what happened was that the elephant was very sick and about to die. He may have been wounded, but more probably sick and very old and, just before he collapsed, he shook his head and, like old men whose teeth get loose, out flew the tusk.

When shooting in the Western Nile district with Mr. Mansfield Markham, we came across the body of a dead elephant he had shot about eight days before, and we were much surprised to see three elephants standing within a few yards of the carcass, which was then in a high state of putrefaction. This is unusual, as generally the smell of a dead elephant will clear all the other elephants away.

Cutting out the tusks from a big bull is an undertaking, as they are buried in a socket covered with bone in the skull to a depth of three feet or more and have to be cut out with an axe by a man who knows the job, otherwise the ivory is likely to be damaged. First, of course, all the flesh has to be removed from around the tusks and most of the head. If the tusks are left in a dead elephant for about five days they become loose, and can then be pulled out with ease.

In the hollow at the base of the tusk there is a nerve similar to the nerve in the tooth of a human being and, on the tusks being cut out, I have noticed a curious thing. The local guide and gun-bearer will nearly always take the tusks away into the bush by themselves before removing the nerve. They do this as they have a superstition that if the hunter sees the nerve taken out he will eventually be killed by an elephant.

The actual shooting of elephant is not so easy as most people imagine, although it is nearly always done at close range, on an average from 30 to 40 yards and sometimes very much closer than that. In these days, soon after the sun gets up elephants nearly always go back into the densest cover they can find. This applies more especially to the old bulls, and how such an enormous animal can conceal himself at such short distance is amazing. His whole body seems to blend with whatever type of bush or forest he may be standing in. I have often told this to sportsmen whom I have been out with, and they wouldn't believe it until they had seen it themselves.

The herds are sometimes met in comparatively open country, but seldom the bulls carrying the big ivory. Gone are the days one reads of of the " old-time " hunters in South Africa who used to hunt elephants on horse-back when the elephant used to roam in the open country but, against that great advantage, they were badly armed with old muzzle-loaders.

I am not going into all the details of the different vital shots, which I have never seen better described and illustrated than in W. D. M. (" Karamoja ") Bell's *Wanderings of an Elephant Hunter* (1923).

The most vital shots are the brain and the heart. The brain is the quickest and most humane and, if reached, the elephant collapses as if his legs had been knocked away from under him. It is always as well to put in a second shot, as he may only be stunned and may remain in that position for quite a time and then suddenly get up and go away, and it will not have any effect upon him.

The brain shot has the difficulty of being a small target. One has to judge the angle from which one is shooting to reach the brain, and this can only come from experience. To reach the brain when an elephant is standing broadside, aim a shade in front of the ear-hole, but if one is standing at an angle, one must shoot more forward or behind the ear-hole according to the angle. It requires a great deal of experience to gain this knowledge.

If an elephant is facing one, one cannot have a better guide than to put a shot between the eyes at the base of the trunk. It is a difficult shot to bring off, as one must also take into consideration how the elephant is holding his head and how close one is to him so as to get the right angle for both these shots.

The heart shot has the advantage of being a much larger target, and allows a larger margin of error, as if it is high it will sever the upper arteries of the heart, but if right will reach the lungs, both of which are fatal. With the heart shot the elephant will go off, as if not hit, for a 100 yards or more before he falls. This also applies to the lung shot, but he seldom gets up again. I have shot elephants with the heart shot which have collapsed in their tracks, but this is not often the case as they generally run some little distance.

If an elephant is feeding with his trunk up a shot in the chest at the base of the neck will also kill him.

When sportsmen who have not had much experience of elephant shooting fire for the heart, in nine cases out of ten they fire too high. This I put down to the enormous size of the animal and also to many people imagining that the heart is situated higher up in the body than with other animals. This is not the case. It is situated in the same position.

There are, of course, other shots, such as just above the root of the tail to reach the spine. This is a cruel shot and should hardly ever be attempted. It is of course fatal, but most difficult. It is much better not

127

to fire if the elephant is unwounded, as one will probably come up with him again and get a much easier shot.

When following elephant I have come up with them when they have been walking down an elephant-path, and all one can see are the hind-quarters and an enormous belly, which sticks out rather like a small-sized balloon if he has been feeding all night. I have often whistled, and the elephant will sometimes stop and turn half round, giving a chance of a vital shot.

Then again, there is the knee shot. Once the leg is smashed, an elephant is anchored and cannot move. I have read of this shot, but never yet have I met a hunter who has used it, or ever attempted it. The answer for the knee shot is simple. In nine cases out of ten one cannot see the elephant's legs, owing to bush, and if by chance the animal is standing in open country, why take such a difficult shot when there are others more easy and vital, open to the hunter?

When accompanying sportsmen on safari after elephants, I have invariably advised them to take the heart shot whenever possible, as it is by far the easiest.

As to the best rifle to use against elephant, this is a never-ending discussion and always open for argument. In my opinion a double-barrelled high-velocity rifle, the heaviest the hunter can handle with convenience, anything from a .400 up to a .577 rifle. A .600 rifle is too heavy and has not the penetration powers of a .577 rifle.

Elephant hunting in these days is nearly always in thick bush and at close range, and with a heavy rifle you can fire quite as accurately, to all practical purposes, as with a light rifle, up to 40 yards. A double-barrelled rifle has the advantage of being able to get off a second shot quicker than a magazine rifle, although some will not agree with this statement. More especially is it more useful in the case of a charge in the " thick stuff," when range is limited and one uses it just like a shot-gun. A small-bore rifle will kill an elephant if in the right spot, but it has nothing like the stopping power, and in the case of a charge, if the brain is not reached, it would probably not turn the elephant. But the same shot from a heavy rifle would bring him to his knees or slew him aside, and give the hunter an easy shot for his second.

That great Elephant-hunter, W. D. M. Bell, shot most of his elephants with a light rifle, his favourite being a .275 bore. But Bell was an exceptionally fine shot and a past-master at finding the brain from any angle. He had the advantage of doing his hunting in an unadministered part of Africa, where elephant licences were unrestricted as to numbers.

Take a magazine rifle, such as a .318 bore, as a second rifle, and then, if you have the luck to come across elephants in open country at a distance and more especially if on the move, I would always use the light rifle. That is, of course, quite a different proposition, but hunting elephants in thick bush with a light rifle—most decidedly *no*!

XIX

LIONS: "MAN-EATERS" AND OTHERS

I WILL not go into all the details of the hunting of lion, as so much has already been written by other sportsmen, but will only touch lightly on some of my personal experiences and certain incidents that have come to my notice.

A lion can easily be killed with a small-bore rifle, and does not seem to have the same vitality as many other animals. In the case of a charge, he must be hit in a vital spot, either the brain or heart, or smash the shoulder which will enable the hunter to get in a second shot. A lion can come at a terrific speed when charging, galloping like a dog. I've only been charged by lion a few times, and on all occasions they had been wounded.

I have heard, and read, that many lions, when about to seize their victim, rear up on the hind-legs, but the people whom I know have been mauled, both white men and natives, have nearly always been bitten about the thigh. The other body and arm wounds have been inflicted when the victim was knocked down and lying on the ground.

Seldom will lion charge from a distance of more than 60 to 70 yards, but I have heard of cases where they have charged from a much greater distance. Once a lion or lioness has been wounded, they invariably make off into the thickest cover they can find, then it is up to the hunter to use every means to finish the lion off. Very often, if you have marked the lion, you can induce him to charge into the open by getting your gun bearer to fire a shot, or other Natives to throw stones.

If you have to follow him up by spooring, then go very slowly, stopping every now and then, and don't bother about the spoor but let your gun-bearer do that. Keep your eyes skinned for the slightest movement, as lions can be devilish cunning. The way they can conceal themselves in patches of grass or bush is astounding, and instinctively they seem to appreciate just the right opportunity to charge the hunter. Not every lion or lioness will charge, even when wounded and followed into bush or long grass. I have personally known them to bolt on several occasions when being followed up. A lioness is far more likely to charge than a lion, and, what is more, they are quicker. Personally, I do not like following wounded lions or lionesses. Once bitten, twice shy! But it is a job which sometimes has to be done.

130

As an example of how lions will await their opportunity to charge, I was hunting with my friend, the late Captain Sir Pyers Mostyn, in the Ngoro-Ngoro Crater during 1921. I had wounded a lion, which had bolted into some long and thick grass, a terrible bad place in which to follow up a wounded lion. As the grass was dry, we fired it. Pyers stood at one end and myself at the other.

I was just on the point of turning round to leave as the grass was practically all burned out, when out came the lion straight for me like a shot from a gun. I was lucky to stop it. When looking over the lion we saw that its tail was badly singed with the fire. A clear case of cunning-ness, for he lay absolutely doggo until seeing me partly turn round to leave. If he had only waited a moment longer, he would have had me for a cer-tainty. I suppose the fire was just too much for him.

I cannot pass this safari with Sir Pyers Mostyn without writing a few yarns about him. Pyers crammed more travels and adventures into life than any man of his years whom I ever knew, until his death at a compara-tively young age, in his early forties. He had served with his Regiment, the Welsh Fusiliers, during the Great War with great distinction, receiving the Military Cross, and, from what I have heard, he deserved something more. Twice wounded, once very severely, and then looking for more, he was knocked out by a blow on the head in the Irish trouble after the War.

He was a grand all-round sportsman, a good horseman, and a fine pilot, flying his own 'plane. A few years before his death he had farmed in the Nyeri district of Kenya, and his chief form of amusement was pig-sticking and " bull-baiting " rhino. That is to say, he would round up an old rhino on his pony which generally ended in the rhino taking the offensive. Pyers told me that on one or two occasions he had all his work cut out to get away from one, even when riding a good pony, which gives a very good idea of the pace that a rhino can move for such a clumsily-made animal.

He had smashed himself up in every conceivable way, pig-sticking, flying, falling through a bridge in Portuguese East Africa in a car on a shooting safari—one of his natives being killed, and he himself stretched out and nearly killed—and on another occasion knocked head over heels by an elephant. Pyers met his death when schooling a pony over a fence. The pony came down with him at the fence and threw him on to his head and fractured his skull. This caused his death shortly afterwards, on February 28th, 1937. The tragic part of it was that the pony, which Pyers was schooling at the time of his death, also killed Capt. Eric Gooch, a well-known and popular settler in Kenya, whilst out pig-sticking. The pony put its foot into a hole, threw Gooch and broke his neck. I am very fond of horses, but I think that pony deserved a bullet for killing two such good fellows and sportsmen.

Pyers was a most quiet and unassuming person, most popular with everyone who knew him, and a great loss to Kenya. He was a man who, I think, had no nerves and one of the very few people who did not know what fear was, and there are mighty few of them.

Now I will hark back to our camp in the Ngoro-Ngoro Crater. We had come up from Arusha with a porter safari. The road was not through to the escarpment in those days and only a Native path led down into the crater. It was our intention, after hunting in the crater, to make our way to the Serengeti Plains, as this was before motors had opened that country up. To do this we sent back our porters to Arusha in order to bring up more *posho,* so that we could make a dump at the crater. Unfortunately we could not carry out this plan as Pyers was feeling far from fit. He had had trouble with his old war wound and was laid up in camp for several days.

At the time there was a Captain Hurst who had built a *banda* (grass hut) and was living in the crater. Hurst was a very keen and experienced hunter, who spent his time in taking photographs of game and studying animal life in the crater. After arrival and making our camp we got into touch with Hurst, and he rode over to our camp on a mule one morning. He told us that on the way over he had wounded a lion, and it had gone into a thick patch of long reedy grass. Hearing that we had a couple of dogs—they were a mongrel breed with a good dash of Airedale in them, most useful in locating and rounding up a wounded lion as they attracted his attention by yapping around him and thus gave the hunter a chance to approach and get a shot in—Hurst asked us if we would care to come and help him round up this lion with the aid of the dogs. This we did. On arrival at the patch of grass into which the lion had gone, we did every-thing possible to locate the beast but without success, so we came to the conclusion that it must have passed through or else gone into some other cover.

As Pyers was not feeling too fit we both returned to our camp about 11 o'clock, but Hurst took the two dogs with him to try another patch of grass on the way back to his camp. As we made for our camp we heard a couple of shots, but thought nothing of it. About three o'clock in the afternoon the boy turned up with the dogs, and I asked him about the two shots. " Oh! " said the boy, "A lion had caught the *bwana,* knocked him down, and he was covered with blood." As Pyers was not fit, I got on to my mule and galloped over to Hurst's camp, taking some dressings and iodine. I found him not nearly so bad as the boy's report indicated. What happened was that Hurst had come on the wounded lion, which had promptly charged and knocked him down, but, luckily for him, one of his shots broke the lion's jaw. Its blood had poured all over Hurst, making

132

him look an awful sight. Hurst was not badly mauled, but had a good number of small wounds and a couple of bad bites in the thigh.

I cleansed the wounds and syringed out the two deep bites with neat iodine. Poor Hurst nearly passed out in a faint from the pain of the iodine, and I must say that I got the wind-up, thinking the iodine business had been overdone. Anyhow it did the trick. The wounds healed without any sort of poisoning, and Hurst was quite fit again within three weeks. The secret is to treat the wounds as soon as possible and to drive some sort of very strong disinfectant right down to the bottom of the wounds. Nine cases out of ten, it is blood-poisoning that kills the hunter from wounds caused by lion or leopard.

Poor Hurst's luck was dead out, as shortly after this he was hunting elephant—I believe in the Mahenge district—and was killed by an elephant which smashed him to pieces. I don't think anyone ever knew exactly what happened. The only evidence came from an African who was acting as gun-bearer to him, and it was all rather contradictory.

Hurst, as I said, was a very experienced hunter and had shot a number of elephants before this. A good sportsman and one who had done very good work as a Scout in the German East African Campaign of 1914-18, for which he received the Military Cross.

Shortly after the first Great War I was on safari with a friend of mine, with an ox-waggon and a few porters. This is a very comfortable way of doing it, provided you have a good team of oxen and a driver who knows how to handle them, but it is too slow for the sportsman in these modern days of hustle.

We were out for a general shoot, but I also wanted to look over the country for the purpose of taking shooting-parties out. We decided on first making for the Yatta Plains, about 60 miles east of Nairobi, and then on towards Kitui and the Tiva River. The Yatta Plains at that time were a much-favoured hunting-ground, but now a great deal of it is under sisal, thus spoiling yet another bit of " Old Africa."

For about ten days we camped on the Yatta Plains, and shortly after our arrival were joined by my wife and my partner on the farm, Captain A. J. Dudley, who came by motor. I was out early one morning and came on five lions on a " kill," but some bad shooting only killed one. Sending out the ox-wagon, I had the carcase brought in to camp where it was skinned and then dragged out of camp for about 100 yards. This was not done until the evening through the slackness of the boys.

In the morning the boys told us that they had heard lion at night and close to the carcase of the lion. We went out and had a look. Not a scrap of the carcase was left, nothing but lion spoor all round and not a sign of hyena spoor. There is no doubt whatever that the carcase had

133

been eaten by its own kind and these lions were nothing but a lot of blinking cannibals. I have read, and heard it stated, that lion will not eat other lion. I often wonder if the lion had not been skinned, whether this would have happened.

There happened to be a party of South African Dutch in the vicinity with their wives and children, trekking about with a couple of roof covered ox-wagons, just as they did in the old trekdays in South Africa. They were out for shooting lions and selling the skins. One of the Dutchmen got very slightly mauled by a lion, and I met him shortly afterwards. He had only a slight wound on a hand, but neglected it and, in consequence, blood-poisoning set in and he died shortly afterwards.

Lions have been shot from a hide-out or *boma*, as it is usually called in this country. The *boma* is built of thorn-bushes with just enough room for a couple of people to lie down, and a small hole is made for a look-out and to shoot through. A small opening is left at the back to allow one to crawl through and blocked up by a good stiff thorn-bush after one gets in. The " kill "—zebra for preference—is dragged up close to the hole through which one is shooting. It is placed not more than about a yard from the point of firing but wants to be well pegged down to prevent a lion dragging it away.

My wife was very anxious to shoot a lion, so one evening we took up residence in the *boma* just when it was getting dark. We also had with us a gun-bearer with a long spear to prevent hyena getting on to the " kill." The first scavengers of the veldt are the jackal, then come the hyena, who clear off the jackal. If any lion are about intending to come on to the " kill," the jackal and hyena clear off immediately. On this occasion, after being visited by jackal and hyena, the lions arrived about eleven o'clock and came in absolute silence. They make a low growling noise when they get on to the " kill," but after that one hears nothing but the crunching of bones or tearing of flesh.

On peering through the look-out hole, it seemed like nothing but a seething mass of lions. After letting them settle down to the eating business I fired first and one lion rolled over dead. The others cleared off at once. After about 20 minutes back they all came, and this went on until about half an hour before dawn. My wife shot two.

Now this was the most astounding part; the lions kept coming back, with dead lions around them, until there were only two left on the " kill." I fired with a heavy double-barrel express rifle and killed one, but, to my astonishment, the other lion never moved off the " kill " and went on feeding as if nothing had happened. I then killed the last one with my second barrel. The blast from a heavy cordite rifle is terrific, and at night one sees about a foot of flame come out of the barrel, and this last lion was lying less than two yards from the lion killed with the first barrel.

In the morning we picked up two lions and three lionesses, the lions having very poor manes. All were dead within a radius of about 20 yards, so we had not the hazard of looking for any wounded ones. That is when all the trouble starts. To say the least of it, wounded lions are apt to be a bit peevish.

That was my wife's first experience of lion, but what with the smell of a two-days-dead zebra combined with the smell of the lions, she said it was quite enough for one night. The only excitement during the night was when one of the lions, after being shot, made a rush at the *boma*, crashed up against the side of it, and came in half way to fall over dead.

This may sound rather like slaughter but, in those days, lions were listed as vermin. They are now quite rightly on the protected list of the game regulations, and shooting from a *boma* is now illegal.

Shortly after my safari to the Yatta Plains, Kitui and the Tana River, I went on safari with my wife to the Southern Masai Reserve beyond Narok, again with an ox-wagon and a few porters. I was doing this to look over the country, as I had a party coming from England for a shoot. Parts of this area are quite lovely and first-rate country for a general shoot.

One morning, while sitting in camp, some Masai came up and said that they had just seen a "troop" of six lions not far away. We left immediately to try and get a shot. At that time I had engaged a boy whose name, I think, was Juma: anyhow, I'll call him Juma. He was the type of boy one would call a "white man's burden," a sore trial to the temper, born lazy and dirty, with as much brain as a rabbit, and always in trouble with the other boys. He was an exception. Most of the safari "boys" are excellent, cheerful and hard-working.

Coming up with the lion, not much more than 300 yards from the camp, I shot one, but, owing to the bush, did not get another chance. They turned sharp left-handed, going off at a gallop in the direction of our camp, but, after a short distance, they settled down to a fast trot. Unknown to us, the bright lad Juma had come out of camp to see what was happening. The country just around there was rather undulating with scattered bush.

Juma received the shock of his life when, owing to the folds in the ground, he was suddenly confronted by five lions. Losing his head and instead of running off at an angle, Juma took the same line of country as the lions, running practically alongside them but slightly ahead. This continued for about 200 yards when suddenly he tripped up and went head first into a thick thorn-bush. The lions passed quite close but took not the slightest notice of him. He had never moved so fast in all his life, and it

135

took him quite a time to recover from the shock. He was greeted with roars of laughter from all the other boys in camp who had seen Juma's performance. That was just the sort of thing which amuses them and is thoroughly enjoyed, for most Africans have a great sense of humour.

When man-eating lions are mentioned, it always reminds me of the famous (or infamous) man-eaters of Tsavo which took such a toll of the Indian coolies working on the construction of the Uganda Railway. Their boldness and cunning have never been surpassed. It got to such a pitch at one time that the Indian coolies refused to work. All this has been graphically described by Lieut.-Colonel J. H. Patterson in his book, *The Man-Eaters of Tsavo* (1906).

I have had so little experience of man-eaters that I will only touch slightly on this subject. During the East African Campaign of 1914-18 I was with a column operating against the Germans in Portuguese East Africa. At this time the column was resting for a day near the Lurio River. About 10 o'clock in the morning, when sitting down and having a chat with my old friend Charlie Mills, a headman of the porters rushed into the camp and told us that a lion had just taken one of the porters who was bathing in a stream quite close to camp. Seizing our rifles, we went to the stream and found about 100 porters in a great state of excitement. They told us all were bathing and washing clothes when, without warning, a lion had suddenly jumped in amongst them and carried off one of their fellow-porters. We followed the lion, which we could easily do as he had dragged the unfortunate porter along the ground, and came on the body about 300 yards away. Half of the neck had been eaten and one of the arms was completely gone. Evidently the lion had heard us and cleared off. We followed the spoor for some little distance and then lost it. As the column had sudden orders to move on, we could do nothing more in the matter. This just shows how bold lion can be, for the porters were making no end of noise, laughing and shouting, and thoroughly enjoying a bathe in the stream.

A friend of mine, who was also out with a column operating in Portuguese East Africa, actually shot a lion standing over a woman it had just killed. All I have heard leads me to believe that man-eating lions are more common in Portuguese East Africa and Northern Rhodesia than in any other part of Africa. There were also quite a number of cases of sentries being taken by lion during the war, both in German and Portuguese East Africa. Cases of man-eating lion going into huts and taking Natives away are quite common occurrences where man-eaters are concerned. Jim Sutherland had a boy, when I was with him, who told me that at night a lion had entered his hut and seized him by the leg—he showed me the lion's teeth marks. He was dragged outside the hut, but

136

luckily for him some of his pals picked up some firewood, threw this at the lion, and made it clear off.

Another instance I came across was in the Mahenge district of Tanganyika Territory during 1923-4, when hunting elephant. A lion and lioness killed 23 Africans before being trapped or rounded up by the Natives, and this was within a period of about two months. This lion and lioness were devilish cunning. They killed in a village, and the next day were 20 miles away, before killing again.

I think the chief causes of lion turning man-eaters are: (a) lack of game, (b) finding that Natives are easy meat in the way of killing for a meal, (c) younger lions follow the example of their elders in that particular line; and, (d) old age, when they find difficulty in killing game.

There are not many instances of man-eating leopards, but they do occur sometimes. An extraordinary case of a leopard mauling five men at Kilimani, which adjoins Nairobi, occurred in the April of 1945. The leopard must have come out of forest near the Ngong Road at no great distance, and an Italian prisoner-of-war who was working with some others, was the first to receive the attack. The leopard suddenly appeared and mauled him in the back, then went for an askari, who had to be sent to hospital, entered a garden and there mauled another askari. In the meantime some other Italian prisoners-of-war had rushed off to Kilimani Police Station and reported the facts to the Inspector, who issued rifles to police constables.

The leopard then entered a house, pursued by the Inspector, and greatly upset the household which included a European lady. He passed through the house into the garden, with the Inspector hot on his heels, and then turned and charged the Inspector. He fired but failed to stop the leopard, which mauled him rather badly about the face. The beast left the garden and then went straight for a Native police constable, also mauling him. The leopard was eventually shot by another Native constable. Not a bad bag for one morning! I can't think why this leopard, absolutely unprovoked, attacked the Italian in the first instance. All this happened in broad daylight and in a built-up area.

I cannot pass over lions without mentioning the famous Serengeti lions, although so much has been written about them and they are known to many sportsmen who have visited East Africa. These particular lions have shown great sense in making their headquarters round the Game Ranger's house at Banagi Hill, for so many years, until the outbreak of Hitler's War, occupied by Captain M. S. S. Moore, V.C., now Game Warden of Tanganyika, and his wife. They are known to all their friends as Monty and Audrey, and are old friends of mine. The lions and the game of Serengeti owe them both — Audrey Moore is also an Honorary Game

Warden—a great debt of gratitude for the way they have been looked after, by way of " Closed Reserves " for lions being made, seeing that the game laws have not been broken by visiting sportsmen and others, and also cutting down the number of lions to be shot outside the " Closed Reserve " to one.

The number of lion to be seen on the Serengeti is astonishing. I should say that in the course of a week's touring about in a car one would see well over a hundred different lions, prides of 15 to 20 being common. Lions can be seen following a lorry towing a dead zebra, pouncing on the zebra and having a sort of tug-of-war with the lorry, and when the zebra is loosened the lions often follow up to play with the rope; all this with people in the lorry taking pictures. It must be seen to be believed. On one occasion I was camped with a party quite close to " Monty " Moore's house. In the night the lions started playing about with the dustbin and at other times chased the cat round the house.

Of course these lions are practically semi-tame, though no undue liberties should be taken with them. A lion *is* a lion; but several people have asked me if they are a different species of lion! The answer to that is let them put a bullet into them, and then follow them when wounded into the bush, and they would very soon find out that these are very much the lion one so often reads about—a raging rampant beast that will eat anything. Some years ago a lion was wounded by a visitor quite close to Banagi Hill and charged him, mauling him so badly that he died shortly afterwards. It goes to show that a lion is a lion, from whatever part of the country he comes. Wonderful photos and pictures, of course, have been taken of them under these conditions. They are about the easiest animals to photograph, but not outside this " Closed Reserve."

I was once out with a party in that part of the country, but did not happen to be with them at the time when they left camp after tea for a short tour in the car. They came across five lions, which at once expected to be fed and followed the car nearly into camp. It fairly put the wind-up these people. I don't wonder, as it is rather disconcerting to have five lions lolloping along close behind the car, and more especially as they did not know that the lions in this part of the country were in the habit of doing that sort of thing. The fact is some of these lions are getting so damned lazy that they won't trouble to hunt for themselves but wait to be fed from a lorry. This, of course, is a bit of an exaggeration.

On several occasions I have known lions to wander right through the camp at night, past all the boys, not taking the slightest notice of anyone, but badly putting the wind-up the boys who make a quick bolt for their tents. Personally, when camping I always sleep with the fly of my tent open, but when in this country either I close the fly of the tent or put some chairs in front. Monty and Audrey Moore's pets, as they call them, are a bit too familiar. Not for a moment do I think that they would tackle anyone asleep in bed, but I strongly object to a lion poking its nose into my tent. With the Serengeti lions one never knows where they will wander. As Audrey Moore says in her most interesting book *Serengeti* (1938), which gives such a good description of the lion and game of the Serengeti, these lions will do almost anything except eat you and would probably do that, too, if encouraged. I expect that after these war years the lions will have to be re-educated and fed from the lorry so as to have their photos taken again, as practically no safaris have been into that country since the war started.

I quote the following incident as related by the Game Warden of Uganda, Lieut.-Colonel C. R. S. Pitman, D.S.O., M.C., and mentioned in his book *A Game Warden Takes Stock* (1942)—an astonishing story, supported by photographic evidence, of an emaciated and mangy lion in Northern Rhodesia which, when prowling round the outbuildings of a Government station, got its head through a lavatory seat and could not get it out. It was shot, with the seat fixed round its neck like a horse-collar.

After this incident, I don't think anyone can tell what lions might do!

XX

DANGEROUS GAME

SO many people often ask the question—which is the most dangerous game species. Personally, I would rather side-track the answer as there are so many different conditions under which the hunter may meet animals classed as dangerous. A hunter may have the misfortune to be mauled by a lion, or smashed up by an elephant or buffalo, and he will, inevitably, be prejudiced in classing the animal by which he was caught as the most dangerous. There are other reasons, which I give as follows, without going too much into details, as it might be a bore.

One might almost include bees and hornets under this category, as they are often met with in bush and forest country. When hunting, if one has the misfortune to be attacked by a swarm of bees, it is no laughing matter, and I have known cases where people, badly stung by a swarm, have nearly died from the effects. On one occasion when I was hunting with porters on safari, a swarm of bees attacked them. Never have I seen porters scatter so quickly, throwing down their loads and bolting in every direction. It was nearly an hour before the bees allowed them to return and pick up their loads, which were scattered about all over the place. Before this, every time they attempted to pick up their loads the bees were on to them immediately.

The animals confined to Africa which I class as dangerous are elephant, rhino, lion, buffalo and leopard. Very few of these animals will charge unprovoked, and they nearly always make way for men. Elephant are more likely to charge unprovoked than any other animal, with the exception of that cantankerous old devil, the rhino. In most cases it is nothing but bluff and they will often swerve aside when within about 20 or 30 yards, but there are a few which mean business.

All dangerous animals vary very much in temperament, just like human beings, and the person who lays down hard and fast rules as to what different animals will do can be written off as having had no experience of dangerous game.

There is no doubt that outside the Game Reserves and in a country where animals have been hunted, they are much more apt to charge than in the Reserves. There is no doubt that the African elephant is not a bad-tempered animal by nature. One has always to remember that

140

elephant have been hunted for their ivory all over Africa, both by Europeans and Natives, from time immemorial and this has naturally made them dangerous.

There is still another factor which, in my view, is the most important of all. That is the type of country in which an animal is wounded. All animals are easy meat in open country, provided the hunter gets as close as possible before firing and makes certain of the first shot which has a more paralysing effect than any shot afterwards on any animal, dangerous or otherwise. Elephant are 70 per cent. more easy to kill in open country than in thick bush, but it is not often that one has the luck to find them in such country. Even the old rhino is no mean adversary in thick bush or forest country, but I do not put him in the same class, from a danger point of view, as elephant or buffalo, as the rhino is so easily killed or turned for such a big animal. Following up wounded lion, buffalo, elephant or leopard in the " thick stuff "—long grass or bush—is a highly hazardous game and they are all equally dangerous. On several occasions I have seen elephant, knowing they are being hunted, double back on their tracks and charge even when not wounded.

There are charges *and* charges from all of these animals. Some are just bluff and are not carried home; others are all out to kill at any price, and they come at a terrific pace. Often a so-called charge in the case of a herd of elephant or buffalo is nothing more than a stampede; granted, that the result may be the same to the hunter as a real charge. One statement which I have so often read in books is that the hunter has avoided a charge by climbing up a tree. I can't understand this tree-climbing business, as nearly all the determined charges seldom start from more than 60 to 70 yards, and so give a hunter no time to climb a tree. There are exceptions, and the rhino is one. If he gets the wind of a hunter in open country, he will often start from 100 yards or more, advancing a few yards at a walk, then stop and shake the head from side to side, then, probably go off again at a walk, but after a short distance, break into a trot, and then, if he really means business, break into a gallop over the last 20 to 30 yards. Yes—granted the hunter may climb up a tree in a case like this. With all other animals they come at such a speed that it would be absolutely fatal to turn and run for a tree.

There is *only* one thing to do, and that is to stand firm and shoot, most important of all, not to shoot at too great a distance but to hold your fire as long as possible. The one animal I think the most difficult to stop in a determined charge is a buffalo, for his vitality is perfectly astounding, and I will give the following instance to show how a buffalo will carry through his charge, though mortally wounded.

At the time I was on safari with the late Rear-Admiral Sir Basil

Brooke. We were camped on the Guaso Nyiro River in the Northern Frontier Province of Kenya and, early one morning, coming upon a solitary bull buffalo, the Admiral fired a trifle too far back behind the shoulder. The buffalo cleared off, going into a patch of thick bush on the gentle slope of a small hill. As we were walking up the hill to get above the buffalo, out he came, full belt and straight for us. Admiral Brooke had a double-barrelled .500 express and myself a double .577 rifle. The Admiral fired first from about 50 yards. I shot immediately afterwards, both shots apparently taking no effect, as the buffalo never faltered in his stride or slackened his speed.

Brooke shot again, and I fired my second barrel at a range of about nine yards, but again the shots seemed to have no effect. The Admiral took a flying leap as the buffalo passed between us, the horns missing him by inches. Then the buffalo turned a complete somersault and fell stone-dead. We both examined him to see where our bullets had hit him, only to find they were all in the chest and every one would have proved fatal. I could hardly believe it possible for an animal to come on like this one did. One might reasonably think that any one of the shots must have brought him down, at least to his knees.

The only time I have ever been charged by any animal unprovoked —except elephant and rhino—was by a cow buffalo. At the time I was with a friend who was keen to get a buffalo and, having had no luck all day, we were returning to our camp along an old game-path. Suddenly, without the slightest warning, a buffalo charged out of the bush, grunting as it came, and not more than 12 to 15 yards away. At the time I was carrying a .318 rifle. I just had time to get it half way up to my shoulder and fire. By a 100 per cent. fluke I hit the buffalo in the spine, dropping her dead at my friend's feet. At the same time as firing, I took a head foremost dive into the bush in a small donga on my left. This cow buffalo had no calf with her. This took place near a settled area and she may have been wounded previously, but we could not find any sign of a wound. These are the only two occasions on which I have been charged by buffalo.

Some may suppose from all the mauling which I have related that big-game hunting is a dangerous game. But it is well to remember that all the incidents related are exceptions spread over a great number of years. Also that the big-game hunter may make himself out a bit of a hero, but he is far from it. One may go on several safaris and have no trouble whatever in shooting these animals, but I do maintain that if a hunter keeps at it long enough he is bound to find himself in some very awkward positions and only straight shooting will pull him out.

Personally, I do not mind saying that I have on several occasions felt very frightened when following dangerous game in the thick bush, because

I know from experience how dangerous these animals can be, and it makes me take every precaution. But when one actually sees the animal one is hunting, this feeling seems to disappear. The novice will often take risks that no old hunter would ever even contemplate, and get away with it, not realising, through lack of experience, what he is up against.

From a purely sporting point of view, I put the animals in the following order. Many hunters, perhaps, will disagree, but everyone to his own opinion.

First, I put the elephant. By elephant I mean the big old tuskers that are getting more difficult to find every year. The reason being that there is always such interest in the spooring and hunting of these animals, all of which I have already described, and so will leave it at that.

Second, buffalo. As one has often to spoor them up, watching the wind, moving with the utmost caution, and in absolute silence when approaching near to get a shot. But you don't have to travel the same great distance as so often when after elephant. There are often occasions when you may suddenly drop on them at any time when in a buffalo country. Often one gets them out in the early morning and evening, when they are feeding in open country. Another factor from a sporting view; one can't use motor-transport for touring about on the chance of seeing them in the open, as in most buffalo country the bush and grass is far too thick for the use of a car. There are a few countries where a car can help you in this way, but that is the exception.

Third, lion. To my mind there is much luck attached to lion, as one never knows when one may come across them. One drops across them in the most unexpected places and in all sorts of different types of country. So many of the lions, these modern days, are not actually shot from the car but seen and located by the hunter, who tours about in the early mornings and evenings. He may see them on a " kill," or else making their way back to a lie-up, and often comes across them lying under the shade of trees, or on the edge of some donga. A good many are killed by driving dongas and long grass near water or a stream, this being done by making the porters walk in line—generally accompanied by a White Hunter—and beating empty petrol tins and shouting. In very few places can one follow the spoor and track them down.

One of the old methods of hunting lion in Eastern Africa was riding them down, the hunters being mounted on fast ponies. This type of hunting, to my mind, could not be equalled for real sport and excitement, but it is now a thing of the past owing to lions seldom being found in open country suitable for riding after them. I do not think this form of hunting lions has been done since 1914. Personally, I have never hunted lions in this way. The following short account is based on what a few hunters

143

have told me and on what I have read.

The lion or lions must be found in open country, or driven into it. The hunters press them hard for about half a mile, so that they get blown and lie down, or they may whip round and charge on getting fed-up with being hunted. The hunters do not follow directly behind the lion or too close, otherwise the animal may suddenly turn round and charge, and this does not give the ponies time to turn round or get into their stride. In that case there is a good chance that the lion will catch the hunter. If the hunters ride to a flank or on each side of the lions when they are pursuing them, in the case of a charge they can then turn their ponies without checking the pace, and gallop out of danger. I should say that the distance the hunters follow the lion or lions is about 140 yards. When the lion lies down—probably after being hunted for about half a mile—the hunter dismounts and takes a shot. I should say it is a highly exciting game, requiring a cool and steady nerve. This type of lion-hunting, I should place in a class of its own; and there were quite a number of maulings of sportsmen from it, some with fatal results.

Fourth, the rhino. So often you come across them in comparatively open country and they are easily killed for such a large animal. If getting the wind right, they are easily approached to within 40 to 60 yards. On occasions I have followed up their spoor about six or seven miles before coming up to them, but that is rather exceptional as one generally tumbles across them without having all that trouble. In thick bush, as explained previously, the rhino is a different proposition and must be hunted with every precaution.

Fifth, leopard. There is even more of the element of luck in coming on to leopard than lion, as they are, to a great extent, nocturnal; but occasionally one comes across them on a " kill " early in the morning. I have seen more leopard on the Serengeti during the daytime than in any other part of Africa. Leopards are mostly shot by the following methods: (a) over " kills " in the morning, and touring the country by car one occasionally comes across them. They, like lion, turn up at the most unexpected times and in all sorts of different types of country; (b) in driving for lion one often gets a glimpse of a leopard, but seldom do they break cover into the open country, nearly always doubling back through the beaters or lying absolutely doggo in thick bush to let the porters pass them; and (c) if wounded and followed, leopard will almost certainly charge the hunter.

Sixth, the hippo. Shooting hippo can't be counted as a sport for, at some times, they are shot in the water from the land. When shooting from a canoe, they can at times be quite dangerous.

144

XXI

GAME COUNTRIES

I HAVE had the luck and opportunity to travel and hunt over more than nine different countries in Africa — north, south, east and west, covering a period, on and off, of more than 40 years, and so can claim to have a good deal of experience. Most of my early safaris were done with porters off the beaten track and in some parts untouched by civilisation. From what I have seen and read, there is nothing to compare in variety and quantity of game, from elephant downwards, with what may be found in Eastern Africa, with its ever-changing and beautiful scenery of every type, from snow-clad mountains to forest and park-like country and last, but not least, a delightful climate.

What changes have taken place in recent years — roads, railways, motors and 'planes! All these have gone to open up new game countries, with the advent of lorries and cars for transport. Many sportsmen of today would think twice if they had to walk with a porter safari for about 200 miles or more to reach some of the good game countries.

The Serengeti, situated in the north-west of Tanganyika Territory, is now well-known to sportsmen and visitors from all parts of the world. The area is justly famous for the number of lions and the vast herds of game to be seen. It is, indeed, a wonderful sight, to gladden the heart of all true lovers of Nature. The Serengeti is a country that varies from plain to bush and park-like country. All of it is practically uninhabited except on the plains where the Masai roam with their cattle, but they do not hunt game or molest them in any way.

I passed through this country with a friend in 1911, and then, of course, it was part of German East Africa, coming on from south of the Central Railway and crossing it at Kilimatinde, thence to M'Kalama and on to Ikoma. I well remember seeing vast herds of wildebeeste, zebra, antelope and gazelle, but I did not realise at the time what a magnificent game country we were passing through. We could do very little hunting as we had to keep pushing on with all speed owing to our being unable to buy *posho* for the porters, as none was to be had anywhere between the German *bomas*.

This country was practically unknown to Britishers before the war of 1914-18 and I think I am right in saying that a good American sportsman,

145

Leslie Simpson, was about the first white man to open up this wonderful game country. This he did by motor transport and cutting tracks through the bush and so eliminating the question of porters and *posho* to a great extent, as well as the water difficulty. On the heels of Leslie Simpson followed other hunters, who gradually opened up the country, and before World War II parties of tourists were taken out for about a week's trip from Arusha to see the wonderful game country and the famous Serengeti lions.

Another marvellous game country, and quite unique in its way, is the Ngoro-Ngoro Crater in Tanganyika, about 75 miles from Mount Meru and about halfway between Banagi Hill and Arusha. The bottom of the crater, which is only about ten miles long by eight miles wide, is covered by short grass cut up by some swamps with long grass. These swamps are fed by springs. The bottom of the crater is about 6,000 feet above sea-level, and surrounded by hills over 7,000 feet high, with in places nearly a sheer drop into the crater. At certain times of the year this place is literally teeming with game, which includes lion, rhino and all the more common game. There are also a few hippo in the swamps. It has been estimated that, at certain times of the year, there are as much as 50,000 head of game in the crater.

I always think that the Ngoro-Ngoro Crater is one of the wonders of Africa, the rim being surrounded mostly by forest and in the distance by rugged mountains. I heard quite recently that they are going to make a motor road down into the crater and also build a hotel. Such are the changes coming over old Africa! For several years the Ngoro-Ngoro Crater, and also parts of the Serengeti Plains, have been Game Reserves, but now both these areas are to be turned into National Parks and so there is no reason why the game should not be preserved in its natural surroundings for years to come, for the benefit of all lovers of the wild life of Africa.

Last, but by no means least, is Amboseli and its surrounding country. This area is situated on the Kenya side of the Kenya-Tanganyika border, and is not far from the foothills of Mount Kilimanjaro. This country is partly the remains of a soda lake, several large swamps covered by high grass but in which there is now little water, and that brackish, and light forest and open rolling plain. In the early mornings you nearly always obtain a superb view of the snow-clad summit of Mount Kilimanjaro.

Since the June of 1945 I have had a permanent Army Welfare Camp at Amboseli, for the main purpose of members of the Forces in East Africa Command being able to spend a week-end at the camp and to see the wonderful wild life in Kenya. These brief week-end parties are immensely popular with the Forces, and there is a long waiting-list of those who have put their names down to go when they can be taken.

I do not believe there is any place in Africa to equal Amboseli for seeing such a variety of game animals in such a small area. Within a radius of less than 10 miles circumference from my camp there are buffalo, rhino, lion, elephant, and some hippo in the swamps. On the plain, or in the light bush country, are giraffe, zebra, wildebeeste, impala, and several other species of antelope and gazelle, and around the swamps, a great variety of wild fowl and other birds, including marabout, white stork and pelican abound.

These safaris can all be done by car. It is scarcely ever necessary to alight, except occasionally when I wish to get the party a really good close-up view of elephants. All the game thereabouts is exceptionally tame, and you can see elephants and rhino right out in open country. It really gives visitors an entirely false impression about elephant-hunting when seeing these animals strolling about in the open country, just like so many cattle, more particularly in the early morning and evening.

Amboseli is unique for the purpose of photographing big game animals. The country is, of course, in the Southern Masai Game Reserve of Kenya and has been a Game Reserve for very many years. As the Masai do not hunt game, the wild beasts have not been molested for a long period, and the way in which elephants practically ignore the Masai and their herds of cattle, even with the wind blowing from the latter to the former is amazing. This does not always apply when they get the wind of Europeans. When out with parties I always take a heavy double-barrelled rifle, just in case it may suddenly be urgently needed.

The tameness of the elephants at Amboseli does not apply with equal force to that bad-tempered and livery old gentleman the rhino. He does not seem capable of learning any sense, so is much inclined to take the offensive if seeing a motor-car anywhere in the vicinity. They will sometimes charge a car without any sort of provocation, other than its presence in their own preserves.

You do not see, of course, all this variety of game on every trip to Amboseli. But one can always be certain to see elephants and rhino, also the more common varieties of game on the plain or in park-like country and, more often than not, lion and buffalo.

As an example of what happens I took out one party, leaving the camp about 6.40 a.m., about 40 minutes after sunrise and brought them back just after 10 o'clock in the morning. In that brief time of about 3½ hours we first saw three rhino, shortly afterwards five buffalo, and then nearly ran on top of two lions in light bush country. Proceeding for about another mile we got a good close-up view of a herd of elephants right out in the open country and also a couple of buffalo standing on the edge of a swamp. On the way back to camp we had a splendid view of a good maned lion and a lioness. In addition, we saw nearly all the common species of game.

If anyone can tell me where can be found a country with that variety of game in so small an area, I would much like to hear about it. Captain A. T. A. Ritchie, Game Warden of Kenya Colony, is now pressing strongly to have this region made into a National Park.

I cannot close this chapter without a few lines on the tsetse fly. The country round Amboseli is teeming with every variety of game but there is no tsetse fly in that part of the country. I personally know of several very bad belts of tsetse fly where there is very little game in the vicinity. Wipe out the game and the fly will range further afield, which has been proved, and will often be driven into a country where before the fly was unknown, often into a cattle country and on to human beings, who suffer accordingly. Where game is scarce it is known that tsetse will feed on birds, such as guinea-fowl and partridge.

It seems to me it is quite impossible to eliminate tsetse fly by the extermination of game, and it's a disgrace to any Government which allows the awful slaughter of game which has taken place in some parts of Africa.

XXII

FERAGI: MY GUN-BEARER

FERAGI BIN SALEM D.C.M., late sergeant in the King's African Rifles, had been my gun-bearer and head "boy" when on safari for 14 years, a seasoned warrior with all the tricks of the old soldier, and what one would call among white men "a real hard case," but a great character in his way. I never met any white or black man who was such an artist at getting money out of anyone with his plausible tales, always "broke" after being paid off, even after a long safari; but with all his faults — and we all have them, white or black — he was a lovable character and a real man.

Feragi was a member of the Atonga tribe, a small tribe who live on the west shores of Lake Nyasa. They have the name of being very independent but most intelligent when in any way it concerns themselves. A great many of them join the King's African Rifles, and real fine soldiers they make, more especially in the field, for they are a cursed nuisance when resting and there is nothing doing.

Feragi had a fine record of war service. Enlisting as a bugler in the K.A.R., as a boy he fought in the Uganda rebellion of 1897, in the Somaliland Campaign of 1902-04, in the expedition against the Nandi in 1905-06, and in the East African Campaign of 1914-18. He was wounded twice, once in the Somali Campaign and very badly in the first Great War, on which occasion he won the Distinguished Conduct Medal.

I met his Company Officer, who had known Feragi well during the War; and at the time he was with me he greeted his late Commanding Officer as a long-lost friend, and also touched him up for a bit of' *backsheesh*! His Company Officer told me all about his doings during the War, said he was a first-rate fellow in the field but a rare nuisance out of it. Feragi rose to the rank of sergeant twice, but was broke again when the Battalion was resting near some *boma,* and reduced to the rank of Private. His one great trouble was women—always the same old story with white and black men. But shortly after this episode when his Battalion joined up with another Column, Feragi distinguished himself in action and was again promoted sergeant, and that is his military career, and a fine one at that.

I gave him to His Majesty the King—when as Duke of York he and

149

the Duchess visited Kenya on their shooting expedition on safari in Kenya in 1924-5—as gun-bearer, and well he did his job. His Majesty liked him so much that he took him up to Uganda when they hunted in that territory. The boys called His Majesty "*Toto ya Kingi Georgi* (son of King George)." Many boys when acting as gun-bearer to His Majesty would be overwhelmed with the responsibility and lost their heads. Not so Feragi; he just carried on as if he were gun-bearer to Mr. Snooks. The King was also touched up for a bit of *backsheesh,* and Feragi had no qualms in asking for it!

His Majesty, so Feragi told me afterwards, had promised him a watch. I never thought anything more about it, but he continued to pester me for several years, each time saying "When is *Toto ya Kingi Georgi* going to send me the watch?" So when in England, I told Admiral Sir Basil Brooke—Comptroller to the Duke of York as he was then—that Feragi was always bothering me about the promise of a watch. Sir Basil mentioned it to His Majesty, who very kindly sent me a very nice silver watch with Feragi's name and the date engraved on it, to give to him, which pleased Feragi enormously.

Feragi was also gun-bearer to H.R.H. the Prince of Wales—now the Duke of Windsor—on several occasions when he visited Kenya on his second trip.

When back on my farm, and when my wife and I were in Nairobi doing some shopping, it was not long before Master Feragi appeared, like a vulture on to a " kill." He seemed to know by instinct that we were in Nairobi, probably getting the news from his pals. He would appear most polite, carrying all the parcels for my wife, looking into shop windows, more especially in the fish shop. He would say to my wife: " That's a nice fish, *Memsahib. Mimi njaa kabisa!* (I am very hungry)." Result, a fish for Feragi, who promptly disappeared. My wife was lucky to get off so lightly, and not be touched for more than a fish. All Coast boys are great fish-eaters. What he really liked was to get hold of my wife when I was not there, as he thought he could do better business.

When funds were running low with Feragi, he used to walk out to our home on the coffee estate—about 6½ miles from Nairobi. When he appeared the conversation was something as follows (in Swahili).

" *Jambo, bwana.*" (Greetings, master!)

Self: " *Jambo,* Feragi! What d'you want?"

Feragi: " I have come to clean your rifles—*Baba, Mama* and *Toto.*"

So called by Feragi which means in Swahili my .577 rifle *Baba* (father); the .470 *Mama* (mother); and the light rifle, *Toto* (child). In due course the rifles would be cleaned and, what is more, perfectly cleaned. He really saw that all my weapons were kept in perfect condition and took a great personal interest in them. After the cleaning of the rifles, Feragi was to be found in the kitchen drinking tea, with no intention of going until he had seen me. I came out again and met Feragi and the conversation continued.

Self: " Well, Feragi, what the hell do you want now?"

Fergai: " Oh, *bwana*, it's only a *shauri kidogo* (a little trouble)."

Self: " What is it?"

Feragi: " Well, it's like this. I've just got a new wife, for my old wife " (he generally had two or more) " is *mabaya sana* (very bad). I want an advance of pay to get the new one."

Self: " I'm damned well fed-up with you and your women. Do you think I'm the ruddy bank?"

Feragi: " Oh no, *bwana*, but this is a very nice young girl."

Self: " Look here, Feragi, you're getting an old man and it's about time you gave up playing about with the women."

Feragi: " Yes, *bwana*. I am getting old but I am very strong."

What generally happened after these occasions was that I was touched up again, and you could not see Feragi for dust *en route* to Nairobi after he had got an advance.

I only once hit Feragi, or in other words, took a flying kick at him, which caught him fair and square. That was in the Western Nile District of Uganda when after elephant; we saw two bulls in comparatively open country and he refused to go up near them; not that he was afraid, but just pure cussedness. The bottom of the matter was that a short time before I had refused to buy him a pair of boots which he had seen at a store at Rejaf in the Southern Sudan, when we were passing through, and he had set his heart on them—he had a perfectly good pair of light boots suitable for hunting—and afterwards he behaved like a spoilt peevish child. After the safari I returned to the farm, and still Feragi was most difficult. I got so fed-up with him that I sacked him and told him to go to the devil. We were not on speaking terms when we next met.

Shortly after this episode my wife and I went Home, and I returned alone to Kenya a few months later only to be met on the platform and greeted by Feragi as a long-lost friend, doing all he could to get my kit off the train; so back Feragi comes to me again.

With all his faults, and we all have them—irrespective of colour—he was a very great help to me in more ways than a gun-bearer. As all Africans are, he was a great judge of character; he was most useful in helping me to get a safari together, in the way of collecting good boys, seldom making the mistake of selecting bad ones. Feragi, also, always remembered every little detail that was required, which just makes all the difference to the comfort and efficiency of running a safari. He spoke

151

about six different Native languages fluently; and that, in itself, was a great help to me when on safari in parts of Africa where the Natives did not speak Swahili.

Feragi was a very great asset in being able to get information that I required out of local Natives, such as where I could get food for my boys, or the best hunting districts, and obtaining local guides in the district I was hunting in. To get information out of the Natives, more especially Natives who are not accustomed to white men, is always difficult. The line I always took was to hand them over to Feragi, and tell him to give them a real good feed and get him to do all the talking. Then in the evening when sitting round the camp-fire or lying on my bed in my tent, I would give the local Native a cigarette and then start the talk. It is wonderful what a cigarette and a good feed will do! Soon Feragi and the local guide would be chattering away like a couple of monkeys. I would then take a hand in the conversation and collect all the information I required as to the best locality to hunt next day, and give orders to the boys to make all arrangements for an early start the following morning.

Another great asset Feragi had was that he was a sportsman and loved hunting for hunting's sake, more especially when after elephant. Very few Natives, from that point of view, have the sporting instinct. They either hunt for meat or money, and when they do hunt, they kill off game regardless of sex or numbers.

When you get good " boys " hang on to them, they can be invaluable; they get to know your peculiarities and trust you, and upon a good staff of " boys " depends to a very great extent the success of a safari; bad " boys " give endless trouble, bad temper and much bad language.

Being somewhat deaf, which is a very great handicap, more especially when after elephant in dense bush and long grass where you can only see a few yards ahead of you, old Feragi would just give me a tap on the shoulder or by other signs let me know that he had heard elephant. On more than one occasion he helped to pull me out of a hole when we got mixed up with elephant.

Feragi passed over the Great Divide, which we all have to do sooner or later, in the June of 1937. I was in England at the time when I received a cable from a friend of mine who was looking after him and paying his retaining fee, to say that Feragi had passed on to another camping ground. On my return to Kenya I made inquiries as to the cause of his death from several of the Natives who knew him. They all said he was suddenly taken ill in his hut and died within two hours. They all swore that he had been poisoned. Personally I think this was most likely true and that some other Native had a grudge against Feragi, probably due to him running after his woman. So that is the end of Feragi, women again the trouble.

One rather extraordinary incident happened when I was in England during the late war. One evening I was showing some cinema pictures of game, mostly of elephants, to some friends. In the dining-room in which I was showing the pictures I had a most excellent painting of Feragi, hanging on one wall, by my sister-in-law, Mrs. Caton-Jones. In the morning when I came downstairs, it was found that the cord of Feragi's picture had broken and that he had turned a complete somersault and landed on the sideboard, resting up against the wall, as if he had been placed there. Nothing was broken. I think the sight of the elephant pictures was just too much for him, and he had to do something about it!

In Feragi I lost a good friend and an excellent gun-bearer.

XXIII

THE WHITE HUNTER AND HIS DUTIES

THE advent of the White Hunter was in 1903 and 1904, when British East Africa (now Kenya) became known to sportsmen as a new and marvellous country for all big game. It was a sportsman's paradise, and it was the big game that attracted many of the early settlers. Sportsmen became so fascinated with the country, its splendid climate, the lovely and ever-changing scenery, that they took up land, settled and made their homes. A great deal of the country, which at that time was waste land and unoccupied by the Natives, was literally teeming with all kinds of big game. These days it is all under cultivation with prosperous farms. This has driven the game farther afield, as settlement and game cannot go together, but it still remains a wonderful game country owing to the efficient control by the Game Department.

White Hunter is a term associated with Eastern Africa more than with any other part and many people have asked me: " What is a White Hunter, and what is his job?" I will try and explain.

His duties are many and varied and can only be learned by long experience. In the first place he is responsible for the control and organisation of the safari, for taking his clients on to the shooting-ground; and for doing his best to see that they obtain all the trophies they require, and that the trophies are brought back in a good state of preservation.

He must also have a good knowledge of all the game countries of Eastern Africa. Now that roads have so opened up Africa, and there are few places that cannot be reached by car and lorries, shooting safaris think nothing of going to the Belgian Congo, the Sudan and French Equatorial Africa. Only a few years ago, such places could only be reached by porter safari and by very careful organisation, the places taking anything from a month to three months to reach, and the safaris often passing through parts of the country that were probably unknown. In these days it is only a question of days or less as, if money is no object, the sportsman can hire a 'plane which will put him down in the vicinity where he can be met by his White Hunter, who will take him by porter safari to the main camp. More often, this can be done by car, the White Hunter having to go on ahead with the safari and make all arrangements.

I may be rather prejudiced having done all my early safaris with porters, but to my mind these accursed motors and 'planes have taken away a great deal of the fascination and sporting element of big game, and if one goes deeper into the subject, what have all these modern inventions done for the happiness of civilisation?

A White Hunter must, of course, be a good hunter. That is, have a great deal of knowledge as to the habits and localities of big game and, above all, he must love the wandering life of a safari apart from any financial gain. It is not necessary for him to be an outstandingly first-class shot, but what is necessary is for him to be able to keep his head under every possible circumstance and shoot straight at close quarters in case of emergency, when a dangerous animal may charge and his client fail to stop it. It speaks well for the recognised professional hunters that there has hardly ever been a case of a client being injured. On the other hand, several White Hunters have been mauled and injured whilst accompanying a safari. Not a client has been injured since the formation of the East African Professional Hunters' Association at Nairobi in 1934; nor have there been any complaints against any of the Hunters as to the running of a safari.

From a shooting point of view the White Hunter may seldom be required, but the occasion sometimes arises when he is wanted badly; more often when a dangerous animal has been wounded and has to be followed up, often in thick bush. That is just when all the trouble starts, as no White Hunter will leave a wounded animal until he has done his utmost to follow up and finish it off. When I have had to follow up wounded dangerous game when out with a safari, the sportsman has nearly always insisted on following up as well.

Going into bush where one can only go in single file a second rifle is of no advantage, in fact the reverse; especially if the owner of the rifle is inexperienced, for the Hunter has continually to keep an eye on him, and the more people, the more noise. Also, when creeping through bush some clients are none too careful with the handling of their rifles. Once, when following up an unwounded buffalo through thick bush, a sportsman poked me in the back with the barrel of a loaded rifle at full cock, as he wished to attract my attention! I told him what I thought about it!

In East Africa the regular safari " boys " are, as a rule, good at their own particular job but, like old soldiers, they are quick to take advantage of any weakness on the part of the hunter. They want careful handling and, at the same time, a firm hand over them. It has been my experience that the " boys " who cause the most trouble on safari are the Native drivers. They seem to get swollen heads as soon as they are in charge of a car or lorry, and to regard themselves as rather a cut above the rest of the " boys," very often complaining about their rations and wanting something extra. The whole secret of a well-run safari is to have a good staff of " boys " who are well-known to the White Hunter and who know him and his peculiarities; and above all things, to have a good cook.

The Hunter must have a rough knowledge of doctoring in the field, such as dealing with wounds and malarial fever. The boys are continually asking for medicine, and seem to suffer more from fever when taken out of their own country into malarial districts. Natives are easily dealt with, but with more drastic measures than with white men. A real good dose of Epsom Salts and about 30 grains of quinine will generally fix a go of fever and set them right again. It is up to the Hunter to keep them fit and cheerful, and to see that they are as well fed as possible.

Another important factor is for the White Hunter to work with the Game Department in whatever country the safari may be, as he really acts as an unofficial Game Warden. He must see that his clients do not break the Game Laws and that there is no unnecessary slaughter. All the White Hunters whom I know are good sportsmen and love big game, and all are against their clients filling up their licences to the maximum. Just a few heads of each species is what they aim at. After all, it is in the interests of the Hunter to help in the preservation of game. I have always found the Game Departments, of several countries, the most human of Government officials and not tied up with so much red tape and officialism as some of the other Departments.

If by chance a law is broken, it is essential to report it and have a talk with the Game Warden. The Game Departments know pretty well what has happened on each safari through the " boys " employed with it, for they tell the news of the safari to Natives who are attached to the Game Department on their return to civilisation. Not that the Natives attached to the Game Department are encouraged to spy upon safaris, but anything unusual that has occurred is bound to be heard by a Game Department. What Natives don't know about people and different happenings is just not worth knowing. They have got a white man beaten every time. This not only applies to safaris, but to the private lives of white people in general.

Some visitors get an idea, not so much in these days as formerly, that the Game Laws are made to catch people out. This is not the case, but they are framed in such a way that, if a Department wants to take action against any particular party who have not been playing the game, such as committing unnecessary slaughter, or hunting game in an unsporting manner, or shooting game from a car, they can always be caught out.

The White Hunter must be full of tact, a bit of a diplomat, and study very carefully the peculiarities of the people he is on safari with. There are certainly some odd people who go out on safari these days, of which more anon. In a month in the bush one gets to know the real character of others more than is possible after living years with them at home.

Many people going out on safari in these days do a great deal of photography of game, so there again it is very necessary to have a knowledge of photography and the handling of a cinema camera. In fact, a White Hunter must be a Jack-of-all-trades, guide, philosopher and friend.

The White Hunters in Eastern Africa are mostly settlers who own farms, as it is by no means an all-time job, and it is very exceptional for a professional hunter to be employed on safari work for more than seven to eight months in the year. Most of the safaris visit Eastern Africa from September to February, and their numbers are very limited, and competition is very keen. Many hunters work for a firm that specialises in outfitting parties, and supplies all the transport, stores, equipment, food and porters. A few hunters do all the outfitting themselves.

Members of the East African Professional Hunters' Association usually receive a salary varying from £100 to £200 a month. They are all experienced hunters and most reliable men, who have had years of experience in conducting safaris, but there are others who can be obtained for much less, men who have just started on hunting as a profession. One often hears that the White Hunters are overpaid, but if the people who make that statement had to accompany some of the people that go on shooting safaris, they would very soon change their opinion. Often the Hunter does not know, when he is engaged, anything about the people he is to accompany, and he has to take the good with the bad.

I know most of the old Hunters in East Africa, and what a real good lot of sportsmen they are. Apart from their hunting capabilities, they are the best of good fellows to be on safari with, and their hearts are much more in safari work than farming; hunting and wandering are in their blood, and I think they find farming rather a dull job; and I quite agree. Once a man gets bitten with safari life, it seems to unsettle him more than anything else and it is terribly hard to settle down to a humdrum existence on a farm. I have often noticed that with Natives, many of the old regular safari " boys " who are most excellent and hard-working when on safari, are often useless at other jobs although they may get just as much pay and not nearly so much work.

So many different types and nationalities visit East Africa to go on safari—Americans and British, Americans predominating, and the great majority are good sportsmen in every sense of the word. Many are the splendid sportsmen and charming characters one meets, and one makes some real good friends. It is a joy to be out with such people who take an interest in the game and their habits—apart from collecting trophies. This makes the White Hunter's job so much easier.

There is nothing more peaceful and delightful than sitting round a big camp-fire on a bright starlight or moonlight night, the silence often broken by the distant roar of a lion or the mournful howl of a hyena. I know, of no other place where people open up and become so confidential and it is always most interesting to get their views on different subjects of life in general, under these conditions.

There is no better job than that of a White Hunter but, like every other profession, it has its drawbacks and there is another side to the picture.

XXIV

SOME ODD PEOPLE ON SAFARI

Who treads the dewy path at morn,
Who bear-leads fools beyond all scorn,
Who wishes they were with the Quorn
Or that his clients were unborn,
The White Hunter.

—The Man and His Job (from *EAST AFRICA*)

December 26, 1935.

HERE is that other side of the picture which I am glad to say does not often apply to the people who visit East Africa for a shooting safari. But there are occasions when they would make the best-tempered saint use bad language and continually quote to himself the last three lines of this little poem with a few more strong adjectives attached to it.

Some years ago I was engaged by a millionaire, whom I shall call X., to accompany him on a safari after elephants, emphasising the fact that he *must* shoot a big tusker. Before his arrival I took all the tents, stores, drink and equipment to an old camp of mine situated on Ithumba Hill in the Ukamba country. This was a good centre for a main camp, as it was situated in the middle of good elephant country and had the advantage that one could get food for the porters. The camp could be reached by cars and lorries over a rough track cut through the bush. The camp itself was open land and free of bush, with some big shady trees to pitch the tents under, comparatively cool and with an excellent view of the surrounding country of endless miles of thorn-bush — a hot, arid and waterless country with the exception of a distant view of the Tana River, outlined by a line of palm trees and green vegetation.

The stores which X. had ordered were enough to last for four months; and as to the drink (champagne, whisky and old brandy), there was enough to make half-a-dozen men continually drunk for six months; all this was for a short safari which was not going to last much over a month. On X.'s arrival, much to my astonishment, he insisted on having another lorry-load of truck stores sent to the camp.

I had engaged a very good fellow, whom I shall call B., to help me with the porters and stores. He was a settler who had done a great deal of safari work. I knew that I should have my work cut out with everything connected with the hunting, without having all the worry and trouble with the porters and messing, etc.

Before the arrival of X., B. and I had engaged porters and sent riding mules to the camp, all to be in readiness for X.'s arrival. I then returned to Nairobi to meet X., leaving B. to make all arrangements for the camp. X. arrived at Nairobi shortly after my return and, after a few days, we both left by car, also with a lorry, as we had to camp one night *en route*, X. taking his white valet and chauffeur along with us.

We spent the first day at the main camp, B. and myself organising the porters and loads for a seven or eight days' hunt from the main camp. Instead of only requiring about 25 to 30 porters, which should have been sufficient, I found out that, after we had made up all the loads (tents, food, drink) which X. insisted on taking, we required over 90 porters. But I did insist on leaving his valet at the camp, to which he agreed.

For this safari I had engaged old M'Kula, whom I have mentioned before. He went through the same performance of placing food on his friend and fellow-hunter's grave before we started on the hunt. After the third day out X. became thoroughly bored with the constant trekking through endless bush, and insisted on returning to the comfort of the main camp. We did several of these short safaris; never would X. stay away for more than four to five days. On one occasion we did get on to the spoor of a big bull but, on getting near it in some thick bush, it got a whiff of our wind and cleared without our even getting a glimpse of it. Things, as you can imagine, were not very cheery, as X. was continually grumbling about the " boys " and the food; in fact nothing ever seemed right. He was thoroughly fed-up with his short experience of elephant hunting. His one and only remark to me was: " When am I going to see a bloody elephant? "

One night after we had made a camp and X. had swallowed a good number of drinks he became most despondent and was rather offensive in his remarks about White Hunters, and I am afraid I rather lost my temper and told him what I thought about him and his outfit. I asked how he could expect B. and myself to get him an elephant when he had nothing but a damned circus trailing behind. In fact things became very strained and diplomatic relations were nearly broken off. I quite expected to get the sack. But this incident had cleared the air considerably, and he became more human and quite friendly. Poor B. had a worse job than myself, keeping the porters closed up when following us through the bush, most times just following us by spoor. It meant endless halts as porters were continually falling out to adjust their loads, and we could never cover any distance.

Shortly after this we returned to the main camp again and X. said that he wished to return to Nairobi. After a great deal of persuasion he promised he would do a full seven to eight days' hunt, but nothing, he said, would induce him to go after elephant again if he did not get one in that time. All the " boys " were thoroughly disgruntled with the safari, no one more so than old M'Kula, who asked me if the *bwana* thought he was hunting chicken and not elephant. Why the comparison of hunting chicken and elephant, I can't think!

The night after our return to our main camp, whilst in my tent which I always have pitched at a little distance away from the people I am on safari with, as " boys " are continually coming to me with some talk or *shauri* (business)—and it is a good plan not to be sitting in each other's pockets all the time, however charming the people may be, as one sees quite enough of each other—a deputation of the safari " boys " came to see me, headed by my old headman Buakari. A word about him. He was a Coast Native who had been an askari and headman on many a shooting safari before the days of motor transport. He was of the old type which now is fast disappearing: honest, loyal, reliable, hard-working, and he is what soldiers would call " a steady-going old file." The rest of the deputation consisted of Feragi, X.'s personal gun-bearer, and M'Kula. They told me they had been having a *shauri* (consultation) amongst themselves and they said that the *bwana* would never shoot an elephant unless I sent for a friend of M'Kula's, who had some good medicine for elephants.

Then we had what one would call a good heart-to-heart talk, as they had finished their evening meal (the one big meal they have in the day), and I had passed the cigarettes round and that's the time one can get at their minds (as much as anyone can get at the back of the Native mind). After all, they are just like ourselves; one can get much more to the bottom of things with white men after they have had a good dinner and a drink than at any other time.

They were all unanimous that M'Kula's medicine-man should be sent for, to which I agreed. Personally I have not much faith in this " medicine " business and I thought our chances of getting an elephant under the present conditions were pretty hopeless but, knowing how much the lives of the Natives are governed by superstition, even the ones who have been brought up by the Missions and who call themselves Christians, I gave way. They are all practically under the influence of any sort of superstition.

The next day M'Kula's friend arrived, not an old man, but a very

161

ordinary-looking Mkamba. The first thing he asked for was my heavy rifle and X.'s. As it was the afternoon X. was having a siesta. He was asleep, so I told his gun-bearer to crawl under the fly of the tent and get the *bwana's* rifle. This he did. Then the medicine-man placed the rifles in my hands, talking a lot of mumble-jumble stuff; after he had finished blessing the rifles, or whatever he was saying to them, he told me to hold out both my hands and then spat into them which rather took me aback. Anyhow I said nothing. After that he told me to rub the spittle into my hair, but I merely rubbed the backs of my hands on my hair, which quite satisfied him. " Now," he said, " the *bwana* will get a big elephant within five more days." All the boys who were present were convinced that we should do so. That was more than I was.

The next day we left on our final hunt and on the third day camped near a dried-up sandy river bed, where by digging one could get most excellent clean water. Up to that time we had not seen any fresh spoor. That evening I told X. that I would be out at daylight and have a look up and down the river bed to see if there was any fresh spoor. The next morning shortly after dawn was breaking I went to the river bed with M'Kula, the two gun-bearers, and our friend the medicine-man. Lo and behold, there was the fresh spoor of a big bull which had been digging for water in the river bed during the night. I sent X.'s gun-bearer back to the main camp at once, with strict orders to get the *bwana* out of bed at all costs (he was not an early riser), even if he had to drag him out. Half-an-hour afterwards X. arrived on his mule; my syce had brought him along.

Following the spoor, which led us down an old elephant path (some of these old elephant paths one could drive a car along in most places), both of us riding as X. hated walking. After going for about an hour and a half, we could see by the spoor and droppings that the elephant was not far ahead of us, so we both dismounted, telling the syces to follow along with the mules at a good distance behind whilst X. and myself followed up the spoor and the gun-bearers. I told X. to keep close up as at any time we might come up with the elephant.

After about one hour I saw the outline of the elephant in fairly thick bush, standing facing us about 40 yards away. He had evidently heard us and suddenly he came straight for us, and as his head burst through the bush about 25 yards from us, I could see that he had two very fine tusks. Thinking that X. would fire, I waited a few seconds but, as he was coming on at full steam, I had to fire, dropping him with a frontal shot. I shouted to X. to fire, and he put a couple of bullets into him, and that was *that!* X. was greatly pleased and embraced me. He could not have been nicer, and thanked B. and myself for all we had done for him, and said he was

162

afraid he must have been a trial to us both. X. had a great many good points but was quite unsuitable for that sort of life and got no enjoyment out of it, in fact the reverse.

On cutting out the ivory and weighing the tusks, we found that they averaged 115 lbs. each. Our " boys " and the medicine-man, of course, were delighted and indeed it was " good medicine " to produce an elephant carrying ivory like this; in fact it was just the dope the doctor ordered in what looked like a hopeless case. I asked X. about getting his second elephant, but nothing doing! He said: " I've got a good elephant, and no more elephant hunting for me. I'm off back to Nairobi," which he was the day after our return to the main camp, leaving B. and myself to follow on with the lorries in our own time after we had packed up the camp equipment and stores.

Whilst I was away on this safari, my wife met Brigadier-General Claude de Crespigny and Jerry Preston, who both offered to bet her £100 that X. would not shoot an elephant, as they said he would never stay the course. Luckily she did not take the bet, as I think she thought I would let X. shoot any sort of an elephant that walked on four legs. De Crespigny was a fine soldier and great sportsman. He had done a great deal of shooting in different parts of Africa but was never a fit man after the first Great War, as he was constantly in pain from an old war wound, and he died as a result of it. Jerry Preston was an American and another first-class sportsman. He also had been on many shooting safaris and spent a great deal of time in Kenya. I was on safari with him in Tanganyika Territory after Greater Kudu and one could not wish for a more delightful companion. He also passed on to another camping-ground at quite an early age, greatly missed and beloved by so many who knew him in Kenya.

Several years ago I was on safari with a man whom I will call D. He had had no previous experience of big game, but was very anxious to shoot an elephant. A man of fine physique and young, I thought he would enjoy the hunting and porter safari life after elephants. For the first two weeks everything went very well; he was full of vim and energy and also seemed to be greatly enjoying life on safari. During this time we came up to elephants on two different occasions, but they were nothing but cows with a couple of young herd bulls with tusks under 40 lb. I would not let him shoot one, as before starting out on the safari he had emphasised that he must shoot big tuskers, also that time was no object to him.

A few days later he became thoroughly disgruntled and fed-up with the bush and trekking. This particular part of the country in which we were then hunting was terrifically hot, and on one occasion when on trek in the middle of the day, I found D. walking along without a helmet and stripped to the waist. On my asking him what the devil he was doing, he said he was having a sun-bath! I pointed out the error of his ways, and told him if he did that sort of thing he would most probably get sun-stroke and would get his back so blistered that he would not be able to bear anything on his back.

A few days after this, when we had made camp, D. came into my tent in the evening and said he had had enough of elephant hunting and wished to shoot the first elephant he saw—whether a bull or cow. He also accused me of not allowing him to shoot one of the bulls which we had seen a few days previously, as he said they were both good tuskers. This annoyed me thoroughly so I said: " You can shoot any kind of elephant you like, provided you write down a statement saying that you wish to do so. I don't want to be accused of helping you to shoot a cow or a bull with tusks under 30 lb. each, which would be breaking the Game Laws." He wrote down the following humorous statement (but he never meant it to be humorous).

" Somewhere in the Backyard of Voi.

" I, D., agree that if I shoot a bull elephant, whether he be full, middle or young grown, within the next 48 hours and its tusks are such as compensate or satisfy the law, so that it may not be confiscated, which law states 30 (thirty) pounds or less, I shall, and am bound to think, believe and know I have had a satisfactory shoot.

"Before God Almighty,

(Signed) D.

" P.S. On thinking this over, I also agree that if I get a bull elephant within the law, I am satisfied with my elephant shoot. I fully expect to get one."

By great good luck we struck a fresh spoor of a single bull the next day, coming up with it after three hours' trekking. D. shot the elephant, which carried tusks a shade over 50 lb.; and that finished his elephant hunting.

D. is another type of the White Hunter's trial and burden.

Many are the amusing incidents or otherwise which occur on a safari when acting in the capacity of a White Hunter. Several years ago I accompanied two sportsmen, whom I will call F. and C., on a two months' safari. F. was a retired business man who had made his " pile," out to enjoy life, fond of good living, middle-aged, fat and jovial, and oozing good nature. His friend C. was a very different type: young, active, keen, and interested in the game and their habits, and one who thoroughly enjoyed safari life apart from the shooting. Neither of them having done any big game shooting before in Africa, naturally they wished to obtain a great variety of trophies.

For a general shoot such as this, there is one outstanding country, and that is in the north-west of Tanganyika Territory, on the famous Serengeti Plains which are now so well-known to big game hunters from all parts of the world. It is a country that is easily reached and has the advantage that cars and lorries can go in any direction without being confined to the so-called roads, which are merely rough tracks made by shooting safaris. All this goes to make it an easy country to shoot in. In most cases very little walking has to be done except to approach the game. The climate is delightful, with ever-changing scenery, and a great variety of lovely camps. This makes it a most attractive and interesting country, more especially to people who are out on their first safari.

Two days before starting out, I met F. in Nairobi just after he had finished a most convivial lunch, and had done himself extremely well. Greeting me as a long-lost friend, he pulled wads of notes out of his pocket which he insisted on me taking in advance of my salary. This I diplomatically refused so as not to give him any offence. If I had accepted the kind offer I should have been paid twice as much as would have been due to me.

We reached the edge of the Serengeti after six days, always making camp early, thus allowing us plenty of time to go for any afternoon or evening shoot. There is no lack of the common game—such as kongoni, and Thomson's and Grant's gazelles—in the vicinity of these camps. It gave them a very good opportunity to get to know the conditions and try out their rifles before they tackled any dangerous species. F. and C. both proved quite good shots after a little practice, but I noticed that F. was a public danger in the way he handled his rifle, always having it at full cock without the safety catch on, swinging it about it any direction without any consideration into whose tummy it was pointed. I told him as diplomatically as I could to be more careful, otherwise he would put one of us in his " bag " as one of his trophies, but it had little effect.

One morning just after we had struck camp and were moving on to another camping-ground, we were all in the car ahead of the lorries. When passing through some rather bushy country, a half-grown rhino suddenly rushed out towards the car, making a blowing and snorting noise in the way they have. Poor old F., who was sitting in the back of the car with his friend, nearly collapsed from shock. Why I cannot think, as there was not the slightest danger of the rhino even hitting the car. Anyhow, he soon recovered and soon became his usual jovial self, so all was well! At this time we had been on safari for ten days and both had collected quite a variety of trophies, and were shooting well, but F.'s handling of his rifle did not improve in the slightest.

On leaving camp another morning we saw a lion lying down under the shade of some flat-topped thorn trees. F. and I stalked up under cover of some clumps of bushes and an ant-hill, getting to within 60 or 70 yards, when the lion evidently hearing us stood up. F. fired, making a first-class shot and killed it stone-dead. He was terribly pleased and so was I, as I thought it would give him confidence. We celebrated the event that evening in camp, F. waxing quite eloquent on the joys of big game shooting.

On another occasion when we were all out together we saw three lions in the distance disappear into some rather long grass. Thinking that they would probably lie up in the grass, we decided to walk them up. Before starting I warned them both that we must all keep in line and close together. Getting half-way through the grass we suddenly put up a hyena, which shook F.'s nerves badly. I turned round to see that he had fallen behind, walking along, rifle at full cock pointing straight at the centre of C.'s back. But never a sign of the lions, as they had passed through the grass.

On another day when out with F. we saw a rhino about 300 yards distant, lying down in fairly open country, settled down for his siesta. As the wind was in the right direction I told F. we should have no difficulty in getting quite close. Getting to within 40 yards, he suddenly got up on his feet, alarmed by the tick-birds which always accompany them. F. fired, bringing down the rhino with his first shot. I walked up, naturally thinking F. would follow close behind me, when suddenly the rhino got up on to its feet and started to come straight for me. The poor old rhino was badly wounded and coming at a slow pace, so I shouted out to F. to fire and finish it off, when I heard shrieks from F., who had not moved forward, saying " I'm scared! I'm scared!" I shot the rhino, afterwards sitting old F. on its back and taking his photograph in that attitude, which greatly pleased him.

F. was now most anxious to shoot a buffalo, and this, I thought, would be a hard test for him as a considerable amount of walking has to be done when after buffalo and F. was incapable of walking any distance. When out with him one morning, we met a local Native returning to his village and questioned him if he had seen any buffalo. " Yes," he said, " I've just passed one lying down in a patch of bush out in the plain."

There were few buffalo in that district, and I thought it extremely unlikely to find one in the middle of the plain, with so little cover about. Personally I did not believe this Native, as he did not seem very intelligent but, as he was so emphatic about it, I told F. we had better go and have a look. On getting to within 60 to 70 yards of the patch of bush, we saw a buffalo lying down. He instantly jumped up on his feet, at the same moment F. fired with both barrels, the buffalo rushed through the bush

166

and fell dead on the other side. As I was walking up towards the dead buffalo, suddenly there was a bang behind me, the blast nearly knocking me over. I turned round and asked F. what the something something he was firing at? He swore blindly that he had never fired, and was in such a state of excitement that he did not know that he had let his rifle off. I told him to open the breech of his rifle, which was a double-barrelled .470, and out flew an empty cartridge. He was a menace where a rifle was concerned!

A few days after the buffalo episode I was up early to see that everything was ready to start off for a day's hunt. I was greeted by F. coming out of his tent looking very dejected and not in his usual good form as he was always most cheery, even in the early mornings. " I've had a terrible time. Sitting up in my chair all the night," he said. I asked what the devil he had been doing not going to bed, and what was all his trouble.

" Well," he said. " It's those God-damned zebra and kudu roaring round my tent all night. I've shot all the dangerous game I want, and am going straight back to Nairobi." At that time he had only been out on safari for just over three weeks.

I had with me a young settler whom I will call K., who was very keen on becoming a White Hunter, a rather wild lad but a very good worker, and an enthusiast where sport was concerned. His job was to look after the lorries and car, also to take turns with myself in taking out F. and C. for a shoot in the evenings. I told K. to take F. back to Nairobi before he changed his mind, as after the buffalo episode, I thought he would finish up by adding one of us to his trophies. F. left with K. for Nairobi the same day. I was really sorry to see the last of him, as there was something very likeable about him, but he was the most dangerous man I have ever seen handling a rifle, and from that point of view I was glad to see him depart.

K. returned from Nairobi to C. and myself after six days. He said F. and he had had a most hilarious dinner in Nairobi to celebrate F.'s return from the perils of big game shooting. Not to be outdone in the way of collecting the rest of the dangerous game, F. had bought a leopard's skin at an Indian duka on his return journey which he said he had shot en route.

C. and I then continued the safari and as I had a licence I completed the specimens that F. had not shot, so he returned Home with quite a good " bag " to show.

It is extraordinary how unsophisticated and ignorant some of the people who visit Africa for a safari are in the ways and habits where game are concerned. I was once out with a very successful business man, who asked me if antelope, such an kongoni and wildebeeste, were carnivorous.

167

I was so astounded at this question that I really did not think he meant it, but found that he said this in all seriousness.

As to lions there are also people who regard the lion as a roaring and savage beast that is out to kill them on sight, and have nightly visions of being dragged out of their tent and eaten alive. Once I was out on safari with a very nice married couple who had come from the Continent. Both were of a nervous disposition. At the time we were in a country where every night lions could be heard roaring, often at no great distance from the camp. As this was their first experience of safari life, they were naturally rather upset by it and in the morning complained of a sleepless night, asking me the next day if there was any danger of lions coming into their tent. I did my best to console them, and said that they were just as safe in their tent as in their own home but, to give them confidence, I told their personal " boy " to place a lighted lantern outside the door of their tent after they had gone to bed. Even this did not have the desired effect, as a lion was roaring on the following night rather closer than usual.

The next morning they dropped me a very broad hint that I should put my bed outside their tent and do a guard over them. I told them jokingly that if I did so, I should be more of a menace than any lion if they woke me up in the middle of the night. Seeing that I could not be induced to act as a guard over them, they solved their difficulty unknown to me, by asking the white man who drove the car and looked after the lorries to sleep outside their tent. He did so. Again we were serenaded by the lion at night and in the morning they told me that they had both slept in the same camp-bed, I suppose for mutual support to their shattered nerves. How they managed to sleep in a single camp-bed I cannot imagine, as both were on the plump side, the husband being rather more than plump, to say the least of it.

Shortly afterwards we packed up camp and left the Roaring Lions.

XXV

SAFARI TO NORTHERN FRONTIER

E ARLY in April 1946 I took out a party to the Northern Frontier Province of Kenya so that they could get photographs of elephants. I was only away from Nairobi for 11 days. I went up there with the heavy transport a few days ahead of the party to select a camping site and to look over the country. The party arrived a few days later and said they could only stay for three days as they had to return to Nairobi on important business. How they thought they were going to get photographs of elephants in that time, I don't know. Anyhow I had the devil's own luck on the first morning. I got the chief member of the party to within about 45 yards of elephant, also the professional photographer accompanying them. After that, on our way back, I spotted four bulls out in the open, one a very good tusker. A big bull was facing us at about 50 yards' distance and we got some real good photographs of him. I saw this bull had good tusks; I put them down at about 60 lbs. each, but I did not shoot him.

After getting back to the camp it poured with rain and the next day, after a devil of a job, I moved the camp as the party were afraid they would not get back to Nairobi in time for the important business. The third and last day, all the party went out, including two ladies, as they wanted to see elephants. God was good to us. We came upon the same four bulls again and then I saw the old big bull once more. I looked him over more carefully and saw that his tusks were short but thick. As this bull started to walk towards us, I sent the photographer some little way behind me, when he took a photograph of the bull and myself facing each other. I did not shoot it.

The members of this party said they would like to see me shoot this bull. I had a licence, so went after him as the bull moved into some thicker stuff; I only walked about 500 yards, with all the party trailing after me, before dropping the elephant. I never had such easy meat in all my shooting career or such an easy job to get a big tusker. But it is money for jam when you get them out in the open like this, though that was the first shot I had fired since 1938 except when on the rifle range of the Home Guard.

When I got back and had the tusks weighed, they were 97 lbs. and

99 lbs. each, with the tip of one tusk broken off. An extraordinary thing happened when we got back to camp, as a local Native brought me the point of a tusk and it weighed 8 lbs.; so that brought the average weight of tusks to just over 100 lbs. each — one was 97 lbs. and the other (with the broken tip brought in to me) 109 lbs. The ivory realised £126 on sale.

XXVI

PHOTOGRAPHY AND GAME

THE camera today is taking the place of the rifle to a great extent, which is all for the good of the game. The good sportsmen who come out to Eastern Africa on a shoot do no harm to the game as they only require a few good specimens of each species. The great offenders to the Game Laws are the Natives with their nets, game-pits and snares. They kill anything that walks on four legs indiscriminately and regardless of sex or numbers.

The fascination in photographing game is that however many photos one takes of the same species of animal, one always gets a different picture. The key to photographing game is the motor-car. Animals do not seem to connect the car with human beings. One has only to take a car up near game and the moment one gets out of it, the game is away. A car can only be used for photographing the plain-dwelling animals or through light bush country.

I should say that 90 per cent. of the photos of lion are taken from a car, for they, in the same way as other animals, do not seem to connect the car with human beings. Rhino can often be taken from a car in a country where they have not been disturbed, as one often finds them out in open country; but here again they show their bad temper and will often charge the car. Very, very few photographs have been taken of elephant from a car, as there are few countries where a car can get through where elephants frequent. This also applies to buffalo to a great extent.

To approach game in a car drive up slowly and not directly towards them, but edging slowly up. If the animals are restless stop every now and then until they settle down. In this way one can nearly always get within easy photographic range of them.

I do not pose as an expert photographer, as it is only recently that I have seriously taken it up. Personally, I do not think you can better the Leica camera with a 13.5 cm. telephoto lens, and have it screwed on to a piece of wood made like the short stock of a rifle; it is then quick and handy. A stock like that was given to me by an old friend, Pat Ayre, whose name is coupled with that of another old friend, Phil Percival, as being the two leading White Hunters in this part of Africa. What they don't know about big game and all the work connected with safaris is not

171

worth knowing.

Like the rifle, the camera should always be ready, as often one comes on an animal unexpectedly, and it is often a question of seconds to get a picture. I have only had a few professional photographers out with me on safari, but it has always struck me they are very slow; they expect the animals to pose for them. To put it vulgarly, they are always messing about with the camera, testing the light and focussing. This does not apply, of course, to the ones who have had a certain amount of practice in photographing game.

So many say, when they see close-up photographs of the dangerous species of game, " Oh! That must be very dangerous, much more so than shooting these animals." That is an entirely wrong idea, for the following reasons. Very few animals will charge you unless wounded, as I have said in a previous chapter. Also, and most important of all, photographs of dangerous game must nearly always be taken in open country to get anything like good pictures. Then if perchance the photographer, who may be covered by a hunter, or if by himself, is charged, well, he gets a good view of the animal and should be able to kill or turn it. It is a very different matter in bush or long grass when hunting with the rifle and following up a wounded or even an unwounded animal; then, if hustled, they will charge occasionally. The animal in a country like this is often nearly on the hunter before he has time to fire. And that's the answer to *that!*

For instance, within the last year I have taken over 100 photographs of rhino, elephant, lion and buffalo, many of them quite close, which I call anything from 25 to 40 yards. On no single occasion have I had to use my rifle. Only on one instance, and that was with an elephant which charged, did I drop my camera and was on the point of firing when it swerved off. The photograph entitled " charging elephant, taken at about 25 yards " was taken at the time. I got a good action photograph of the start of that charge, but she still came on in a most resolute manner. At a distance of roughly 25 yards she was enveloped in a cloud of dust and still coming " all out " at me, but I took another photograph (scarcely daring to hope it would show more than a cloud of dust), then hastily dropped the camera and grabbed my heavy rifle. I had not the slightest wish to shoot her, even in self-defence, but it did look as if this would become an imperative necessity. Suddenly, however, the cow swerved aside from me and made off to rejoin the herd. Thereafter she caused me no further anxiety. It is difficult to account for that cow's sudden display of violent dislike to my nearby presence but, quite possibly, she had recently been crossed in love. I am unable to suggest any other cause.

Personally, I only know of three accidents when taking photographs of dangerous game, all of them, unfortunately, being fatal for the hunter. One was from a lion, which incident has already been related, another was with an elephant, which charged the photographer, he being covered by two other men with rifles (a bad show and one which should never have happened); and the third an instance of an old hunter being killed by a rhino, of which I know nothing about the details.

And finally I say, everyone to his own opinion, but personally I do not think there is any life, even in these days of motor transport that can compare with life on safari in Africa with rifle and camera.

In conclusion, if the reader has followed me so far, I will say: *"Asanti. Kwa heri, bahati!* (Thank you. Goodbye and good luck!)"

THE END